Philosophy and Education

VOLUME 14

SCOPE OF THE SERIES

There are many issues in education that are highly philosophical in character. Among these issues are the nature of human cognition; the types of warrant for human beliefs; the moral and epistemological foundations of educational research; the role of education in developing effective citizens; and the nature of a just society in relation to the educational practices and policies required to foster it. Indeed, it is difficult to imagine any issue in education that lacks a philosophical dimension.

The sine qua non of the volumes in the series is the identification of the expressly philosophical dimensions of problems in education coupled with an expressly philosophical approach to them. Within this boundary, the topics—as well as the audiences for which they are intended—vary over a broad range, from volumes of primary interest to philosophers to others of interest to a more general audience of scholars and students of education.

Moral Education

Beyond the Teaching of Right and Wrong

by

COLIN WRINGE
Keele University, U.K.

 Springer

A C.I.P. Catalogue record for this book is available from the Library of Congress.

ISBN-10 1-4020-3708-2 (HB)
ISBN-13 978-1-4020-3708-5 (HB)
ISBN-10 1-4020-3709-0 (e-book)
ISBN-13 978-1-4020-3709-2 (e-book)

Published by Springer,
P.O. Box 17, 3300 AA Dordrecht, The Netherlands.

www.springeronline.com

Printed on acid-free paper

Printed in the Netherlands.

FOR GABEY

CONTENTS

INTRODUCTION

Casual reference to moral education or the manner in which young people should be brought up to behave may provoke a range of responses depending on the context and the personalities and ideological perspectives of those present. In the past, these responses sometimes included a Rousseauesque assertion of the inherent goodness of all human beings, which only needed to be left to emerge uncorrupted and undistorted, with the help of infinite loving-kindness on the part of teachers, all with the patience of saints. More extreme versions of this view may have comprised vehement protest at the very idea of the state, through its educational institutions, concerning itself at all with such matters, which were felt to be properly the province of the family or religious organisations, if not a matter of individual choice for young people themselves when they were grown up. Explicit proposals for moral education were invariably at risk of being perceived as indoctrination or an abuse of children's rights of freedom and autonomous development.

More frequently these days, the response may be a succinct list of the speaker's own choice moral prescriptions, an assertion that these need to be inculcated in a clear and unequivocal way to all young people of whatever age, inclination or social experience and, often enough, a statement of the sanctions to be applied to those who do not or will not conform.

Whereas the older responses were both sensitive and relatively well informed, they have often been criticised for offering little practical assistance to those parents and teachers attempting to make something of young people not only destined to grow up but already living in a less than perfect adult world. By contrast, the more recent reaction seems unsentimental, pragmatic and down to earth. It certainly receives the all but universal support of the popular media and politicians and other public figures of a certain stamp as well, of course, as vocal sections of the general public. Since the publication in Britain of the *Consultation on Values in Education and the Community* (School Curriculum and Assessment Authority 1996b) and the printing of its conclusions in the Primary and Secondary Teachers' Handbooks of the National Curriculum, this response must even be regarded as having official support. The *Consultation on Values in Education and the Community,* of course, makes no reference to sanctions but many official publications and pronouncements place upon teachers responsibility for 'insisting' that standards of behaviour be respected.

It must be said that the above response in no sense represents a formula for moral education. That some kinds of behaviour are undesired by adults, whether parents, teachers or the authorities, will tell young people little they did not know already. That certain demands or prohibitions reflect values, themselves grounded in God, human nature or consensus is likely to carry as much, i.e. as little, conviction with the majority of young people as it does with thinking adults. Threats of sanctions may deter, but only as long as young people are, in fact, young enough to be intimidated by them. To young males they may constitute a challenge rather than a deterrent. Where successful, the result will not so much be obedience to proper authority, as it is sometimes described, as subordination to power, insofar as learners may, depending on the way this brand of instruction is delivered, have no way of genuinely accessing the rationale of many of the things that are said to be required of them. The process may habituate some future adults to behave in a visibly law abiding manner, but it is difficult to see how it could make them moral, or even understand what moral conduct involved. How, indeed, should it be supposed to do so?

Talk of ethical theories is scarcely at a premium in current debates about morality and moral education, yet these are no more than attempts to make explicit the reasons why some things are considered good and others bad; to go beyond the simple commands 'Do this' and 'Don't do that, or else'. Few would suggest that anything resembling a formal course in Ethics would provide an answer to our current problems. Nor is it naively supposed that the young, or for that matter the not so young, are invariably disposed to follow the good and eschew the bad once they have fully appreciated the reasons for doing the one and not the other, especially when the rewards of misdemeanour, including the all-important reward of peer approval and admiration are so great. Adult vigilance and even the threat of sanctions may sometimes need to be thrown in to tip the balance in favour of the good.

Conforming behaviour alone is an inadequate goal of moral education, even if it doubtless possesses a certain social utility. It is essential to our understanding of morality that, for instance, people we regard as moral consider the consequences of their actions for themselves and others, respect the rights of others and are conscious of the limits of their own rights, scruple to manipulate or simply to use others for their own ends, strive to achieve certain admirable qualities of character, respect the values and practices of their own and other groups and communities, care for those who depend on them, and so on. They may also feel that their moral commitments extend beyond the realm of their private conduct and include an obligation to appraise and, as far as they reasonably can, influence the conduct of public affairs and the actions of those who govern in their name.

These habits of thought and action reflect the key concepts of a perfectly ordinary moral understanding. Given the nature of the world in which we live, there are sound reasons why they should be available, at a level appropriate to the young people concerned, to all who are expected to live as morally responsible adults. In the pages that follow, it will be argued that to be deprived of such an understanding diminishes the educational process by omitting a major facet of our human intellectual heritage. It is to entirely lose out on the rich store of moral wisdom that has been accumulated in experience, hard thought and passionate debate over the centuries. Self-evidently, this is something more than the banal interpretations of the simplistic slogan that the young should be taught the 'difference between right and wrong' to which I shall shortly have occasion to refer. For someone's moral education to be limited to such an aspiration is for them to be culturally impoverished, somewhat in the manner of those generations in the past whose induction into other great disciplines of human thought and feeling was restricted to that which was thought necessary for them to fulfil their lowly roles to the satisfaction of their betters.

In the central chapters of this book I shall have something to say about many of the things that have been thought, said and written in the past about the appraisal of human conduct and their implications for current moral education. First, however, I shall need to deal with two issues that so often frustrate attempts to make progress in discussion of the nature of the moral education to be offered to the next generation, namely the relationship between morality and religion and the question of whether moral imperatives can have absolute validity or must be seen as essentially relative to context and individual perspective. In later chapters I consider how it may be possible to avoid, on the one hand, entirely endorsing a particular and inevitably one-sided view of morality and, on the other, falling into either stultifying relativism or the patronising expedient of presuming to 'clarify the issues' for readers, while leaving them to reach their own conclusions. I attempt to offer a tentative solution to this problem, but with the hesitancy and caution appropriate when, as must of course ever be the case, our conception of the well lived life continues to evolve. In later chapters I discuss a number of issues of particular relevance to the moral education of the young in the modern world and, finally, presume to offer some comments on the task of moral education in practice.

PART ONE

PRELIMINARY CONSIDERATIONS

CHAPTER 1

RESPONDING TO A MORAL CRISIS

In a remarkable television interview some years ago the British dramatist Dennis Potter revealed that when he first became aware of the symptoms of the pancreatic cancer that was eventually to cause his death, his initial response was to take aspirin. Such a reaction is natural, indeed rational, enough. Why look for trouble beyond that which thrusts itself upon us or attempt to take remedial action that turns our life upside-down or extends beyond what seems to be immediately required? Such will certainly be the response of politicians or heads of public bodies expected to find rapid solutions to problems, rather than confess themselves impotent before their complexity.

It is therefore perhaps not surprising if, faced with concern about rising rates of largely petty crime and anti-social behaviour among the young, occasionally highlighted by particularly shocking actions by individual young people, politicians should simply and straightforwardly locate the root cause of the problem in the failure of schools to be sufficiently energetic in teaching children the difference between right and wrong. If the supposed shortcomings of schools in teaching other things also happen to be in the news at the time, such a reaction will be all the more predictable. The particular moral lessons which schools were supposedly required to teach by one British Secretary of State for Education included regard for proper authority, loyalty and fidelity and the development of a strong moral conscience (Haydon 1997). Other writers, deploring the apparent 'loss of virtue' (Anderson 1992) in our age have urged the teaching of 'two extra Rs' , 'Right and Wrong' (Seaton 1991) teaching the 'virtue of diligence' (O'Keeffe 1992), and 'respect for perennial human values' (O'Hear 1992). Phillips (1997) blames many of our social and educational problems on the failure of parents and teachers to lay down the law on matters of right and wrong and deplores the fact that parents no longer feel able to call upon the supreme authority of God and the Bible to back up their commands, while numerous authors writing under the Institute of Economic Affairs impress (Murray 1996, Himmelfarb 1995, Dennis and Erdos 1993, Berger 1993, Davies 1993) are unanimous in attributing the emergence of what they term 'the underclass' to a decline in such simple Victorian virtues as honesty, industry, independence, sobriety, thrift and chastity.

Of more direct concern to teachers in schools has been the publication in Britain of two documents by the School Curriculum and Assessment Authority (SCAA), namely *Education for Adult Life; the Spiritual and Moral Development of Young People* (School Curriculum and Assessment Authority 1996a) and *Consultation on Values in Education and the Community* (School Curriculum and Assessment Authority 1996b). The first of these is the report of a conference emphasising delegates' concern at what is described as the malign influence of 'relativism' and calling for a process of consultation to arrive at a consensus on a framework of moral values, which schools would have the confidence and authority to 'instil' into the young. The second document reports the outcome of the resulting consultation by a 'forum' set up in the wake of the conference and consisting of some 150 members of various faiths and some of none at all involved with young people in various ways. The forum's conclusions are presented in the form of four 'statements of values'.

These relate respectively to Society, Relationships, the Self and the Environment. That relating to Society asserts 'We value truth, human rights, law, justice and collective endeavour' and that concerning Relationships "We value others for themselves, not for what they have or can do for us. The statement headed 'The Self' begins 'We value each person as a unique being' and that under 'The Environment', 'We value the natural world as a source of wonder and inspiration and accept our duty to maintain a sustainable environment'. The statements of values are each followed by a number of 'principles for action' expressed in the form 'On the basis of these values we should . . .' Thus, on the basis of the statement of values relating to Society, for example, it is said that, among other things, we should 'understand our responsibilities as citizens and be ready to challenge values and actions which may be harmful to individuals or groups'. In a slightly modified form, these conclusions are printed in *The National Curriculum Primary/Secondary Teachers' Handbook* (Qualifications and Curriculum Authority 1999)

In themselves both statements of values and principles for action are mainly enlightened and uncontroversial. Of more significance in the present context, however, is the manner in which they are presented. The source of such values is uncomplicatedly identified either as 'God' or as 'human nature'. The document is, furthermore, said by the Director of SCAA (*Daily Telegraph* 30.10.96) to be a 'statement of what we as a society are authorising schools to pass on to the next generation on our behalf', capable, if such were the will of Parliament, of being inculcated 'in a straightforwardly didactic way.' Disconcertingly, one official is quoted as referring to a further consultation process involving a public opinion poll and a representative sample of 3200 schools, enabling people to say whether they want 'something stronger' and a representative of the National Association of Schoolmasters/Union of Women Teachers is said to have demanded something more relevant to 'teachers battling to restore and maintain sensible discipline'. Elsewhere, writing in a joint publication with Marianne Talbot (Talbot and Tate 1997) the former chief executive of SCAA suggests that we should instil '*our* values', namely 'the values to which every person of goodwill would subscribe' (emphasis original).

Talbot and Tate note that of some 1500 adults included in a MORI omnibus poll approximately 95% actually did endorse the views agreed by the SCAA forum. We are told nothing of the 5% of parents and other citizens who presumably did not.

The particular values being advocated here are not our present concern. Of greater import is the underlying conception of values and their relationship to moral conduct embodied in the paper and implied by some of the comments upon it. Essentially, the model is that of values derived, if not from God or human nature, then from consensus or something else capable of fulfilling a similarly authoritative function, justifying a range of prescriptions which may be of a harmless and general nature open to a range of interpretations, or may be sharpened up into 'something stronger' which teachers may be 'authorised' to pass on to the next generation, 'didactically' if the government of the day should so will.

We have here the basis of a crudely inculcatory approach to moral education in which prescriptions are enunciated and assertively enforced. Such an approach is objectionable for two main reasons. First, it is inadequate to the needs of a world in which the precise application of moral values is subject to interpretation, even if consensus on a particular verbal expression of them were possible, and in which the permanent public monitoring of individual conduct is no longer possible. Second, it profoundly misrepresents the nature of moral judgement and its relation to action, and deprives this mode of human experience and expression of its due place in the educational programme.

In the United States similar calls for focused and uncomplicated programmes of 'character education' instilling such apparently simple 'core' or 'basic' qualities as 'honesty, empathy, caring, persistence self-discipline and moral courage' have been made by the Character Education Partnership, the Character Counts Coalition and the Communitarian Network. (Lickona 1996). Character in this sense has been defined by one widely influential writer in uncomplicated terms as that 'psychological muscle that allows a person to control impulses and defer gratification which is essential for achievement, performance and moral conduct.' (Etzioni 1993).

In the United States as in Britain there is widespread agreement that certain social evils - violence, drug and alcohol abuse, marital infidelity, vandalism, teenage pregnancy, poor time-keeping and work performance and the failure of good citizenship - are the direct result of the failure of schools to instil these values or desirable character traits (Lickona, loc.cit). In neither country does there appear to be any acknowledgement on the part of those advocating these views, either that the values or character traits themselves are problematic or that failure to teach them effectively results from any cause more complex than a failure of will and commitment and good sound commonsense on the part of schools and others in the adult world.

That moral standards are not what they were and that something urgent needs to be done has ever been the complaint of the older generation against the young and there have certainly been some who have doubted that we have cause for moral panic or, indeed, whether we can even know whether we are currently suffering a moral decline. Straughan (1988) demonstrates neatly that this would be difficult to show empirically and doubts that it can be an empirical claim at all. The most we can hope to show is that particular kinds of misdemeanour may occur more frequently at one time than at another but if some increase while others decline we are hard put to it to draw conclusions about overall moral standards. White (1997) argues that survey data showing that 48% of 15-35 year olds did not believe there were definite rights and wrongs in life might as plausibly be taken as evidence of a wholly desirable increase in moral sensitivity and sophistication as of a decline in moral standards.

Nevertheless, at a superficial level, there is certainly a widespread perception that, at least in terms of traditional indices, things are going morally wrong. The impression is sometimes given by the media of whole residential suburbs where the young are irremediably enslaved to narcotics and hell-bent on a desperate regime of larceny to fund their addiction. The publication of statistics of (mostly) rising crime is a regular event, particularly in the fields of burglary, street violence and indecency. It is also the experience of the older generation that the young are less deferential, less conforming to the adult norm in their dress codes and disturbingly free and easy in their relations with the opposite sex. 'Where will it all end?' is a question often asked by members of the older generation. White suggests that we may be inclined to scapegoat the young for our moral and social ills but the adult generation is also commonly represented as having taken leave of its moral senses in reports of the pointless mass murder of school-children, acts of terrorism, child-abuse, financial fraud or casual political skullduggery. The phenomenon of apparent moral chaos, as Smith and Standish (1997) point out, is not confined to the Western world but is also to be observed in South Africa, China and Eastern Europe where, it is sometimes suggested, the whole framework of law and order may be in danger of breaking down.

Possibly this whole perception may simply be an example of Flew's (1975) Buggery in Bootle Effect in which increased vigilance and detection creates an impression of the increased incidence of certain events and should be regarded as an encouraging rather than a worrying sign. Undoubtedly, certain misdemeanours such as rape and assaults by adults on children, not to mention financial and sexual deviancy on the part of the rich and powerful, were much under-reported in the past. It may be, however, that we nevertheless have good reason to carry out some assessment of the moral state of our affairs and that this naturally has important implications for our approach to moral education. We may need to define certain specifiable acts of wrong-doing, whether by adolescents, businessmen or politicians as unequivocally beyond the pale and deal with them promptly and energetically when they occur. Such a response, however, is no more than an emergency palliative which, if overly relied upon, may do as much harm as good in the long term, besides preventing a true diagnosis of the situation. The model suggested by the simple remedies considered at the beginning of this chapter is, to risk working the medical comparison to death, that of a society basically in a state of healthy functioning but occasionally requiring a dose of disagreeable medicine, maybe the lancing of a boil or at most some minor if locally painful surgery and then all will be well and we may carry on as before.

To doubt this complacent response is not necessarily to imply that our present malaise signals some deep-seated social or moral cancer. Other explanations are possible. One may be that, analogously to adolescent growing pains, our difficulties, if they are real at all, simply reflect not so much a sickness but the problems of adaptation to naturally changing circumstances and conditions. It has been said ad nauseam that our society is in a state or rapid change and it would therefore not be surprising if our ways of coping with life in it had somewhat lagged behind. If this is the case, the danger most obviously to be feared is not the malady itself but the malign effects of a regime seriously and increasingly inappropriate to the needs of the situation. What would be required would be a measure of readjustment and a greater degree of sophistication in the mode of moral thinking offered to the young and embraced by ourselves, rather than an energetically enforced regression to the so-called core values or 'basic' behaviours of an earlier developmental stage.

That doctors should not only differ but also seek to impugn the theoretical basis of their rivals' prescriptions is no new experience. It is therefore unsurprising if more thoughtful approaches to both morality and moral education come up against what has been called the anti-intellectualism of conservative spirituality (Blake 1997), attempts to ground values in such explicit foundations as the will of God or the facts of human nature, or preemptive attacks on the supposed relativism of those who suggest that traditional values may be in any way problematic. Significantly those blamed in this connection for directly or indirectly corrupting the youth have included such moral innovators and progressive educators as Rousseau and Dewey (Phillips, op. cit.) who were markedly sensitive to the moral evils of their times and the impoverished educational practices by which they were not mitigated but encouraged.

To suggest that changing social, cultural and therefore, ultimately, economic conditions may be partly responsible for our moral ills or grounds for abandoning older inculcatory brands of moral education is not necessarily to excuse bad behaviour. Far less is it to suggest that moral judgements are necessarily relative, at least in Tate's interpretation of the term (School Curriculum and Assessment Authority 1996b) as being purely a matter of taste, so that serious attempts to arrive at conclusions about right and wrong are a waste of time. On the contrary, to suggest that there are no good reasons for preferring one course of action or one mode of conduct to others seems a patent absurdity, though there may be much disagreement as to the nature of those reasons and how they should be weighted in relation to each other. The conditions of modern life, however, greatly increase the burdens morality has to bear and consequently the importance of a suitable and effective moral education. Thus, far from moral education being unnecessary or something to be relegated to the margins of the curriculum as now so often tends to be the case, it will be argued that the conception of moral education we have encountered so far is simply inadequate to the task it has to perform.

Responsibility for providing a rigorous account of the changes that have rendered the simple moralities of prescription and prohibition unequal to the needs of the present day must necessarily be left to social scientists. The purpose of the following remarks is simply to call to mind broadly recognized trends that are common knowledge, in full recognition that it is always hazardous to draw idealised pictures of a more restricted, stable and innocent past. It may nevertheless be possible to imagine a time in the indefinite but not too distant past, when our lives were lived in close proximity and often in full view of those with whom we were united in bonds of affection, family ties or material dependence. Our conduct could be monitored by our elders and superiors, who not only felt entitled but also obliged to admonish us for our shortcomings. Our misdemeanours were their dishonour in closed communities from which there was no escape and in which reputation was both a social and a material family resource. Within the bounds of one's community, gossip was ubiquitous and memories were long. Social penalties for wrongdoing or unseemly behaviour were harsh and legal penalties for actual breaches of the law even harsher. Temptations were relatively few and life choices limited. With luck, a fulfilling life could be achieved by following a limited number of uncomplicated prescriptions reinforced by childhood sanctions and scoldings, the conventional wisdom of daily conversation or more formally the weekly sermon, or by emulating the conduct of one's elders or respected others in the community.

In terms of social cohesion and control, it will be unnecessary to labour the differences between such a condition and our own. Outside our strictly nuclear family our relatives know of us and our doings only that which we choose to tell them. We may know nothing of even our immediate neighbours except, perhaps, their names. We are unlikely to know anything of their lives before we or they took up residence in our present homes, or of their fortunes or the character of their relatives. How we spend our time outside our working hours is no business of our colleagues or superiors and even enquiries after our health or well-being are usually no more than conventional courtesies. To give a serious or informative reply to such enquiries is normally a solecism. Much of what we do is invisible to those who may have an interest in knowing about it and deception, or at least impression management, is a common and essential social skill.

Our paths in life are not laid out before us by status or tradition, and of this any liberal must be glad. If we do not consciously choose how to live, we may at least follow our inclination with more or less deliberate direction, more or less discipline, control or yielding to whim or immediate desire. Our elders are no longer our models. Few young people aspire to resemble or occupy the position of their same sex parent at the same age and many parents would not wish it so. Other young people may see little prospect of matching the levels of status and security achieved by their parents and regard the advice or more explicit moral injunctions of their parents as out of touch and irrelevant to their lives, either now or in the future. In this they are mostly right, for neither their experience nor the social and moral world in which they have lived the corresponding part of their lives bear much resemblance to the present or foreseeable future. When the future is no longer easily predictable or clearly present before our eyes in the shape of our elders, delayed gratification may seem a dubious strategy compared with enjoying now and facing the consequences later.

With us, furthermore, innocence is no longer protected by ignorance. Actions and ways of life that once scarcely entered the realm of fantasy are now daily presented in the media, not only as fiction but as reality. It is no part of the present argument that media images are literally the cause of wrongdoing but it must be said that patterns of deviancy and rebellion which were formerly unthinkable have now palpably become an option for many young people. A further consequence of losing the protection of ignorance is that nowadays the have-nots are aware of the material and symbolic goods the haves possess and, in committing acts of deviancy, are able to see themselves not as flouting the will of Providence or rebelling against the natural order of things but, with a greater or lesser degree of self-deception, as the victims of injustice venting their legitimate resentment.

Unlike ourselves, few individuals or moral authorities in the past had to deal with the moral or intellectual issues of difference and exclusion. Little was known of foreignors, mostly living far off in distant lands. If they appeared as enemies they could be fought against, killed, hated, despised or ridiculed without equivocation. Non-standard sexual practices or family patterns were straightforwardly abominated. Differences of belief were accommodated by social separation, or dealt with by pogrom or the faggots without supercilious intellectuals or intrusive media raising doubts about the legitimacy of such treatment in the minds of ordinary people. The poor and socially excluded could be either reabsorbed as the recipients of charity, driven out as beggars and vagabonds or publicly condemned as robbers and outlaws. Though such groups may have been seen as a threat, we may suppose that their presence united society against them rather than provoking moral dilemmas or controversy

Without wishing at this stage to prejudge the general issue of moral relativism it will be clear in the light of the above that many of the explicit maxims of prudent or virtuous conduct will greatly vary from context to context. The level of truth-telling and generosity appropriate among cousins and erstwhile village playmates would be foolish naivety in the modern city. In a closed society, studied deference to social superiors in general is not only a courtesy but a moral obligation, since failure to show it may materially disadvantage other members of one's family. Elsewhere it is, at most, optional and may even be seen as a moral failing or sign of social ineptitude. Ambition for one's own sake or that of one's dependents is at least permissible if not a positive virtue in the modern world. In a more stable society where it can only be achieved through ruthlessness, the denial of one's origins or the desertion of one's kinsfolk, it is likely to be condemned as a vice. Sexual conduct capable of leading to tragic consequences in the past may be of little moral significance in the modern world

These circumstances demonstrate the inadequacy of conceptions of moral education that seem to imply that the so-called difference between right and wrong may simply be 'taught' by one generation to the next in the way that we might teach the dates of historic battles or the capitals of foreign countries. Whatever kind of knowledge moral education may involve, it is clearly something different from the knowledge of other curricular subjects which may be presented propositionally, memorised and stored for later regurgitation in the examination room and which, if not properly learned, risks being forgotten (Ryle 1958). For it is unlikely that those who burgle houses, mug old ladies, drive under the influence of alcohol, or falsify their tax returns have simply forgotten the difference between right and wrong as we might forget Ohm's Law. The problems that beset us in regard to moral education are not merely problems about means, as if the desired behavioural outcomes of moral education were, as Talbot and Tate suggest, perfectly known and agreed so that all that was required was to train and motivate teachers to efficiently put into effect the most expeditious manner of achieving them. The very least that is required is an appreciation of why some modes of conduct are to be preferred to others and how this may properly vary in the light of such considerations as likely outcomes, details of the specific situation or our relations with others.

Much has been written and publicly said on this topic. Collections of short articles (Halstead and Taylor 1996, Smith and Standish 1997, Inman and Buck 1995, Gardner and others 2000, Halstead and McLaughlin 1998) contain much that is insightful and convincingly critical of simplistic or more traditional approaches to moral education but in, the nature of the case, are not able to explore fundamental issues relating to the governance of conduct in any depth. Certain influential longer works (Carr 1991, Pritchard 1996, Noddings 1984 and 2002a and at an earlier period Hirst 1972, Straughan 1988 and Wilson 1972) stoutly advocate particular points of view but pay little regard to alternative perspectives. Then there are, on the one hand, major works in the field of Moral Philosophy (MacIntyre 1982,1988, Slote 1989, Williams 1985 and Gert 1998) in which educational concerns are at most a minor consideration and, on the other, quasi official documents such as those from SCAA already referred to and the ad hoc pronouncements of politicians, journalists and others recorded in the press.

The existence of such a plethora of utterances and publications would seem to require rather than render redundant an attempt to arrive at a critical synthesis of the various perspectives which currently contribute to our moral understanding and relate these coherently to our thinking about moral education. In the following chapters, therefore, it is proposed to consider in some detail various approaches to the whole question of morality and its nature and the justification that may be given for particular moral claims. The underlying argument of this book will be fourfold. Firstly, it will be held that good and valid reasons may be given for doing and expecting others to do some things rather than others. The relativist view that no such claims may be validly and confidently asserted will therefore be rejected as, however, will some claims to the absolute validity of certain injunctions and the grounds upon which they are supposedly based. Indeed, our second underlying argument will be that although good and valid reasons for action may be given, there is no single, overriding principle grounding all moral claims and that, in many cases the application and weighting of various considerations will ultimately be a matter of individual judgement, wisdom and experience. Any satisfactory scheme of moral education must therefore give consideration to a range of moral perspectives. Thirdly, an attempt will be made to apply our general conclusions to two specific areas of moral concern in the modern world, namely those of sexual conduct and family life on the one hand and the obligations of citizenship and public life on the other. It will be suggested that, though often matters of deeply held personal or religious conviction, sexual behaviour and the conduct of family life are subject to the same kinds of moral consideration as other areas of conduct and, like them, are to be judged in terms of their contribution to the satisfactory lives of individuals. In relation to citizenship, it will be proposed that in democratic countries, the moral obligations of individuals relate not only to their private conduct but also to their status as citizens, bound sometimes to abide by laws of which they disapprove and collectively able to influence the actions of government, both domestically and in the world at large. Fourthly and finally, it will be argued that, though various means may be employed to further the moral development of the young, these only truly advance such development when they lead to the doing of what is right in the light of moral understanding and genuinely moral judgements.

CHAPTER 2

THE SCOPE OF MORAL EDUCATION

It will have escaped few people's notice that much of the recent panic about the moral shortcomings of the young has concerned what we may term palpable misdemeanours, of the kind commonly committed by the young, and most frequently though by no means solely by the young and excluded: acts of vandalism, burglary, random violence, disorderly public behaviour and the abuse of alcohol and drugs. Other equally palpable and socially undesirable acts, such as speeding, driving while under the influence of drink by middle-aged motorists, white collar crime which may deprive honest folk of their life savings, commercial practices which, though legal, cause massive damage to the environment or viciously exploit vulnerable workers at home or abroad, are rarely discussed in the context of moral education. Indeed, if they are discussed in moral terms at all it is by those of a distinctively progressive inclination, who are a quite different group from those who most frequently express outrage over the shortcomings of moral education. To this extent we may almost say that morality and moral education are presented as something applying predominantly to the poor and the young. This being so, one may be tempted to see both morality and moral education as no more than a means of social control or 'symbolic power' (Bourdieu and Passeron, 1970) achieving, when effective, that good social order which may otherwise need to be effected by the more costly means of heavy policing or military force.

This functionalist deconstruction of morality is not entirely without relevance in sensitising us to the implications of any pattern of supposed moral education aimed at achieving conformity to traditional norms of behaviour. The suppression of palpable misdemeanours, actual crime or acts of more or less undisputed wrong-doing, ranging from mass murder at one extreme to childish naughtiness at the other will not be central to our present discussion of moral education and in many cases does not fall within the purview of moral education as it will here be understood at all.

Children who misbehave at table or cause classroom disruption at school, adolescents who vandalise public property or terrorise old people, adults who commit fraud or abuse or harm the vulnerable may be perfectly aware, not only that what they do is wrong but also why it is wrong. The problem here is scarcely one of

12

not knowing the difference between right and wrong, however these terms are construed. Sometimes, of course, the problem may be pathological, in which case the solution falls within the field of medical treatment, and therefore outside the competence of traditional educators, such as parents and teachers. More often, the deficiency is one of surveillance and enforcement rather than the agent's understanding, a failure of containment rather than education. If learning is involved it is learning, not that certain actions are wrong, but that they will not be tolerated. Relevant moral issues here, however, do not concern the child's or young person's knowledge of right and wrong but the proper use of punishment in an educational or reformative context, appropriate levels of restriction and liberty appropriate to the young, the proper balance between the convenience of the mature and the exploratory needs of children and empirical questions about the most effective ways of socialising the young without producing obsessive conformity or resentful rebellion.

The answers to these latter questions will in turn be dependent upon further questions as to why it is that misdemeanours at various stages of development occur at all. We may be reluctant to talk about the 'causes' of deviancy or crime in even incipiently rational beings but it is certainly true that deviancy, at least in regard to publicly recognised norms, occurs more frequently in some social milieux than in others. It is unlikely that one explanation fits all or that the apparent requirement of justice notwithstanding, the same manner of treatment or the same degree of moral condemnation is always appropriate for two apparently similar anti-social acts.

For moral education to have been successful it is not only important that the learner's actions should normally be socially acceptable. This will hopefully be one result, and in itself no small achievement, but this is far from being the only or even the central goal of moral education. There are, furthermore, considerable problems about spelling out the requirements of good conduct in terms of specific injunctions of the form 'Always do this/never do that' given that purposive actions in a complex environment cannot readily be characterised in terms of their externally observable exponents. As with the outcomes of all genuinely educative processes, actual behaviour is but the external or symptomatic expression of inner cognitions or other states of mind which, by their very nature, have no one to one entailment with the world of material action. If specific acts or abstinences are sought, it is not moral education but some other more directly controlling process that is required.

There are, however, a number of more obvious and down to earth reasons why moral education couched in terms of specific injunctions is inadequate. It is difficult to imagine that any such list could ever be complete or not liable to change over time or according to circumstance. This is not just a contingent empirical matter. It is simply impossible to imagine actions of any category that may not in some circumstances be harmful, damaging or even downright wicked. It is a commonplace of ethical discussion that actions generally regarded as forbidden may in certain circumstances be permissible or even positively desirable. The circumstances which render actions right or wrong can also not be spelled out explicitly in advance. Even if this were possible in principle, which it is not, attempts to do so undermine the very simplicity which is the main argument in favour of explicit commands and prohibitions as the basis of moral education.

What is or is not moral may also be contentious or arbitrary. Public nudity or semi-nudity, the use of mild intoxicants or minor breaches of the law as a means of serious and conscientious protest would be obvious examples, yet these are some of the activities that most arouse the anger of those who complain of the laxness and ambiguity of current moral standards among the young. Such a simplistic conception of morality and moral education also fails to touch the serious moral choices with which individuals are faced in the conduct of their lives. The fact that conceptions of morality based on simple injunctions are characteristically negative makes them restrictive and controlling rather than encouraging positive moral aspiration. One could perhaps conceive a set of corresponding positive injunctions but these would raise even greater complexities than negative ones, insofar as prohibitions are necessarily less complex than positive instructions.

More seriously, any such list of prohibitions or commands necessarily raise but does not answer the question 'Why should/shouldn't I?' To be effective even as a simple mode of social control, moral education needs to engender commitment to some more general set of principles or sentiments. The learner needs to see, understand and above all acknowledge the reasons why some actions are to be undertaken and others not, for without such an understanding learners cannot adapt their conduct to the complex and changing circumstances of the moral life which, in most cases these days will go far beyond the horizons envisaged by their mentors.

There is one further important consideration. Moral judgement and evaluation upon whatever basis is one of the more important, fruitful and illuminating ways we have of appraising our own actions and those of others. It is part of humanity's intellectual and cultural heritage. Opinion may be divided as to whether such a mode of thought was bound to arise, or arise in the form in which we have it, or whether its development has been culturally fortuitous. Conceivably there could be sophisticated cultures which lack the conception of morality as we understand it but human life would arguably be the poorer without it. Someone with no moral understanding (if such an individual can be imagined) is excluded from the mainstream culture of the modern world and someone whose understanding is restricted by a simplistic conception of morality is correspondingly deprived.

It is an assumption, perhaps no more than an assumption, for the doctrines of predestination and determinism continue to have their proponents, that human actions are the result of choices, or may in principle be so. We act for reasons upon more or less reflection. In the absence of such an assumption most of our educational, political and juridical institutions would make no sense. Unlike the caterpillar which must eat and eat of its prescribed food plant until nature determines it is time for it to pupate, we not only have the opportunity but often cannot escape the necessity of choosing how we shall respond to our situation, what course of action or even what way of life we shall pursue. If there are societies or even social milieux in our own society in which the range of options is less extensive than in others, it is nevertheless inconceivable that any life is entirely constrained from minute to minute, though it may be largely prescribed by human convention.

For human beings, the option of rejection and disobedience always remains, however harsh the penalties may be. Like it or not we are constantly forced to choose, though often the choice may seem easy or obvious enough.

Choices that relate purely to the agent's advantage are choices of prudence. But other choices concern not only the agent's advantage but recognise what some postmodernists (Levinas 1978) have referred to as the essential otherness of the Other. The making of an important class of choices recognises that the world, the world of other human beings and also the animal and material world as Midgeley (1994) convincingly argues, do not exist simply to serve the interests of the 'I' but have their own separate existence. In the case of human beings, these include their own legitimate interests that, along with the aims interests and desires of the agent him or herself, may ultimately constitute reasons guiding the agent's acts. If the distinction between the moral and the prudential is sometimes less sharp than is supposed it has, nevertheless, been a central focus of traditional ethical concern throughout the post-classical era.

The making of reflective choices necessarily entails the consideration of reasons. It is the nature of those reasons and their implications in practice that has traditionally constituted the study of Ethics. Though moral education is something very different from the study of such bodies of theory, not to say commitment to the conclusions of any one such body, it will be argued that without some acquaintance with such ideas, at however elementary a level, no supposed programme of moral education can fully justify the name.

Human actions are susceptible of a number of explanations, some of which are subjects of moral appraisal and some not. At one end of the scale are involuntary movements. To call these actions at all is something of a misnomer. The (literal) knee-jerk reaction, jumping when startled, twitching, belching, hiccoughing and so on fall into this category. There may be some obligation to control these in some circumstances, such as at a funeral, or during an orchestral concert and dignity, self-control and consideration for others may be important moral qualities, but in themselves these 'actions' raise few moral questions.

More controversial are those actions which are said to be the results of pathologies, obsessions or addictions. Could the woman have refrained from shoplifting, the man from drinking or the priest from interfering with young boys, or not? Are we here in the presence of moral actions for which censure and sanctions are appropriate or medical conditions, which demand therapy and compassion? Sadly, but perhaps inevitably, our legal system tends to favour the former. At a social and human level, our moral education will affect the way we handle our own obsessions. It will also affect the way we respond to the results of obsessions, addictions and so on in others.

Other actions may be explained in terms of emotions. The agent was angry, frightened or jealous, overcome by pity, disgust or ambition. The way in which the emotions are handled has perennially been one of the central topics of moral discussion, particularly in relation to the moral education of the young. The emotions, many philosophers have argued, should be controlled, subject to reason and the will, even eliminated from consideration altogether as motives for our actions. Whatever is happening elsewhere, upper lips, especially in young males of the elite, have been expected to remain unwaveringly stiff. Yet it is clearly not the experiencing of emotions that has been so roundly condemned, but the yielding to them, and even then our judgements are ambivalent. To be called a cold fish is no compliment but an expression of contempt. The person who sometimes yields to emotion is often forgiven or even actually preferred to one who never does. We may be tempted, like a good Aristotelian, to suppose that those whose moral education has been successful would permit an appropriate degree of influence to their emotions or even that the function of certain literary works (Aristotle *Poetics)* was to allow individuals to, in some sense, purge or adjust certain emotions so that they were properly directed and experienced in due measure. But paradoxically, someone who attempted to ascertain just the right degree to which his or her emotions should be given reign and then acted in precise accordance therewith would be insufferable.

Along with emotional responses, tradition, custom or habit may also provide non-rational explanations for our actions. Miss Jones may take coffee at 11 and on Sunday afternoons Major Smith may walk round the village and return via the churchyard in time for tea. In themselves such habits, customs or whatever may have no moral significance or may be socially useful ways of imposing regularity on our activities, or enabling people to know what to expect. The school may have a full staff meeting in the first, sixth and penultimate week of term. One writes the date at the head of a letter and the signature at the bottom. Work in the office begins at 9 and the flower show will be on the second weekend of August.

Habits and customs are not, however, exempt from moral appraisal or irrelevant to moral education. As the derivation of our word 'moral' suggests, adherence to custom may be no morally neutral matter. There have been writers enough (Burke 1790, Oakeshott 1962, MacIntyre 1982) who have regarded tradition as a value in itself, an essential ingredient in a way of life and the identity of those who follow it, which it is of the essence of morality to preserve. People may speak approvingly of those who follow the old-fashioned ways and avoid those they find too modern, though examination may suggest that old-fashioned ways have other, more obviously moral virtues, such as simplicity, honesty and straightforwardness, while those that are characterised as 'modern' appear to exhibit the corresponding vices of deviousness and unreliability. Reference to 'time-honoured customs' may appeal to the authority of our elders or to rose-tinted views of times past but it is also a reminder that those customs have served well enough up to now and that the reverberations of change are unpredictable. It is a moral issue whether the mere fact that something has been regularly done in the past is a reason to continue doing it in the face of evident disadvantage or injustice to which it gives rise, or whether the peace and good order which changeless ways preserve simply serves to perpetuate established privilege.

Changes to what has long been done and is well understood may give rise to confusion and misunderstanding. Over time people come to rely on things being done in a certain way and change may result in the disappointment of legitimate expectations. The expectation that things will be done as they have been done before is often a tacit assumption in many of our personal and family relations, as well as in more formal, e.g. financial, arrangements where it is assumed that established custom and practice will prevail unless otherwise specified. Even the following or flouting of convention in lesser matters such as dress codes or the adoption of formal or informal manners or modes of speech may be of greater moral significance than the acts themselves may suggest. Such behaviour may signal the acceptance or rejection of more significant social practices or relationships, notably those of authority and respect upon which, in the not entirely unjustified view of some, good social order may depend.

Unlike habits and customs, actions deliberately undertaken in pursuit of our conscious goals or interests have, to a perhaps excessive degree, often been the central concern of moral theorising. What personal goals are desirable or permissible, what means to their achievement are justifiable and to what degree they should accommodate the goals and interests of others or take account of other considerations, must be a key part of any well founded process of moral education. Addressing such issues in the current social and educational climate is, however, no easy matter. Given that rational choice is central to any discussion of appropriate conduct, such discussion implies a measure of intellectual rigour, discrimination and abstraction which may be at variance with what some currently regard as good educational practice. The patronising assumption may even be made that such matters are beyond the capacity or foreign to the interests of many future citizens. The view that some goals or ways of life are preferable to or more worthy than others or that some ways of achieving them, even when they fall within the law, ought to be avoided is all too easily represented as authoritarianism or the indoctrination of merely social preferences. It will be an underlying assumption of the pages that follow that a consideration of the grounds upon which both ends and means ought to be chosen must be central to any programme of moral education that is anything more than socialisation or training in conformity.

Finally, some attention must be given to the notion of 'values', a term which has achieved some currency in educational contexts, to the extent that Values Education is now commonly used as the more fashionable synonym for Moral Education. Our values are essentially attitudes of admiration or approbation towards certain ways of behaviour or aspects of our way of life, which we regard as important to preserve or be guided by. We may speak of our own democratic values of freedom and equality, the heroic values of the Roman soldier, the Victorian values of thrift, hard work and respectability or, indeed, the macho values of the street gang. When we speak of the values of an individual or group we typically speak descriptively rather than evaluatively. To say that someone's actions or words reflect their Victorian, public school or Christian values is, in itself, neither to commend nor to criticise them and social scientists may refer to their subjects' values or value systems without compromising their own ethical neutrality. It is, therefore, perfectly possible to teach about 'values', those of our own society or others, without having it as one's central intention to improve the learner's moral character or conduct. This potential for objectivising and thereby relativising judgements of value may account for the distaste for the term shown by such writers as Himmelfarb (1995) when discussing morality and moral education. This descriptive characteristic of the term is also present in the name of the so-called 'values clarification' approach to moral education in which the aim was to enable students to understand certain value positions and their implications while, as far as possible, refraining from influencing their value choices.

Talbot and Tate (1997) pose the question 'Which values should we teach?' and reply ' *Our* values of course?' Attempts to discover what 'our values' are by means of a survey followed by the announcement that these are the values which 'our' society authorises schools to inculcate is, despite these authors' explicit rejection of relativism elsewhere, a prime example of the objectivising and relativising of values. Values, on this view, are not up for appraisal in their own terms but are to be inculcated because they are ours and are 'authorised' by consensus. The assumption is that the values of our society are what they are and that is all there is to be said. Moral reflection becomes a matter of matching our actions or intended actions to what our society's values are supposed to be and acting accordingly. There is no possibility of standing outside the supposed value system of our society or attempting to criticise that system itself.

Such a pessimistic view is unconvincing. It may be true that, as Bradley (1927) says, we owe the whole of our cultural and intellectual apparatus to our society but this does not mean that we cannot turn this apparatus on our society itself, far less that we cannot turn our powers of critical scrutiny upon one aspect of our society, namely the evaluative attitudes of its members. There is much to be said for knowing what values are or were held in our society, in particular parts of it or beyond its borders. This is certainly part of the younger generation's social education and may even be helpful in enabling them to develop the values that will guide their own conduct and shape their own characters and aspirations. But that something is held to be true by a million housewives, ninety per cent of all car owners or a representative cross section of society is no guide to validity in morals any more than it is in any other form of enquiry.

Values, therefore, though fundamental to the moral education of future citizens, cannot be exempt from critical scrutiny. Questions such as 'What values are most worthy?' and 'What should someone's most fundamental aspirations be?' cannot be baulked or replaced by the easier question of what values are held by other people, and are as crucial to any consideration of moral education as those other traditional moral questions 'What should I do?' and 'How should life be lived?' It is enabling learners to respond to these questions in a considered and well-informed manner, rather than in terms of simplistic reactions to one's own or other people's choices, actions, attitudes or beliefs that is moral education's central aim.

CHAPTER 3

MORALITY AND RELIGION

Those who complain most bitterly about the moral condition of the young are often inclined to blame what they term the moral relativism of our age. We have supposedly lost confidence in our previous moral certainties and hesitate to assert them confidently and unambiguously, with the result that the young are given no firm sense of moral direction and may reply to statements that some things are right and others wrong by saying 'Who says so?' or 'That's just your opinion' or in some other way express doubt either about the statement itself or about the meaningfulness of such statements in general.

It would certainly make life easier in the eyes of some if we could say that morality, good citizenship or whatever consisted of a round number of Thou shalts or Thou shalt nots which could be propositionally expressed, given to be learned and tested in the manner of course or lesson objectives as they are sometimes currently conceived. In itself this would not entirely satisfy those who see moral education as a means of controlling the masses. To know that something is in some sense 'wrong' is no guarantee that it will not be done. At very least our list of dos and don'ts would need to be backed up by a rigorous regime of conditioning, systematic expressions of praise and blame or unmistakeable modes of reward and punishment. But for such a regime a clearly articulated, unequivocal and readily understood list of injunctions is a sine qua non. A firm framework with wriggle room is required so that learners 'know where they are'. The approach is spelled out clearly enough by the proponents of so-called assertive discipline or 'character building' in the modern American interpretation of the term.

In the next chapter it is proposed to consider in detail the whole question of moral relativism versus absolute moral values. First, however, it is convenient to deal separately with one supposed source of absolute moral values and moral commands, namely religion. Many but by no means all of those who characterise effective moral education in terms of explicit and supposedly irrefutable moral injunctions, may base their claims on religion and attribute the supposed deterioration in the moral condition of society to the decline of religious belief. Such people may see a revival of religious belief as a means, possibly the only means, of solving the moral problems of society.

There are usually two claims involved in this position: first, that religious belief and observance would have a profoundly beneficial effect on behaviour, particularly that of the young and second, that God's will is the source of moral values. These two claims are not synonymous. It is perfectly possible to hold that belief that God wishes certain things to be done or avoided would have a beneficial effect on conduct while thinking that any such belief, or indeed any religious belief whatsoever, is false.

So what of the effects of religious belief upon conduct, regardless of whether or not it is true? We may draw a veil over the many acknowledged atrocities carried out in the name of religion, whether by cynical manipulators who have used religion for their own ends or, more tragically, by sincere believers, carried away by fervent idealism or motivated by the hope of reward or fear of eternal punishment. Such has too often been the stuff of shallow anti-religious polemic. Even those who, like the present writer, have no religious belief are, in all honesty, bound to recognise that the Judeo-Christian religion embodies many of the most admirable of moral values. With the prohibitions of the Old Testament commandments that we should not kill, steal, covet, bear false witness, commit adultery and so on, it is difficult to quarrel. The same is true, only more so, of the virtues enjoined in the New Testament, notably in the Sermon on the Mount. Who can doubt the moral insight of Him who commended humility, mercy, the making of peace, mourning for the sorrows of others and a general hungering and thirsting after righteousness when the prevailing values were, as some might say they still are, those of war, violence, wealth, power, arrogance and pride. The command that we should love our neighbour as ourselves quite simply seems to say it all, particularly if, like the good Samaritan, we see all as our neighbours whom we encounter or simply pass on our way through life. No doubt similar claims may be made for other religions and if no mention is made of them here, this simply reflects the writer's disinclination to speak of that with which he is but superficially familiar.

That the moral virtues of love, mutual support, compassion and forgiveness are honoured and not infrequently practised in many religious communities and that undertakings of great humanity world wide have been inspired by religious faith therefore goes without saying. It is also highly plausible that if many simple and some not so simple folk can be led to believe that a loving and powerful being takes an interest in our conduct and is pleased by our good deeds and saddened by our shortcomings, or at a cruder level, that our virtues will be rewarded by eternal bliss and our failings punished by the unspeakable sufferings of eternal hell-fire, this may have some small influence on how we behave. There are, however, some obvious objections to basing our moral education on the promotion of a return to religion and the validity of a set of explicit and absolute religious commands. These objections apply irrespective of whether or not belief in God is true.

To begin with, not all human virtues and excellences are readily compatible with religious belief as it has traditionally been understood. Like the Greeks, we value a certain measure of proper pride and self respect, an appropriate measure of confidence in one's worth and achievement. We also value doubt, enquiry, criticism and independence of mind, and may even see these as central to our culture. It simply is the case, and for reasons that are not entirely contingent, that these qualities lead many, though not all, to reject religious belief. If we have made moral commitment too dependent on religious belief it is hardly surprising if, when belief in God is rejected along with belief in Santa Claus, some are inclined to say with Nietzsche (1885) that if God is dead all is permitted and then with Saint Paul, 'When I was a child I thought as a child but now that I am a man . . . . ' . To simply suppress disbelief would imply a level of oppression, propaganda and persecution unacceptable even to thoughtful believers.

It similarly just is the case that there are a variety of religions in the world and there would appear to be no philosophically reliable way of deciding which, if any, is true. To suspend belief while disinterestedly seeking to discover whether one's own religious tradition is the true one would be unacceptable to the faithful of many religions, yet tolerance of belief, if not of conduct, is an important virtue, at least in the liberal West. It appears to be a characteristic of religious belief that it depends on belief in its total truth and has historically often been incompatible with the possible truth of other religions or even internal heresies. The stronger our belief, the greater our commitment, the more we are encouraged to crucify our reason particularly when, like Abraham (Kierkegaard 1843) we find ourselves apparently commanded by God or those whom we must believe to speak in his name, to do what our reason tells us is the most heinous of crimes. Exclusivity is essential to religious belief which so sharply distinguishes between believer and infidel, saved and damned, the chosen people and the sons and daughters of the uncircumcised. Mutatis mutandis, the same may doubtless be said for the various religions of the world. Outsiders may not only be seen as less worthy of beneficence than believers but even legitimate objects of hatred.

To make religion the basis of morality is to make obedience the supreme, indeed, the only virtue. It is often represented as a virtue by the powerful and seen as an essential element in the characters of good children, soldiers and wives. Yet it is far from clear that obedience is really a virtue at all. It may seem to be so in certain situations when there is no time for reflection or argument, in the heat of battle or on the high seas, but in these cases it is not the obedience that is the ultimate value but utility and the greater good that may depend on prompt and unquestioning compliance.

One can scarcely doubt that, historically, belief in God's power to reward virtue and, more especially to punish vice in the most terrifying way, has been seen as a most effective way of enforcing good behaviour. Given this, it is difficult to see how anyone who thought there was the remotest chance that belief in such a God might be true could live a life other than one of the most virtuous strivings and the purest of thoughts, yet there appear to be some who are both believers and sinners. As the victim of any armed robbery probably knows, it is prudent not to anger someone who wields absolute power. The Greeks, whose notion of the good life was somewhat different from our own, distinguished very clearly between virtue and the will of the all-powerful Gods. The stories of Hippolytus, Prometheus and especially

Arachnee all concern individuals who anger the Gods by exhibiting qualities we are bound to admire. This is particularly true in the case of Arachnee who continues to defy the angry goddess even after she has been turned into a spider, by continuing to spin a thread more fine than could be produced by any human being, or by the Goddess herself. There is also much to despise in the action of the God who brings Abraham to the point of committing the most dastardly of all acts as a test of his faith. If ever there was a moral truth, it is that might is not right and that power is not moral authority.

The threat of harm or promise of great reward may perhaps excuse the performance of some acts that would otherwise attract censure. Not only can the power to punish or reward not make wrong or morally neutral acts virtuous however. It may actually deprive otherwise good actions of their virtuous character by making them self-interested. Paradoxically, in a world in which all actions are known to a rewarding and punishing God, the only truly virtuous acts would be those of mercy and loving kindness or whatever which, like the sparing of the three women of Jericho, were performed in defiance of God's will. Some who repudiate the notion that believers act virtuously out of fear of punishment or hope of reward may claim that it is virtuous to obey God's commandments simply out of love for him, or gratitude for his creation of us. This is, at least, a more reputable version of the Divine Command theory of morality than that considered above but it has the philosophical disadvantage of making gratitude and love virtues independent of God's will. To reply that love and gratitude are virtues because God commands them would, of course, get us no further forward at all.

Any uncomplicated body of guiding doctrine raises problems regarding the interpretation of its explicit injunctions. Thou shalt not kill. But what, precisely is to fall within the definition of killing? Self-defence? War? Acquiescence in one's society's use of capital punishment? Economic arrangements that result in the early death of workers in the Third World? Does the prohibition apply only to human beings, or to all sentient creatures or indeed, to the whole of creation. Similar problems of interpretation arise in relation to stealing, the bearing of false witness, the commission of adultery and so on. One branch of the Christian religion resolves the interpretation problem by conferring the ultimate right of interpretation upon a specified individual, but why should we believe this to be justified? The right does not appear to be conferred in the recorded utterances of Christ himself but to have been claimed later by others who, to say the least, may have had a political interest in doing so.

There is also the problem of legitimate exceptions. It is not difficult to imagine situations in which it would seem legitimate or even obligatory to lie, steal, kill, fail to honour father or mother or even, as in the case of Noah's daughters, commit incest. Certain breaches of divine prohibitions seem more serious than others, but upon what basis can such a judgement be made, since all are forbidden. We can scarcely haggle with God if what is to be morally justified is determined by his command. Pascal (1657), in his letter concerning the Jesuit practice of casuistry, warns us of the danger of interpreting divine commands too specifically so that all that is not explicitly forbidden is, however morally obnoxious, regarded as permitted.

Readers who remember the days of apartheid in South Africa may recall hearing eminently devout white South Africans protesting in all sincerity that since the prohibition of discrimination on grounds of colour is not scriptural, it is no more than a matter of opinion or personal preference, not to say of political propaganda.

However, the final and most telling argument against the Divine Command theory of morality is brought out by the question, already raised by Plato in the *Euthyphro,* of whether certain things are good because they are commanded by God or whether God commands them because they are good. The first possibility seems to raise quite insuperable difficulties. If good simply means that which God commands, then to say that God and what he wills is good is circular and meaningless. Of course, that which God wills is willed by God, but we have learned nothing new. We cannot meaningfully praise God for his goodness. We can only grovellingly glorify him for his power or pour out our gratitude for his forbearance in not condemning us to instant destruction, an act which would instantly become 'good' if He were to will it.

Christians, at least, believe that God commands that we love each other. We instantly recognise the sublime goodness of such a command and when we obey it we do so with a clear conscience. But supposing God had taken it into his head to command us to hate one another or to hate certain particular groups of others, Americans, Jews, Albigensians or whoever? Believers, of course, will quickly point out that God could do no such thing. But why not? Because God is good, obviously enough. But until God has commanded one way or the other nothing, on the Divine Command theory of morality, is either good or bad. From this it will be seen that Divine Command theory is, in fact, a form of nihilism. In this it resembles the consensus view of morality or notions of morality based on the pronouncements of a particular guru or charismatic leader. For it asserts that nothing, love, hatred, mercy, cruelty or whatever is either good or bad of itself but only becomes so when it is designated as such by someone's say so.

The above pages have not in any way been intended as an attack on religion, merely an attempt to show that in a thinking age we cannot rely on a return to religion as our primary basis for moral education. The implication of the above remarks is to assert the autonomy of moral judgement from religious belief, which makes it perfectly meaningful for a devout person to believe that God exists and loves us and wishes us to follow the good and eschew the evil, and even that His explicit commands reaching us through the human understanding of His prophets and priests, point us in the right direction. Such a view would not seem inconsistent with the belief that a merciful God to whom all our thoughts and desires are known, would approve our sincere efforts to understand and do what is right, even when this exceeds the boundaries of what is laid down by historical understandings of His desire that we should strive to be good, or its necessarily limited human expression in the words and understandings of our contemporaries. What is more difficult to accept is the Gnostic view, expressed by Kierkegaard among others, that God makes certain awesome demands on human beings which cannot be known as a result of human thought or striving, that such efforts constitute arrogance, and that we must await the enlightenment of God's grace or follow the literal word of His scriptures or their interpretation by His ministers.

Both believers and non-believers may also concur in the admission that both individuals and societies may make ghastly errors with regard to what ideals it is worthwhile to strive for and what price is worth paying in their pursuit. If, subsequently in a quiet moment, in a lull of peace after some a senseless conflict or disaster brought about by greed, misguided ambition or long standing hatred, there is a moment of regret, remorse, reconciliation or quiet reflection and a determination to live differently in future, and if some wish to describe this moment as a moment of God's grace, so be it.

CHAPTER 4

THE STATUS OF MORAL JUDGEMENTS

To reject religion as a source of absolute moral values does not take us very far towards an answer to the question of whether such statements as 'You ought not to do that','That is the right thing to do' or 'This is a better way to live' can in any sense be regarded as objectively true. When the Chief Executive of the School Curriculum and Assessment Authority (SCAA) (1996b) declared that a prime task for moral education was to 'slay the dragon of relativism' the identity of the beast he had in mind was not entirely clear. Strictly, moral relativism is usually taken to be the view that moral standards vary from time to time and place to place. The relevant locus classicus is the story of Darius, narrated by Herodotus, who noted that the Callatians customarily ate their dead fathers and were appalled to learn that the Greeks burned theirs on funeral pyres, and vice versa (Ladd 1985). Certain practices of the Inuit, killing off their old folk when they became too old and feeble to make the long annual migratory journeys and the fluidity of their conjugal arrangements, are also often cited in this connection.

It is unlikely, however, that the Chief Executive was concerned only with moral relativism in this technical sense. The whole history of moral ideas has been a series of intellectually impressive assaults on the notions of absolute moral truths prevailing at different times over the centuries. From the time of Socrates to the end of the Middle Ages, history is littered with the corpses of those who challenged such ideas and the authority of those who promulgated them. Typically, such challenges were met not with argument but repression and in many cases torture and death. The Reformation challenges the notion of authoritative moral pronouncements backed by religion by insisting on the rights of individual conscience and individual access to and interpretation of the scriptures. Fundamental to Enlightenment thinking is the right to doubt and seek certainty through evidence and reason. At this point the notion of absolute truth, including moral truth, remains intact insofar as lay philosophers continued to believe that reason would reveal something that Hobbes (1642) likens to Newton's 'idoneous principle of tractation' (i.e. the force of gravity), a general principle which would allow moral questions to be resolved with the specificity and assurance of physical science. This route to certainty is, however, cut off by Hume's argument that neither empirical facts nor analytic inference can ultimately ground moral injunctions. If our moral sentiments are emotive responses they provide no guarantee of validity or consistency between individuals, let alone between individuals widely separated by time or space. Hegel (1807) certainly acknowledges an ultimate moral reality to which the Spirit or, as he calls it the 'Idea', embodied in successive human civilisations, is supposedly tending, but for him the moral foundations of any particular society are a product of time and place.

It is a short but significant step from this to the likening of moral talk to expressions like 'Hurrah' and 'Boo' (Ayer 1967) shouted by the supporters of opposing sides in the rowdy shindig of moral dispute. Those attempting to support absolute moral values are further assailed by rebellious youth armed with stories of the disreputable genealogy of morals as supplied by Freud, Marx and especially Nietzsche. This latter is particularly unhelpful to moral educators in his claim (Nietzsche 1885) that the noble and admirable have no regard for morality. As Dostoevsky's Raskholnikov puts it (Dostoyevsky 1881)'Great men do not fear to be criminals.' Or, in the modern idiom 'Only wimps are goodie-goodies.' Foucault (1973) takes the argument of disreputable genealogy one step further with his claim that all discourse and not just moral discourse is concerned to define reality in support of power and others such as Baudrillard (1989) and Fish (1989) argue that we are prevented by prevailing discourses from gaining a reliable picture of reality, let alone making meaningful moral judgements. Meanings, contexts and perceptions change from instant to instant so that, it is claimed, even the notion of continuously existing individuals making judgements and acting upon them cannot be sustained. Rorty, (1989) having earlier rejected the possibility of objective knowledge of reality on either analytic or empirical grounds (Rorty 1979) maintains, but does not attempt to demonstrate, that different moral views are simply 'different ways of speaking' and that there is nothing more to be said.

Given this intellectual tradition it would be absurd, in the context of Western culture, to think that, as with the decisive stroke of a hero's sword slaying a noxious beast, we can cast aside our doubts about the possibility of basing the moral education of the young on a specific set of supposedly absolute truths. Many of these doctrines, and more especially certain garbled versions of them, are heady and exciting to the intelligent young who will be impatient of simplistic and, in any case indecisive, arguments in support of supposedly absolute moral injunctions. Many young adults of an age to be in a position to be involved in the education of children will be aware of these currents in our culture, even though they may be unable to articulate them for themselves, and necessarily be uncomfortable about asserting moral injunctions as if they were indubitable.

That the Chief Executive of SCAA should not have troubled to distinguish between these various attacks on the objectivity of moral judgements is unsurprising for he was clearly not interested in a point for point academic refutation. Indeed, elsewhere he himself (Talbot and Tate 1997) fairly conspicuously declines to defend the objectivity of moral values. The focus of his interest is not in any of the above forms of 'relativism' but in their opposite, a set of supposedly authoritative value statements that can be enunciated and inculcated without equivocation, deviation or hesitation. If they cannot be grounded in 'God or human nature' they may be established by consensus as 'our' values, which the public 'authorises' its employees teaching in schools to inculcate in their name, a statement of moral relativism, not to say nihilism, if ever there was one.

To the educator as opposed to the mere moulder of public opinion and conduct, however, the status of moral utterances is of cardinal importance for to be educated in any form of understanding is not merely to have learnt the content of its discourse or even to follow its injunctions and recommendations, but to understand both their sense and their significance. If they are true, what is it for them to be true, with what degree of certainty may they be asserted and upon what grounds? Without this information individuals are not able to employ criticism in pursuit of their own further moral development in the light of later experience and reflection. In short, individuals are inhibited in their further autonomous moral growth as they would be in their independent scientific or historical development if they were simply inculcated with the conclusions of Science or History (or 'our' Science or 'our' version of History) and denied an introduction to the methods and manner of scientific or historical thinking.

If our understanding of morality is not in some sense true, it must seem unclear by what right we impose it on the next generation with all the prestige and authority of the educational system, or attempt to inculcate it by means of rebuke and sanction. Given the propensity, indeed the intention, of moral utterance to control the actions and influence the judgement of others, moral claims, not to mention whole programmes of moral education, not based on some such presumption, appear distinctly disreputable, not to say politically dangerous, given the opportunities for uncontrolled manipulation of educational programmes. There are particular dangers in using consensus as a way of deriving a set of authoritative moral values given the inconstant and fickle nature of public opinion in moral matters, and the fact that so many of the grosser moral atrocities of the nineteenth and twentieth centuries were so plainly committed with the consensual support or acquiescence of the communities that perpetrated them. Moral education may, of course, be delivered in a value-free way: 'These are the values of the society in which you will grow up and you will need to know about them if you are to operate successfully and to your advantage in that society'. Moral education on this view would simply be a social or vocational skill.

A number of somewhat unconvincing arguments have been put forward on both sides of the debate between moral relativists and the proponents of absolute moral values and depend on such simplistic formulations of the issue as 'Is relativism true or false?' or 'Are there any absolute moral truths?' The first of these allows Talbot (1999) to envisage asking an avowed relativist whether relativism is absolutely true or only relatively so. Either way, like the man who is required either to admit or deny that he has stopped beating his wife, the relativist seems caught in the trap. Relativists who claim that relativism is absolutely true seem to be denying their own relativism but to say that it is only relatively true seems like an admission that some moral truths, somewhere, are absolutely true. But, of course, the whole point of relativism is ultimately to deny that the very notion of moral claims being true or false is meaningful at all, so that the question of whether their supposed truth is relative or absolute cannot arise.

The term 'absolute moral truths' may also conceal a number of ambiguities. Of particular interest here is that between the particular and the general. We may, for example, believe that the statement 'You ought not to steal' may be false under some circumstances as, for example when Hugo's Jean Valjean (Hugo 1862) steals bread to feed a starving child, or that there could be societies in which our concept of property and therefore of theft do not apply. This, however, need not prevent us from believing with absolute conviction and justification that it would be wrong to steal this young man's wallet here, now. In order to believe this we need not first believe that some such general proposition as that acts of stealing are always and absolutely wrong. Talbot's use of the self-referring argument in this connection may seem to score a knock down ad hominem debating point against the relativist but has, in fact, little purchase on the many serious reasons that have been given for doubting various proposed brands of absolute truth propounded over the centuries

It must equally be said that the often quoted argument from cultural variation cuts little ice. As Talbot and others quite rightly point out, cultural variation may simply embody different ways of expressing the same underlying moral value. Eating the dead or solemnly burning them on a funeral pyre may both be ways of showing reverence and respect and the Inuit way of dealing with the old and infirm may show as much responsibility and compassion for the old as our own practices. But the fact of cultural variation does not demonstrate that all practices, let alone all actions, are equally good or bad. Some cultural practices may be and no doubt are the result of cruelty, mean mindedness or the desire of some groups to dominate and abuse others. That we should not judge other societies or cultures is, of course, a perfectly valid scientific rule of social or anthropological investigation. This, however, is something quite different from a substantive moral conclusion. To say that, as a matter of fact, different groups embrace different values or hold different moral beliefs is quite different from claiming that no customs, practices or actions can validly be judged preferable to any others. Such a conclusion would render illusory all claims to social or moral reform and plays into the hands of cynical conservative critics who argue that efforts to bring about a fairer or more equal society are ultimately without moral justification. If evidence of cultural variation is of interest to the moral educator, it is because it enables the significant distinction to be drawn between those differences in custom and practice which are of no moral moment and should not be viewed judgementally and those which indicate important differences of attitude towards persons or the world in general and may properly invite reform, either in the other culture or in our own.

A slightly different version of the attack on the possibility of objective moral judgements, usually referred to as subjectivism, is to suggest that the source of such judgements lies not in the world but in the emotional response of the person who judges. It is, of course, the case that the rightness or wrongness of actions seems to have no existence in observable fact but this does not show that no good reasons at all can be given for preferring some actions to others or that these reasons do not often relate to those actions' observable or predictable consequences. These reasons refer to the real world and are objective in the sense that they are unaffected by our wishes and emotions (Rachels 1999). If we respond to some actions with emotions of moral indignation or delight, these emotions are not the grounds but the consequence of our approval or disapproval.

Alongside the history of critical attacks on various notions of absolute moral demands, there have been influential bodies of moral theory which set out to replace traditional and discredited views of morality by philosophically more defensible foundations for moral judgement. Anscombe (1958) and MacIntyre (1981) among others have dismissed these as attempts to replace the moral laws of traditional religion by moral laws prescribed by the new religion of reason. Various of these attempts will be discussed in detail in the chapters that follow, where it will be argued that these may often furnish sound and valid reasons for approving some particular actions and rejecting others, but that each falls short of providing a comprehensive account of all moral judgements. In the absence of some divinely authorised list of prescriptions which may be relied upon to govern the lives of individuals, it may be tempting to seek some comprehensive general principle to which individual cases may be referred, but this is to mistake the nature of moral reasoning and to commit Hobbes' error of seeking an 'idoneous principle' on the model of a scientific law enabling us to account for all moral phenomena, to legislate for all moral situations. Equally, however, it is a misapprehension of the nature of morality to hesitate to guide and encourage the young to develop the capacity for making moral judgements on the grounds that no such principles can be found. Those who respond in this way, like those who reject notions of good and bad because they seem to have no existence in empirical fact, resemble those scientists who used to reject religion on the grounds that they could find no proof of the existence of God comparable with the evidence for the inverse square law, or those more ancient philosophers who rejected the evidence of their senses because, unlike Mathematics, they were not rooted in irrefutable logic. Such thinkers are not so much looking in the wrong place for the solution to their problems but, rather, do not know what they are looking for.

We earlier saw how discovery of a source of absolute moral values would, in principle, enable us to develop a pure transmission model of moral education in which the educator was the agent of an authority, divine, personal, collective or abstract in which the educator was knowledgeable and pupils essentially ignorant or prone to backsliding. That such a source was rational rather than transcendental would not affect the issue, for those who could demonstrate the link between their demands and the overriding principle would win for themselves the moral right of absolute command. Nor would such a conception of morality and consequent view of moral education necessarily involve an exclusively didactic style of teaching. Pupils could be set work enabling them to 'discover' the correct answers to the sorts of moral dilemmas they would be likely to face in their lives by working out which conclusions could be linked back to overriding principle and which could not. A discussion-based approach to Personal, Social and Moral Education might all too easily be conceived in such terms!

Perhaps, in some stable, primitive societies such a morally authoritative relationship between the generations may have existed and even been advantageous. There may have been times when the old could plausibly say to the young 'What we have been, you are now. What we are now you will surely become. We pass on to you the experience we have gained in life, that you may better follow the path we have trodden before you'. The maxims and ecomiums of the successful and socially approved life may have been passed on without too much concern for the nature and status of justification other than prudence or tradition themselves. If life was ever thus it certainly is so no longer. If the older generation are often inclined to abdicate the guidance of the young, it may not be because they are infected with relativism but simply because they have no guidance to give. They know only too well that the young have a better understanding of their own life conditions than they have and that the certainties they thought they possessed are not so much misguided as no longer apposite. Under these circumstances 'Well, you have your own lives to lead. You must decide for yourselves what you do' is not an expression of relativism but an honest recognition of the limits of one's experience. It is also a singularly appropriate moral stance to take when one has exhausted the satisfactions of life to the limits of one's invention and strength and accepts that the young are also entitled to probe the potential of their own lives in their own generation to the full.

But we do not need to make the question of guiding or even socialising the young more agonising than it is. Though the adult generation may doubt its former moral certainties, it is still entitled to protect itself and others against anti-social acts. Throwing food on the floor, interrupting adult conversation, damaging or taking other people's property, driving while drunk, issuing fraudulent accounts, blowing up buildings full of people . . . Such actions may be condemned and if necessary punished confidently and without inhibition. Our justifications for doing so are immediate and obvious: 'because it ruins the carpet, because Daddy and Mr. Jones are enjoying their conversation and you are spoiling it, because you might injure someone, because fraudulent accounting may leave people with nothing to live on in their old age' and so on. What further reasons could be required? We do not have to add that such actions are "wrong" because they give rise to more pain than pleasure, cannot be made a universal maxim, or infringe the fifth commandment. Such considerations are not without significance in the moral education of the young but do not properly belong to the context of reproving or sanctioning particular and manifestly anti-social acts. Equally, philosophical relativism, the fact that we are a multi-ethnic, multi-cultural society or that conflicts between individual rights and collective utility cannot be conclusively resolved and so on are also of little relevance here.

The development of intellectual and critical aspects of moral judgement, however, cannot be ignored. Though we, unlike Hobbes, may accept that there is no single principle of moral explanation, such principles play an important part in the reflective moral life and must therefore be an important ingredient in moral education. That an action or policy will bring more pleasure than pain is certainly a reason in favour of undertaking or implementing it, but may or may not prove conclusive. We may, for instance, decide to reject it because it infringes the rights of a small number of individuals. But very great benefits may, with due moral circumspection and recognition, sometimes justify overriding relatively unimportant rights, even though rights they undeniably are. Preserving caring relations between individuals may sometimes outweigh the strict demands of justice, sometimes not. The magnitude of the injustice and the extent of the harm to caring relationships will be significant but there is no precise criterion to indicate when one should take precedence over the other. Similar remarks apply when various undisputed virtues conflict with each other, or with any of the considerations mentioned above. An understanding of these issues and the perfectly valid considerations to which they refer is necessary if we are to discipline and sift our responses to various situations, the ability to do which must be an important ingredient in moral education. That we cannot identify a single overriding principle of moral appraisal does not mean that we have to accept that cruelty, meanness or exploitation are somehow alright because their contraries are simply the values of our society and may not be esteemed elsewhere. Cruelty is bad because of the suffering it causes. An act of generosity is good because of the caring relations it fosters and demonstrates. The equilibrium of just employment is commendable because it does not treat human resources simply as resources tout court.

Future citizens need to be able to make such judgements, not only in their personal lives when a certain course of action seems attractive, superficially worthy or even noble. In a democracy they will be responsible not only for their own actions but for judging the behaviour of those who act in their name. It is a common experience that politicians and others who manage our affairs are inclined to describe their proposals and account for their actions in positive terms and many of the twentieth century atrocities we have already referred to were described to those who committed them in the attractive terminology of inspiring philosophies and noble ideals such as purity, heroism, justice and equality, the defeat of evil. We must nowadays also fear (Chandler 2002) that even the ideals of human rights may be used in this way.

The critical discussion of actions, characters and modes of justification are a crucial part of moral education and this must include the recognition that though the search for absolute generalisations may be demonstrably fruitless, certain actions may justifiably be enjoined or praised with confidence and others just as unequivocally condemned. Paradoxical as it may seem in the face of arguments by Hare (1963), not to mention Kant (1785, 1788), many of our most persuasive moral maxims are conspicuously lacking in universalisability. Attempts to remedy this by specifying the circumstances of individual acts more closely (it is only permissible to do x if a, b, c or n) risks leaving us once again with a collection of individual acts requiring individual evaluation. There is no contradiction between this and the conclusion that, taking account of all considerations and circumstances, certain specific actions merit unequivocal condemnation, even though the educated moral consciousness will remain aware that wider knowledge and greater enlightenment may subsequently cause us to revise our judgement. We cannot always know the full circumstances, motives or likely consequences of an action which we, and those with whose upbringing and education we are charged, may be called upon to pronounce judgement. While stopping short of the debilitating admission that Moral Relativism is 'absolutely' true or insisting that the distinction between worthy and unworthy acts is entirely dependent on the circumstances in which they occur, we might nevertheless enter the caveat that acts may be seen differently from different perspectives or on the basis of different experiences or commitments.

Encouragingly, such an attitude would appear to provide a rationale for a feasible and defensible, but far from simplistic, programme of moral education which those responsible for the upbringing of the young would most likely follow if not inhibited by the niggling insinuations of relativism or the cruelties and perversions of various moral absolutisms. Some actions may be discouraged and punished and the immediate reasons given. Others, such as those which are generous, courageous or honest, may be admired and enjoyed and our admiration of them shared with the young as we also share our contempt for those that demonstrate mean-mindedness, cruelty or shiftiness. There remains a further range of actions which are sometimes admired: those demonstrating ruthlessness, arrogance, cunning or power, which may require hard-headed and critical discussion and examination from many angles before their character is seen in its full light. We do not need to disguise, but should rather delight in the subtle shades of grey where the less sophisticated might demand clear borders between, say, avarice and thrift, cowardice and prudence, arrogance and decent self-regard, insincerity and tactful courtesy. We do not need to deny that others may perceive these boundaries differently or that circumstances or temperament might justify or excuse them in doing so. But such a recognition is not to deny the moral difference between obvious cases of avarice and thrift, cowardice and prudence candour or deception.

Since moral judgement addresses the individual conscience to which each of us has unimpeded access in our own case, it is not constrained like the formal process of law making, where legislators have to fear that shady lawyers will cynically turn the absence of clear definition to advantage. It is central to the achievement of an educated moral understanding that there are sound and defensible grounds of moral appraisal, even if it is also true that in doubtful cases the proper course of action is to proceed with caution, deference and maybe even sincere expressions of apology and regret to those whose interests are disadvantaged by the outcome of our deliberations. The reasons at our disposal for living and acting thus and not otherwise are many and varied. It is also part of our predicament that they may sometimes clash and that the situations to which they apply cannot be specified in detail in advance. Moral responsibility is partly a matter of being aware of this and accepting it in our own lives and in appraising the lives and actions of others.

CHAPTER 5

THE DEVELOPMENT OF MORAL REASONING

In earlier chapters we have seen the inadequacy of a view of moral education as the transmission of certain specific injunctions (often of a negative kind) and attempting to enforce these by sanctions of a greater or lesser severity. Rejection of such a crude traditional approach, however, places a requirement upon us to propose an alternative, to say what, in our view, moral education should be about, what ultimately should be its aims. Clearly, we are concerned that the young should come to be good children, good pupils, good people and ultimately good citizens, but we are then thrown back on three further questions. First, can we say anything helpful of a general nature about what it is to be good? Second, can we say anything about how children are to be induced to be good, bearing in mind that, particularly in education, the question of means is often not contingent upon ends but intimately bound up with them. Third, we may also ask whether securing a measure of appropriate conduct is all that is required or whether talk of moral education implies some further aim which, though perhaps not entirely independent of the task of trying to ensure good conduct, nevertheless requires its own separate emphasis. Does moral education, for example, imply some understanding of morality or the process of moral reasoning, over and above the minimum required by someone who is acknowledged to behave well?

That it does so was the underlying assumption of progressive movements in moral education in both Britain and the United States in the 1960s and 1970s, which merit some discussion here, both because of the genuine educational advance they represent over traditional transmission approaches and also because they form the point of departure against which more recent, contrasting approaches have been developed and expounded. A transmission approach in any subject supposes that the adult world is in full possession of the content that is to be taught and is the only source of knowledge as far as the learner is concerned. This content is typically communicated verbally and given to be learned. Motivation is characteristically extrinsic, in the forms of reward and punishment. An objectivist epistemology is implied. Things are supposed to be unequivocally as they are said to be and the learning task is to listen and remember. By contrast, the aim of encouraging pupils to develop their powers of moral reasoning is compatible with both subjectivist and objectivist epistemologies. The objectivist may suppose that since truth is there to be discovered, those competent in the skills of reasoning will eventually discover it without the support of the teacher's authority. For the subjectivist, if there is no moral truth to be discovered, all have a right to reach their own conclusions in their own rational, autonomous and defensible way. Both views are to be found among those who advocate the development of moral reasoning through participation in the discussion of moral issues. The notion of the morally neutral teacher who does not impose his or her own views on learners was central to both the *Schools Council Nuffield Humanities Curriculum Project* (Schools Council 1971) in Britain, some of whose materials, techniques and assumptions continue to inform much Personal and Social Education and also to the recently much criticised Values Clarification approach in America (Raths and others 1966).

Various strands may be traced in the origins of this approach which sought to encourage learners to reach their own moral conclusions through a process of discussion. First there was the across the board reaction in the nineteen sixties and seventies against traditional models of teaching. Teaching as telling was in general disfavour by contrast with so-called discovery, particularly discovery by doing. If they are to come to know that taking other people's things is wrong, let them not be told 'Thou shalt not steal' but come to this conclusion for themselves, not only in the light of their own experience but also by discussing that of others. Learning acquired in this way was supposed to be more effectively learned and understood and to become part of the learner's understanding of the world in a way that didactically imparted verbalisms do not. Why should not this child-centred assumption apply as validly to the moral world as to any other branch of learning? This is not, of course, Aristotle's learning to be virtuous by performing virtuous acts but it may well seem to be an example of learning the skill of moral reasoning by reasoning about moral issues. Like all examples of progressive educational practice, it represents learning as coming from within the learner as learners become autonomous explorers of the world. The increasingly despised notion of the teacher's authority was conspicuously being rejected in the moral as in the material world. What does not well up within the learner as an individual is acquired as a matter of 'social learning' in the peer group, the ability of which to promote learning was increasingly coming to be recognised (Gagné 1770).

The unpopularity, indeed the disrepute, of the notion of the teacher's or rather the adult world in general's authority, particularly in the field of morality, is part of a general loss of confidence in traditional values. This was an age of satire. All figures of authority, not only teachers but clergymen, military officers, judges, policemen and politicians were figures, not so much of fun as of extremely pointed ridicule, at best bungling fools, at worst hypocrites. Cultural diversity was the latest hot intellectual discovery. Sociology was the vogue intellectual pursuit. Traditional values were objectified as middle class and, in the language of Marxist moral criticism, morality was, like religion, part of the oppressive apparatus of the dominant class (Bourdieu and Passeron 1970). If sexual intercourse did not actually begin in nineteen sixty-three as Philip Larkin' poem suggests, this period certainly marked the beginning of sexual liberation. Traditional taboos relating to sex outside marriage, as well as between same-sex couples, were under attack, both intellectually and in practice and the same was true of traditional gender roles, in the home as well as in the workplace. If moral reasoning was to be the vehicle of moral education there were certainly plenty of moral issues to reason about. In fact, if moral issues were to be addressed in education it is difficult to see how, at that time, it could have been done at all other than through the medium of some form of ostensibly open discussion.

Of particular significance in the present context was the way in which the progressive and child centred concerns of the nineteen sixties and seventies were, as before in the nineteen thirties, expressed as a concern with Developmental Psychology. Building on Piaget's (1932) *Moral Judgement of the Child,* Kohlberg (1968) attempts to show how the manner in which moral injunctions are perceived by the child develops according to supposedly invariant stages as between cultures. Two assumptions were essential to this understanding of moral development from a pedagogic point of view. First, it was assumed this process cannot be brought about by explicit instruction or didactic explanation. At the same time, the process was not to be viewed as a spontaneous or maturational process from within but took place only under the influence of cognitive stimulation in which choices and decisions of the relevant kind are made in a situation of social interaction with others. In this regard, the development of moral understanding was seen to be of a piece with the development of understanding of other kinds.

In the context of the 1960s and 70s the pedagogic appeal of the above insight is obvious. As individuals progressed through Piagetian/Kohlbergian stages they were regarded as becoming progressively more rational and for many of the more notable philosophers of education of the time (Dearden and others 1972) the achievement of rationality was a crucial educational aim, if not actually definitive of education itself. As children moved from dependence on the immediate stimulus to the independent following of the rule and thence to the ability to view the rule critically and see it as capable of modification in the light of higher order principles, they were apparently becoming increasingly autonomous, capable of choosing their own values, way of life and political principles as they were of forming their own hypotheses and reaching their own conclusions in other areas of knowledge.

From a practical classroom point of view, the approach provided the rationale for dealing with moral and other controversial issues in a non-authoritarian way. It provided a way out of the kind of situation in which, if moral education were offered at all, it was in the form of teachers holding forth with sincere passion about their heartfelt beliefs while some, no doubt, listened and believed and others simply sat and let it wash over them. Teachers were released from the often impossible responsibility of convincing pupils of the importance and validity of what they felt they had to put over. The age of compulsory school attendance had only recently been raised to sixteen in Britain and here was a chance to show respect for the relatively new brand of compulsory school attenders by listening to them instead of preaching at them, and by allowing them to express their views on serious and controversial matters of the day that the teaching profession had previously tended to regard as no concern of pupils, at least below the sixth form.

Essentially, the methodology derived from the above approach, and still used quite widely in Personal and Social Education lessons and also in the rehabilitation of offenders by the British Probationary Service, consisted of conducting discussion on the basis of stimulus material – photographs, writing, invented moral dilemmas, subject to certain rules. These were principally:

1. All members of the group should be encouraged to speak, all points of view should be considered, criteria of rationality (relevance, consistency, non-arbitrariness) should be followed. Moral considerations were considered to comprise consideration of interests and respect for persons.

2. The teacher as chair, in addition, of course, to preserving good order and ensuring that all received a hearing, was to ensure that the rules of moral debate referred to above were followed as rigorously as possible but was to strictly abstain from expressing his or her own views on substantive matters, let alone of course, offering them as authoritative conclusions.

The process of discussion and the learning of the rules of rational debate rather than the conclusions reached were all important and, in the *Schools Council Humanities Curriculum Project* the teacher/chairperson was enjoined to avoid group consensus as far as possible.

The approach raised, and continues to raise a number of philosophical issues. The first of these to appear among philosophers of education, concerns the supposed obligation of teacher chairpersons to remain neutral. This requirement derives from the assumption that society is irredeemably pluralistic in value terms, that reasoning can do little to bring about a rapprochement in basic value positions and that maybe it would be wrong to attempt to do so. Any such attempt might be seen as a failure to respect the point of view of others. Arguably, all are entitled to their separate views, while each individual needs a coherent set of personal values in order to conduct his or her own life. Bailey (1975), who clearly holds that at least some higher order moral principles possess a measure of objective validity, sees this as no more than an attempt to preserve diversity for diversity's sake.

It is perfectly possible to encourage the development of moral reasoning by means of discussion without requiring teachers to be quite so coy about their own views. Nowadays, both teachers and pupils may be more sophisticated than in the past, so that teachers are now able to reveal something of their own views without feeling that they have to secure the assent of their pupils, while pupils may now be able to hear the different views of their teachers without regarding what is said as any kind of authoritative pronouncement that good pupils are required to take on board. The extent to which this situation is the result of a generation of Moral Education or Personal and Social Education based on open discussion is a matter of conjecture.

One criticism of the notion of the neutral chairperson advanced both by Bailey and by a number of other philosophers at the time of the *Schools Council Humanities Curriculum Project* appears to indicate among some philosophers of education, some confusion between two similar sounding but actually quite different notions. On the one hand, there are the procedural principles of moral discussion (relevance, non-arbitrariness, respect for persons, consideration of interests), which supposedly govern the terms of the debate but, again supposedly, cannot issue in substantive moral conclusions. On the other hand, there are so-called higher order moral principles, which serve as the justification of individual moral claims. For Kantians, these higher order moral principles will include the prohibition of using rational beings purely as means to ends or the requirement that moral injunctions should be capable of forming the maxim of a universal law. For utilitarians, the requirement to promote the greatest good of the greatest number will play a similar role. It is not proposed here to pursue the issue of whether Peters (1974) and others were guilty of attempting to make Kantian principles definitive of morality as such. It is, however, quite clear that a number of philosophers of education supposed that controversial moral issues could be rationally settled by the application of such higher order principles and that the aim of classroom discussion of moral issues was to develop in young people the ability and propensity to do just that (Hirst 1974). More recent researches in the field of ethical theory enable us to appreciate the naivety of this assumption more readily than may have been possible at the time. Interestingly, Bailey's article (op. cit) contains a short diatribe against existentialist criterionless choices. For Bailey, rational moral decisions are a matter of discovering the relationship between the issue at hand and the appropriate higher order principle and deciding in the light of it. In this context Bailey refers to Sartre's character who must decide between leaving home to fight for France against the Germans and remaining to look after his widowed mother. Though Sartre may be wrong in supposing the answer to lie in the young man's being true to his authentic self, he is right in claiming that no higher order moral principles will help him. His problem is precisely that such principles as may be relevant are in conflict. The real answer lies in the particularities of the case. What, for example, does the mother think about it? What other support is available to her? How essential is the man's contribution to the war effort, and so on? These considerations must be weighed in the light of the facts of the situation, not comprehensively validated or dismissed by the application of one higher order principle or another, which is not, of course, to deny that an understanding of these principles will be helpful in the process of weighing. To set up the moral issue in such a way that the kinds of detail mentioned above are, ex hypothesi, unavailable is to misrepresent the way in which our moral decisions are embedded in the complexity of human life.

There are a number of further problems in the view that an apparently dispassionate or neutral chairperson is either necessary or effective in enabling young people to reach a state of uncoerced moral autonomy. First, young people are generally capable of sussing out the general positions of those who discuss matters of any importance with them. We all do this on the basis of tiny verbal and bodily clues and this is an important social skill, which we need in order to know who it is we are dealing with and how to respond prudently, courteously or sensitively. To deliberately withhold this information is to risk one's position being misinterpreted, or given a cruder and less flexible interpretation than is appropriate.

Of more philosophical significance is the suggestion that the form of any mode of discourse represents an exercise of power, which is not without influence on the conclusions that may be reached within that discourse. Without going so far as to accept the postmodernist view that this is necessarily the case, it is fairly clear in the present context that to insist on certain forms of argument involving non-arbitrariness, respect for persons, consideration of interests and so on, must all but inexorably lead to certain naively progressive or liberal conclusions. Under these conditions, many valued social practices, customs, hierarchies and economic arrangements become all but indefensible without a measure of sophistication and argumentative skill that most adults, let alone most pupils, do not possess.

Traditionalists have felt, not without a measure of justification, that the very notion of morality that people, especially the young, should be free to discuss and decide upon for themselves, is not only dangerous and bound to lead to disorder, but is also a logical absurdity. Despite our cultural diversity, they may hold, we live in a society which is only tolerable because certain rules are, in fact, widely respected and people can rely on this being so. Life as we know it could scarcely go on if we could not, on the whole, count on people telling the truth, doing what they have agreed to do, not molesting or attacking other people, not taking or damaging our possessions, caring for the children they have brought into the world, using intoxicants and driving vehicles responsibly, and so on. These practices, it may be argued, are actually and unquestionably in place and they, their importance and their function simply need to be taught and insisted upon, if not in the home, then at school.

This, again, is an objection to the manner rather than the principle of using discussion as a means of promoting moral development. Though accepting that some modes of conduct play an important part in making life tolerable, one may take issue with the extreme traditionalist position that these need simply to be inculcated and that is that. Established practices which make life tolerable for some may ensure that it remains less so for others. It seems entirely proper and perfectly consistent with the continuance of social good order to encourage young people to discuss such matters as whether the present distribution of property in the world is entirely equitable, whether there may be occasions when accepted property rules may be ignored, when it is permissible to be economical with the truth in the interests of courtesy or commercial or legal strategy, whether religious or legal marriage is the only context in which children may be brought up, which mood enhancing substances may be used, by whom and under what circumstances. Although there are certain assumptions and practices that we need to be able to rely on if life is to be tolerable at all and which, therefore, ought not to be blatantly or irresponsibly flouted, these are necessarily subject to a measure of interpretation according to context and circumstance. More importantly, it is likely and in some cases highly desirable, that over time, the interpretation of some of these should change and it is upon the present younger generation, that the task of bringing these changes about will fall.

Managing the discussion of moral issues in such a way that both the point and purpose of established practice and the way in which these are subject to variation in the light of time and circumstance, necessarily entails rather more guidance on the part of the teacher than many values clarifiers and moral educators brought up on the assumptions of the *Schools Council Humanities Curriculum Project* would have been prepared to accept. The case for such guidance would, however, seem difficult to deny, given that such a perception is unlikely to be reached by a group of inexperienced young people without assistance.

A further traditional anxiety about too much discussion of moral issues more centrally concerns the activity itself rather than the manner in which it is carried out. However insistent teachers are in guiding their classes towards responsible conclusions, the mere fact of their being discussed identifies them as matters for argument which may already seem to represent a weakening, if not a subversion, of the reliable social order. If discussion is truly open so that unanticipated considerations may be introduced, outcomes cannot be predicted or controlled. Even for the progressively minded, this may sometimes prove embarrassing as when discussion seems to lead to a hardening rather than a weakening of undesirable, for example, racist or nationalistic views. It is also the case that, with the best will in the world, many controversial issues are all but undecidable and must of necessity remain a matter of individual judgement, particularly if teachers see it as part of their role to actually head off any tendency on the part of the group to reach any kind of consensus. Should this happen too often, there is an obvious danger that the impression will be given that moral discussion is always inconclusive, that there can be no moral certainties and that, consequently, anything goes. Modern critics are not the first to anticipate problems when serious issues are discussed by the young, though Plato may, perhaps, be thought to have erred rather on the side of caution when he advised that this activity should be delayed until the age of thirty.

One final and fundamental criticism of moral education conceived in terms of the development of moral reasoning by means of more or less open discussion, is that it is simply not calculated to meet the perceived problem of declining moral conduct among the young and may actually have contributed to this tendency by undermining belief in clear and unequivocal moral obligations and prohibitions. It is also arguable that, in the nature of the case, it cannot be expected to be effective in improving moral conduct. Warnock (1993) argues that many of the controversial issues discussed by pupils with the aim of promoting their moral reasoning lie outside their experience and do not relate to their own choices and conduct. She would prefer discussion to focus on more immediate issues, such as their own conduct in school. This view rather persists in seeing the young as children in school rather than as future adults and citizens. Education is not for school but for life and it will later be argued that the ability to develop and articulate considered and reflective views on matters that may be outside the range of one's own experience and conduct is an important element in the education of responsible future citizens.

Be this as it may, Plato's claim that no-one knowingly does what they ought not cannot literally be true unless we write more into the notion of knowing than is usual or interpret that which someone ought not to do in a prudential rather than a moral sense. Like Saint Paul, in this if in nothing else, our pupils may see and approve the good while failing to pursue it. Hume notes that, like facts about the material world, the conclusions of moral reasoning do not impel us to act morally. More recently, Bond (1983) and others have been hard put to it to bridge the gap between grounding reasons, which justify what we ought to do and motivating reasons which move us to do it.

Certain more philosophically fundamental reservations arising from a rejection of the very notion of morality as a system of obligations arrived at through moral reasoning and of the notion that the application of higher order moral principles such as justice represents the pinnacle of moral development will be addressed in relation to the alternative conceptions of morality considered in later chapters. In the meantime, it suffices to say that in a society in which social and political conditions change rapidly, which becomes increasingly complex and hopefully increasingly democratic, the procedures and skills involved in rationally discussing what ought to be done and in appraising the actions, of others, particularly those that claim to act on our behalf, become increasingly important. In deciding both individually and, more especially, collectively what ought to be done the alternatives to rational discussion are obedience to authority, the uncritical acceptance of tradition, the use of rhetoric or crude coercion. In one respect at least discussion, provided it is genuine, disciplined discussion and not manipulation or naked bigotry, is bound to lead to moral advance by leading to greater clarity and therefore greater responsibility in relation to the implications of our actions. It should also lead to greater flexibility and tolerance in enabling us to understand the position and reasons of others.

Furthermore, whether or not it affects conduct, the practice of discussing how people ought to behave in an open manner relying on reasons rather than authority is a long-standing one and an important part of our heritage. It has an important part to play in both our response to contemporary events and our co-operative relations with others and as such must form a central element in the educational experience of young people. It is difficult to see how the younger generation could be supposed to have received an adequate moral education without some understanding of the reasons according to which both private actions and public policies are to be judged right or wrong. Part of that understanding is the extent to which these reasons, when they are expressed in terms of general principles, are both limited and provisional. Arguably, one effective means of promoting this understanding is the use of discussion, at a level appropriate to the age and abilities of the pupils concerned, whether in the ordinary course of school life, at times set aside for the purpose, or as they arise in relation to other subjects of the curriculum.

PART TWO

MORAL THEORY AND MORAL EDUCATION

CHAPTER 6

MAXIMISING HAPPINESS

The conclusion that developing moral reasoning may form a significant element in moral education leads naturally enough to a discussion of the kinds of reasons that may be given for doing some things rather than others and, more especially, what measure of validity such reasons may possess. Traditionally, reasons for acting thus and not otherwise have been taken to be of two kinds: those relating to the likely results of what is to be done or avoided (consequentialist arguments) and those that claim that what is proposed conforms to or infringes some supposed rule or duty (deontological arguments). It is sometimes assumed that the two approaches are mutually exclusive. Either one is a consquentialist of some kind, concerned to bring about some particular kind of good, such as happiness, like Bentham (1789) and Mill (1861) and their many Utilitarian followers, or one is concerned to do what is right, come what may, like Kantians who see morality in terms or rules about how rational beings should behave towards one another.

If one takes one or other of these views, one may be tempted to try to explain all moral insights in terms of one's favoured theory and it is certainly the case that many of our specific moral assumptions may be justified in both consequentialist of deontological terms. Acts which we see as evil are likely to have bad consequences for someone or something as well as infringing certain rules of rationally justifiable behaviour. It is sometimes tempting to suppose that the two modes of justification are interchangeable, as when we condemn the breaking of a promise either because of its consequences in, for example, destroying trust, or because it breaks the rule that one ought not to lie or deceive others. But sometimes the two approaches conflict as, for example, when someone lies in order to prevent a major disaster or someone's rights are ignored for the sake of a major social benefit. An attempt will be made in Chapter 11 to deal with such dilemmas and their educational implications. In the meantime it is proposed, in this and the following chapter, to consider the rationales and shortcomings of two widely advanced versions of consequentialist and deontological moral theories respectively.

One is taking a consequentialist line whenever one backs up the view that something should be done or not done because of the likely consequences. 'Don't do that, you'll spoil the carpet', 'Go to work by bike and help save the planet', 'Take your litter home and keep Britain tidy.' The appeal is to consequences which speaker and listener are both supposed to desire or approve. In more academic contexts the appeal may be made to some single overall good or summum bonum in terms of which all injunctions may, by shorter or longer chains of potential consequences, be justified: the good of the state, the building of the city of God on earth, the classless society or whatever. Utilitarianism, the view that right action is that which, in the long run, brings about the greatest sum of happiness or the least amount of pain, is an attempt to find a single overall good upon which a comprehensive system of justification may be based

In common sense terms the approach is appealing. In deciding what to do, any rational person is bound to think first and foremost about the consequences. Most of the things we do deliberately after reflection are done because of the consequences we hope to bring about and if we refrain from doing something, it is because of the predictable undesirable consequences of doing it. One important element in moral education must therefore be to ensure that young people acquire sufficient knowledge of the world to be able to think through the consequences of their actions. Mostly, and perfectly properly, we are thinking of the consequences for ourselves when deciding what to do. Our reflections become moral when we also consider the effects upon others. In the context of moral education, the consequentialist doctrine of Utilitarianism particularly merits critical discussion, not only because of its apparent common sense appeal but also because its underlying assumptions are so frequently at the base of popular moral judgements. A person's life is often considered successful if they are happy in their work, say, or in their marriage. Happy endings in films are commonly judged to be satisfactory endings. In the field of public policy and legislation, the original focus of Bentham's concern, policies which produce widespread satisfaction even at the price of some minor or temporary discomfort, are generally reckoned to be good policies. Many other personal aspirations and public policy aims such as economic prosperity, security, employment or other meaningful activity, the esteem of others and so on may also assume happiness as their further justification, even where this is not explicitly stated. Indeed, if it is not stated, this will often be because it is felt unnecessary or naïve to do so. It must also be said that an apparent appeal to utilitarian considerations may also be made, often with some plausibility, in favour of actions which we may regard as morally suspect. Petty pilfering, especially from large organisations, small scale tax or insurance fraud, fare dodging and so on may be thought relatively innocent in that they seem to harm no-one in particular and may give the perpetrator considerable satisfaction, as well as some material benefit.

Utilitarianism has had and continues to have its staunch supporters, including Smart (Smart and Williams 1973), Singer (1993), Barrow (1991) and many others. It is, however, not without its critics, one of whom (Scruton 2002) goes so far as to deny that it is an ethical theory at all. Scruton's point appears to be that a valid ethical theory serves to help us give shape to our lives. This, Scruton argues, Utilitarianism cannot do insofar as there is no kind if action which it cannot under some conceivable circumstances, be used to justify. It is characteristic of debates about Utilitarianism that its defenders have quite often been able to refute objections made to it at a superficial level but either fail to take on board the true nature of the objection or, in doing so, give the theory an interpretation which actually detracts from its truly utilitarian character, at least in its pure form in which the maximisation of happiness is the only reason for regarding actions as good or bad.

A prime example of this is Barrow's attempt to reply to Moore's (1903) famous 'open question' argument. Moore, it will be recalled, points out that if someone attempts to justify an action or a policy on the ground that it will make someone happy, we may always ask whether happiness is necessarily good, which we certainly could not do if happiness and goodness were synonymous. The argument has a certain validity against the writer, moralist or politician who, having demonstrated that a certain course of action will bring more happiness than grief, complacently assumes there is nothing more to be said. Barrow quite rightly argues that Moore has only demonstrated that happiness is not synonymous with goodness. But this, Barrow argues is not what the utilitarian claims. What the utilitarian claims is that happiness *is* good and upon this claim Moore's argument supposedly has no purchase. In fact, however, it has the effect of forcing the utilitarian to choose between justifying his claim that happiness is good, or openly declaring that he regards it as self-evident. Barrow appears to choose the latter course insofar as he seems to provide no justification of this claim at all. Mill (1861) had earlier rather fudged the issue, as he does elsewhere in his defence of Utilitarianism, by arguing that happiness must be desirable because everyone desires it. But in fact the justification is presented so perfunctorily that one cannot but feel that Mill does not imagine that anyone will deny that happiness is the supreme good, or think any serious justification necessary.

This is the most fundamental theoretical problem for Utilitarianism which it shares with any consequentialist theory, namely that of bridging the gap between the consequence being aimed at and moral obligation or value. It is far from clear that any of the recent attempts to overcome Hume's discontinuity (Hume 1748) between is and ought have been entirely successful without recourse to non-consequentialist principles or, certainly in the present case, to principles other than the claim that the maximisation of happiness is the one and only criterion of obligation. To state, as Bentham (1789) does, that duties that bring no benefit to anyone are purely sterile and therefore invalid as duties, simply states what the utilitarian is required to demonstrate. Exceptions to this notion of sterile duties or virtues are not difficult to imagine. Murdoch's woman (Murdoch 1970) who comes to think more positively of her dead mother-in-law and thus becomes a better person, even though neither the mother-in-law nor anyone else stands to benefit from the change of view, would be a case in point. Processes of moral self improvement we undertake may bring no calculable benefit either to ourselves or others but are morally more estimable than mere acquiescence in self neglect, which must be a consideration of some importance for the moral educator.

Barrow's is not the only attempt to defend Utilitarianism that ultimately involves abandoning the doctrine's central principle. It clearly is not obvious that everyone always seeks to maximise pleasure and minimise pain or is unquestionably correct in thinking it right to do so. Those who accept hardship for the sake of some worthwhile goal or self-sacrifice for the sake of something they consider a duty are obvious examples. Of course, utilitarians may try to co-opt these people for their own cause. They may ask what these duties are, for which people are prepared to sacrifice happiness? If they are not examples of Bentham's sterile duties, they may, in utilitarian terms, quite properly be chosen because the hardship to the agent may be more than outweighed by the increased happiness or reduced suffering of the beneficiaries. Where these arguments fail, utilitarians may fall back on others inherited, in many cases, from classical writers, often more interested in the prudential well being of the agent than that of others. By performing certain irksome duties now one may be avoiding the pain of remorse and regret later. Perhaps, too, the happiness that comes from the achievement of a noble good may be greater or of more value than the vulgar pleasures of idleness and ease.

Unfortunately, all of these replies either raise further complications, forcing utilitarians to construct further defences abandoning the simple common sense plausibility of their original position or simply sell the pass altogether. There is, for example, a problem as to why anyone should regard the happiness of others, particularly strangers, as of equal importance to one's own, or to that of one's own family or friends, or indeed of any consideration at all. Eighteenth century writers, Hume among them, had recourse to the idea of natural sympathy to explain our concern, but even given that we possess such sympathy, this does not prove that we are right to follow its promptings. Such sympathy as we have may serve to explain but does little to justify our moral inclinations.

When Bentham stipulates that each should count for one and none for more than one, this is offered as an axiom rather than as the conclusion of a chain of argument. It may serve as a principle of public policy and legislation among equals, as Bentham clearly intended, in an intellectual environment in which it was still necessary to establish an egalitarian ethos against the claims of privilege, tradition and established religion but the principle of equality itself can scarcely be justified in utilitarian terms. There can be no certainty that the adoption of such an assumption will in fact produce the greatest aggregate of happiness, however measured. Recourse to deontological principles regarding the treatment of others or the non-self generally, appears to be required to supplement the utilitarian principle.

That we sometimes carry out irksome duties now in order to avoid later pain can have no place in the justification of utilitarian moral theory for this is a matter of common prudence, rather than morality. Avoiding the pain of remorse, regret or feelings of guilt is also difficult to reconcile with the utilitarian view of things. To see them as motivation to act virtuously in future fails to do justice to such feelings, for they are felt most intensively when no reparation can be made. It is one of the gravest objections to Utilitarianism as a comprehensive moral theory that it skates with gross insensitivity over the whole area of our moral life which is concerned with judgements of our past actions as opposed to making rational decisions about what to do next.

That the happiness to be achieved through the pursuit of our ideals and commitments may be greater or better than that resulting from self indulgence raises the whole issue of qualities of happiness with which Mill struggles so unconvincingly. Whereas Mill attempts to follow the classical Epicureans in distinguishing between the coarse sensual pleasures of the flesh and other more cultivated 'higher' pleasures, Bentham is more consistent in that he will have no truck with such differences between, to put it anachronistically, the pleasures of high and low culture. If happiness alone is the criterion of value, that derived from refined pursuits is in no way superior to that derived from other more trivial pastimes. It will once again be of significance to the moral educator that, if duration and intensity alone are significant, it is not obvious that these are greater in the case of nobler and more cultivated activities.

Many of the problems of Utilitarianism, along with those of other attempts to construct a comprehensive moral theory, arise from the very manner in which moral theory is conceived. There is much talk among Post-Enlightenment moralists about the 'science' of morality and its potential contribution to the improvement of the human lot, along with expressions of regret that the science in question should be so little advanced in comparison with the sciences of the physical world. Bentham's project is to remedy this shortcoming by producing such a science, and a quantitative science at that. Happiness is the unit of hedonic calculation in managing our social and interpersonal affairs. Moral decision is to be solely a matter of hard-nosed calculation, rather than the amateurish and subjective processes of moral judgement. Happiness, however, is not a homogeneous stuff, quantities of which can be measured, calculated and compared. Nor is it produced by events in the way heat is produced by friction or pressure by measurably decreasing the volume of a container. Eating, drinking and physical contact with another body may give rise to a sense of physical well-being and certain physical deprivations may produce discomfort and pain and possibly measurable comparisons may be made in these fields. But the happiness that comes from the achievement of our projects and commitments and the pains of humiliation and frustration that follow our failures are only contingently connected with the physical if they are connected at all. Utilitarians are frequently ridiculed for supposing that quantitative comparisons can be made between different kinds of happiness but what is more fatal to their position is that our successes and failures bring pleasure and pain not because of their physical effects but because we value them. We think them worthwhile, desirable because of the achievements, the approaches to perfection in ourselves or in the world, which they represent. To see them as valuable because they bring happiness to ourselves and others is to put the cart before the horse. On the contrary, they bring happiness because they are seen as independently valuable. Were they not so, they would bring us no happiness. To argue that anyone who achieves anything, particularly through the performance of some disagreeable duty, is in some sense necessarily happy as a result is to make Utilitarianism true by definition and to fly in the face of our everyday perception that many actions are chosen and approved independently of whether they will lead to greater happiness or not, even though many morally desirable actions may, in fact, do so.

Two final and not entirely unconnected criticisms and corresponding defences of Utilitarianism remain to be considered. The first is that, applied consistently,

Utilitarianism seems to demand too much of us. Whatever someone is doing, especially if they are doing nothing in particular or just amusing themselves, there is probably something they could be doing that would make someone a lot happier at no great cost to themselves. If comfortably off people gave away a significant part of their fortunes to a suitable charity this would probably save a number of lives. This might, to some extent, diminish the donor's happiness and well being, but relatively little compared to the loss of life. Some other moral doctrines, including that of Kant which we shall consider in the next chapter, enable us to distinguish between duties of perfect and imperfect obligation; between things one must do or refrain from doing because of incurred or role related obligations or because someone might suffer unmerited harm as a result, and duties of imperfect obligation, acts of supererogatory virtue which, if one does them, show merit but which may be omitted on particular occasions without incurring blame, though one must sometimes do them to be a benevolent, generous or charitable person. This distinction is not easy to justify in utilitarian terms, particularly given that Utilitarianism stipulates only that we should maximise the aggregate of happiness in the world but seems to say nothing about how that happiness is to be distributed. On grounds of simple Act Utilitarianism, the doctrine that the moral value of each individual action is a matter of felicific calculation, there is no moral distinction between the happiness of some unknown individual in some distant part of the world and that of one's closest relative or friend.

We might perhaps advance a utilitarian justification for not spending every minute of the day or night in maximising the happiness of others by pointing out that if we did so we should soon be in a state of collapse, incapable of contributing to the happiness of anyone. There may therefore be good utilitarian grounds for limiting the extent of our obligations to certain important acts, omissions and persons for which or for whom one has particular responsibility, relying on the needs of others being met by those correspondingly close to them. One ought not to forget one's spouse's or one's child's birthday but one does not always feel obliged to contribute to charity the sum one is told will save a child's life, though one is to be commended if one does so. Yet, on utilitarian grounds, there are no reasons for regarding the surely lesser pain of a forgotten birthday as more important than the greater one of starving to death, even though the person who starves to death is unknown to one.

This brings us to our final failed defence of Utilitarianism. It is frequently observed that aggregate happiness in the world may be brought about by actions we have no hesitation in regarding as wrong. We referred earlier to acts of petty dishonesty, which bring benefit to the perpetrator and maybe to others but do significantly less harm to their victims, if indeed they do any noticeable harm at all. Certain acts of manifest injustice or rights infringement may also seem to bring about benefits greater than the pain caused. To give an oft quoted example, if in cold weather, a small boy is seen wearing a large coat while a large boy is scarcely protected from the icy blast by a small coat, the happiness of the large boy might be greatly increased and that of the small boy not so much diminished by forcing them to exchange coats. Some fairly arbitrary forced confiscation and redistribution of property might have the same effect, as might the occasional humane dispatch of elderly and wealthy invalids with needy heirs. A common utilitarian response to this argument has been the doctrine of Rule Utilitarianism which argues, firstly, that ethical doctrines are, by definition, required to deal not with individual acts but produce consistent bodies of moral rules which may or may not provide guidance as to how to act in individual situations in the real world (Barrow op. cit.). Secondly, it may be argued that though it may sometimes be beneficial to pilfer, prevaricate or even murder, there are good utilitarian reasons for having rules forbidding such actions, even when in individual cases they seem positively happiness promoting.

The defence is unconvincing and the doctrine of Rule Utilitarianism incoherent. If there are already inconsistencies in simple Act Utilitarianism because, for instance, of problems about the nature of happiness, these are compounded rather than diminished by the suggestion that we should require consistency within Utilitarianism's derivative rules such as truth telling, property rights, the prevention of harm and so on. Whereas it may be possible to predict the immediate effects of particular acts (their long term effects may pose more problems) it is harder to predict the consequences of following general rules. More seriously, when faced with the option of observing or breaking a particular moral rule there will always be an issue, for rule utilitarians as for others, as to whether or not it will do more good and less harm to obey the rule or to ignore it. If obeying the rule brings more happiness than misery there is no problem, but in this case the move from Act to Rule Utilitarianism has served no purpose. But if obeying the rule brings more misery than joy, the rule utilitarian has to fall back on the deontological principle that rules ought to be kept. It is no use arguing that, on the whole, obedience to rules brings more happiness than sorrow. The rigid and inflexible application of rules certainly does not bring more happiness and less sorrow than applying them with good judgement and discretion. Rule utilitarians might attempt to safeguard their position by proposing a further 'rule', if such it can be called, that rules should be followed flexibly and should be waived or ignored when this would bring more happiness than sorrow. But this is not Rule Utilitarianism at all but Act Utilitarianism restated. Of course, the consequences of not obeying the rule must include the effect on others of seeing the rule kept or broken, which would seem to oblige moral educators to be particularly assiduous in passing on that all important eleventh commandment, 'Thou shalt not get found out'. This Warnock (1971) seems to concede when he says he would have no great qualms of conscience about breaking a rule not to walk on the grass in tennis shoes after dark when there was no-one about.

If one takes any kind of morally desirable act or attitude it will no doubt contingently be the case that, with a bit of ingenuity, one can find good utilitarian reasons why they should be encouraged and their opposites discouraged. If morally admirable actions or attitudes in themselves do not actually benefit someone (as in the case of Murdoch's imaginary daughter-in-law) the tendency to do or hold them may always be said to have the potential for doing so. As with the much debated issues of promise keeping and truth telling, however, other moral accounts referring, perhaps, to obligations of trust and respect between rational beings, provide a far more straight forward and plausible explanation of why they should be so explicitly picked out as objects of approval.

What, then, should be the attitude of moral educators to Utilitarianism? How far is it an approach to moral issues that should be communicated to pupils, given that, as was argued in the previous chapter, moral education has to have a measure of cognitive content as well as aiming simply to ensure acceptable conduct? We have argued here that it is inadequate as a totally comprehensive account of morality and may sometimes even seem to sanction actions that are reprehensible. As against this, it has a number of merits. The effects of an action upon oneself and others are undeniably relevant to our decisions about what to do. As a way in to thinking about one's own conduct and that of others, including public policy makers, it has the advantage of being relatively accessible. For all its flaws, it represents an advance on the blind following of tradition, habit, obedience to established authority or simply keeping one's head down and staying out of trouble. It is also preferable to the sheer egoism of doing whatever one can get away with and directs attention to the consequences of one's actions for others as well as for oneself. Often enough, the balance of advantage to all concerned will be a reasonable and proper ground for doing one thing rather than another.

It is, however, not the case that any course of action whatsoever, which will give more satisfaction to more people than another ought always to be chosen or that the greatest happiness of the greatest number satisfactorily accounts for all our acts of moral evaluation. In Chapter 11 it will be argued that we have no fully satisfactory comprehensive account of morality and certainly no single principle that will enable all moral issues to be definitively resolved without challenge on the basis of alternative moral conceptions. This, it will be suggested, is inherent in the diverse nature of moral situations and therefore of morality itself.

CHAPTER 7

RIGHTS AND RATIONALITY

In contrast to consequentialist theories, of which Utilitarianism is a prime example, are those approaches which claim to evaluate conduct not according to its results but according to certain rules or principles, notably those that relate to the way human beings, or indeed any rational beings, should be treated. These rules or principles are held to apply regardless of the consequences the agent's action may bring about. In the present chapter it is proposed to examine two such approaches, both achieving eminence if not actually originating in the Age of Enlightenment as thinkers strove to free themselves from traditional sources of moral and political authority. Both of these approaches remain very much part of the way in which we approach moral issues today in the contexts of both public and personal conduct, and may furthermore, be regarded as central to the modern, liberal democratic cthos. Of these approaches, one is concerned with the notion of rights as embodied in the theories of Natural Rights, the Rights of Man or, more recently, Human Rights and developed by such writers as Hobbes (1651) Locke (1689) and Paine (1791) in Britain and Rousseau (1762) in France. The second concerns the manner in which rational beings, human or otherwise, are morally bound to treat each other, as developed by Kant (1785, 1788) and others in Germany.

RIGHTS

Discussion here is principally concerned with moral rights and reference will only be made in passing to legal rights, which may or may not correspond to the moral rights people have. Fundamental to the notion of moral rights is the fact that we enter the world without obligations of subordination to others. As Locke puts it we are 'promiscuously born without evident sign or superiority one to another', though we are bound soon to incur many obligations as a result of our natural dependence on others if we are to survive. That no-one is born innately subject to

51

obligations of obedience to others was an important point to make in a age when the natural authority of the aristocracy and even the Divine Right of Kings were still widely accepted. The point being made was that human beings are at least born free and equal and that any obligations we acquire to parents, country, government, spouse, and employer or to the law of the land, must be seen as, in some sense, the result of our consent. Occasionally this consent may be explicit, as when we make a promise or enter into a contract of employment but normally we are supposed to consent tacitly to many of our social and personal obligations. For example, if we willingly benefit from the fact that others obey certain social and moral norms we are supposed to tacitly indicate our assent to those norms and our willingness to be bound by them ourselves. Locke argues that if we accept the benefits of living in an orderly society we incur the obligation or enter into a social contract to obey its laws and moral conventions. This has sometimes been described as a contractarian view of morality. If we don't like the rules of such a society, Locke suggests, we are free to go and live somewhere else. Later writers have suggested that people tacitly consent to obey laws enacted by democratic government when they take part in elections, or voluntarily abstain from doing so.

Our rights as citizens are infringed, on this view, if government restricts our freedom in ways that we may not reasonably be expected to consent to, does not allow proper elections or locks people up without a proper trial. Subject to certain exceptions, it may require us to join the armed forces to defend our country in time of war, since everyone is supposed to profit from the country's defence but it may not press us into the forces to increase the personal wealth of the monarch or his or her generals. It may not override our deeply or sincerely held convictions, or require us to adopt or give up a particular religion. People not only have rights against governments and civil authorities but also against each other as individuals. We cannot usually be supposed to consent to have our property stolen or damaged but we do consent to pay for goods we buy and to hand over articles we have agreed to sell. We cannot be presumed to consent to being attacked, abused or publicly humiliated. We may always waive our rights. Individuals waive their normal rights not to be manhandled when they agree to take part in a game of rugby. Someone may also forfeit some of their rights by committing a crime. For example, one forfeits one's right to freedom by committing a crime knowing that the penalty may be imprisonment. Law breakers do not, however, forfeit their rights to a fair trial, to a punishment that is proportionate to their offence or to proper treatment from the police or prison staff.

Our modern understanding of rights prescribes certain conditions under which our consent, explicit or tacit, must be given. We no longer accept, as Hobbes argues, that prisoners of war may legitimately be enslaved because they may be presumed to consent to this rather than be put to death or that fathers are entitled to absolute obedience from their children because they could have destroyed them at their birth, (Hobbes makes no mention of mothers) or that employers may expect workers to labour under foul or dangerous conditions for a pittance if the alternative is starvation. This last argument of supposed freedom of contract was long used in Britain and America to oppose decent labour legislation and what conditions employers are entitled to impose on employees remains a matter of political dispute. Public educational institutions are no longer considered to have the right to impose unreasonable restrictions on students as a condition of entry and, of course, women are no longer considered to consent to give up all their rights and submit to all manner of violent and abusive treatment from their husbands in return for the benefits of marriage.

Historically, rights theory has tended to concern itself with the so-called bourgeois rights of freedom, property and political participation. More recently, attention has turned to so-called welfare rights to receive the indispensable necessities of a decent life, such as food, basic health care, shelter and education, from society at large if they are unable to obtain them for themselves. Until very recently such rights were considered controversial and regarded as a matter of charity rather than rights. Arguably, however, the distribution of the world's material goods upon which access to these things depends is arbitrary in the extreme and there is no reason why those whom this distribution places at extreme disadvantage should consent to abide by the law, if to do so is actually life threatening or leaves them without the conditions of an acceptable life. According to Natural Rights theory, supposed consent to obey the law implies that we are better off living in a law governed society than in an unregulated state of nature but if one is deprived of the very necessities of an acceptable life, not to say of life itself, one might reasonably think one could not be worse off outside society. In the light of this, the provision of minimal welfare rights may seem to be a minimum condition of the willingness on the part of the least well provided for members of society to obey the law and abstain from, as Hobbes puts it, 'shifting for themselves' by helping themselves to the resources of others.

Since were are, in Locke's terms, promiscuously born, that is, born free and equal, we cannot be supposed to agree to any form of social stratification or discrimination based on morally irrelevant grounds. We may accept that someone may be refused the post of brain surgeon because he or she has not obtained the necessary medical knowledge or has proved incurably ham fisted but not on grounds of race, gender or social origins. Recently, we have come to see that disability should also not justify social or professional exclusion, and that people suffering disabilities have the right to expect that institutions will take reasonable steps to ensure that, as far as possible, they can participate in the same activities as other citizens. The progress of social justice has been a story of the successive recognition that first one and then another of the differences between people, such as class, race, gender, and so on, is irrelevant to the way they are treated and the respect in which they are to be held.

For the moral educator the concept of rights is of particular importance for historical reasons, because of its fundamental importance to the ethos of a democratic society and because of its currency in contemporary debates on social and political issues. Without an understanding of this concept, many of the judgements about the way people behave or are treated in today's world would be incomprehensible. The concept is, however, readily misunderstood, leading both to many invalid or even absurd rights claims being made and to their being criticised and rejected on equally invalid grounds. Declarations of the Rights of Man or of a state's citizens have played an important part in French and American revolutions and the underlying concept was fundamental to the struggles of the English Civil War as well, of course, as to the whole notion of liberal democracy world wide. The related notion of Human Rights as embodied in the 1948 *United Nations Universal Declaration of Human Rights,* in addition to extending the scope of the rights of individuals to the area of basic welfare, has also empowered the international community to bring pressure to bear on individual states to remedy abuses within their borders.

It is of the nature of a right that someone who is deprived of a right is being wronged and is therefore justified in demanding that the matter be rectified not as and when it is convenient or reaches the top of someone's social or political agenda but forthwith. This has sometimes led to a measure of indignation when rights have been demanded by relatively powerless, traditionally underprivileged or socially ill-regarded groups, from whom a measure of deference has customarily been expected. The stridency with which some rights demands have been expressed has done little to allay the atmosphere of contention that often surrounds the discussion of claims to rights. Not all rights claims sometimes expressed in these vituperative terms are justified. Some of the rights claimed for children in the 1970s may seem to have paid insufficient attention to the rights of adults such as parents and teachers or to the duty of protection which young people are owed by the adult world (Wringe 1981). It is sometimes properly, if contentiously, asked whether certain claims to welfare rights by people who suffer hardship as opposed to serious harm are entirely valid. Some rights, such as the right not to be subject to unnecessary suffering may, perhaps, be ascribed to animals but claims to protection for inanimate objects may be best expressed in terms other than those of rights.

Some commonly used arguments for rejecting rights claims are equally suspect. This includes the frequently heard argument that some groups have no rights because they have done nothing to earn them, do not contribute to society or are not fully rational. We do not need to earn the right not to be hurt or humiliated or unduly restricted in our movement. The concept of rights has, however, also been attacked by more serious thinkers. Weil (1957) for example, sees it as an inherently individualistic, egoistic, bourgeois notion. It is true that it has been misapplied in the past in defence of property, established position or privilege or as in the infamous notion of 'freedom of contract' referred to above. Establishment of the notion of welfare rights has gone some way to lessen the force of this criticism. It is certainly individualistic. If someone is, for example, discriminated against because of his or her (let us say her) gender it is her personal right that is being infringed rather than those of womankind as a whole, though the victim may feel some solidarity with and receive support from other women who stand to be discriminated against in the same way.

It is true that support for rights, particularly rights against governments, implies a commitment to the values of a liberal society. It is possible that in some circumstances it may be more advantageous to waive one's personal rights to, e.g. freedom of speech, movement or political participation in the interests of the collective struggle but there is no reason, in terms of rights theory, why the individual should feel under any moral obligation to so. The popular communitarian Etzioni argues (Etzioni 1993) that we should be more inclined to waive some of our rights for the sake of the community as a whole. In view of recent events his example of the supposed right not to be subjected to suspicionless searches at airports seems particularly pertinent but scarcely a criticism of the notion of rights itself. It has always been part of the concept of Natural Rights that we give up part of our initial freedom for the sake of the common good provided others are prepared to do the same. It seems quite reasonable to suppose that we tacitly consent to the minor inconvenience of a search rather than risk being hijacked or blown up in mid air. MacIntyre (1982), a communitarian of a rather different stamp, rejects the concept of rights along with the whole notion of modern Ethics based on moral rules, in favour of a view of morality to be discussed in Chapters 8 and 9, based on the virtues appropriate to particular societies or practices that contribute to a flourishing human life. He points out that rights may conflict, as indeed they may, and argues that this constitutes both a theoretical and a practical problem for defenders of the concept. MacIntyre, however, rather exaggerates the extent to which rights may conflict (Wringe 2001) and fails to point out that virtues may also conflict with each other.

It is, finally, sometimes argued that talk of rights is inappropriate in contexts such as the family or indeed schools or even wider communities which ought to manage their affairs in the light of love and concern rather than legalistic notions of rights. This is partly true. Life in an environment in which people stood upon their rights and gave or did nothing that could not be demanded as a right would be impoverished indeed. But equally, the notion that we may ignore the rights of those bound to us by ties of affection or friendship would be monstrous. What is essential to a civilised society is that we should at least ensure that we respect each others' rights. If, then, out of love, neighbourliness or collegiality we waive some of our own rights, or in meeting each others' rights we ensure we give good measure, heaped up, pressed down and running over, so much the better. In such a community, rights need never be mentioned, but only because there is a common understanding that they, and those who hold them, will be implicitly respected.

This, perhaps, is a further reason why the concept of rights is of particular importance to the moral educator and all interested in the personal development of future adults. That one has rights, perfectly legitimate expectations of others that one may, if necessary, stand upon is essential to one's self respect (Feinberg 1970). This is particularly so in the case of young people from groups who have not traditionally been accustomed to make demands of others on the basis or privilege or status. In this regard, rights are a truly moral concept in the sense denied by Scruton to Utilitarianism, in that a consciousness of one's own rights and those of others may serve to guide someone through life and be formative of his or her character. Rights are, however, to be seen in the context of other moral values such as love, generosity or the common interest. They may also conflict, as when someone makes mutually incompatible promises to two different people. One should not make such errors or commit such dishonesties, but rights are created by the two promises just the same and at least require reparation when one or other of the promises is broken. Rights are not absolute but are limited by the rights of others and sometimes by wider interests. It is not always wise or courteous to refer explicitly to one's rights, but young people may sometimes need to do so in a world where others are not always disposed to deal with them generously.

RATIONALITY

Like the theory of Natural Rights, Kant's theory of moral obligation also represents an attempt to break free from traditional or religious authority and put forward a conception of moral conduct and its justification on the basis of reason alone. Writers like Hobbes, Locke, Rousseau and others started from certain assumptions about human nature, human needs and so on and then argued for a moral and political system which would ensure that those needs were met. Human beings, it was assumed, were naturally capable of managing their own lives but, given their vulnerability and the natural competition for resources, needed some arrangement to enable them to manage their co-operation efficiently and provide protection against attack from without and disorder and mutual strife within. The particular arrangements they proposed depended on their assumptions about human nature or, as they explained it, the way human beings would behave in a state of nature. For Hobbes, for example, the state of nature was one of mutual fear and war of all against all, necessitating the absolute rule of an uncontested sovereign. Locke and Rousseau took a more optimistic view of human nature and were able to propose more liberal views based on ideas of mutual consent and devotion to the common interest.

By contrast, Kant, whose conclusions are in some ways strikingly similar to those of the rights theory considered above, is in some respects more radical, attempting to dispense with all reference to the contingencies of human nature and the human condition and deduce a moral theory a priori from the nature of rationality alone. The grounds of such a theory would take no account of human needs, shortcomings, desires or inclinations but apply, in principle to all rational beings whatsoever and wherever. Only in its application would it need to take account of the particularities of human nature. Essentially, his argument, as summarised in the *Fundamental Principles of the Metaphysics of Ethics* (Kant 1785) is as follows.

We need to found our theory in something that is absolutely good and requires no further justification. Only a good will, a determination to act morally irrespective of consequences and outcomes, meets this criterion. Kant was certainly familiar with British and other contemporary philosophers and we may see this as an explicit rejection of the consequentialist assumptions he will have noted in their work. How then, he asks, are we to characterise a will to act morally if it is to have no reference to outcomes or the satisfaction of human needs or desires? It must be essentially a will to obey the moral law and it is of the nature of a law to be universal in its application. If one's act is to be moral, the rule or maxim under which it falls must be capable of being a universal law without internal contradiction or incoherence. It must also be the sort of thing one could wish to be a universal law. Kant gives two examples, promise breaking and suicide, which could not possibly be universal laws without self-contradiction. He also gives two further examples, failure to develop one's talents and failure to be benevolent which, though logically possible candidates for universal laws are not ones that anyone could, in their own interests, wish to be followed by others. To act irrationally and therefore on Kant's view immorally, is to wish the rules which the above actions break to be universal laws but to seek exceptions in one's own case.

Kant distinguishes between the rules of skill and prudence (hypothetical imperatives which we must obey if we wish to achieve certain ends) and the categorical imperatives which we are obliged to obey without reference to the outcome. He provides the following account of this categorical imperative and the reasons why are we obliged to obey it. The non-rational contents of the universe, animals and things, are he explains, subject to the physical laws of nature, as are human beings when they act in accordance with their instincts, desires and inclinations. Insofar, however, as they are rational, human beings are free to act according to the moral law. For rational beings, things are only good as means to their ends. Each rational being, however, sees him or herself not as a means but as a source of ends and, in order not to make rationally unjustified exceptions in his or her own case, is rationally bound to view other rational beings in the same light. It is therefore rationally and morally obligatory always to treat other rational beings as ends in themselves and never solely as means, or as it is sometimes more succinctly put, as persons not as things. The rationally chosen ends of one rational being therefore set limits to the freedom of all other rational beings and his or her legitimate ends are similarly limited by theirs. This is an elaboration of the moral law that the rational agent must be able to will that the maxim of their actions should be such as they could will to be a moral law. To this extent, all rational agents, insofar as they choose to act rationally and morally, become legislators identifying maxims of action that are binding both on themselves and upon all other rational beings. It is possible to conceive of what Kant calls a 'kingdom of ends' as a sort of parliament of all rational beings promulgating universal laws both binding on and chosen by themselves. As rational beings they must not only obey universal rules but necessarily also choose to do so. Though subject to the law, they are also autonomous and possess the dignity of the autonomous legislator because the law they obey is of their own choosing and their own making. To act morally is, therefore, to act in such a way as would render the kingdom of ends possible.

In fact, Kant provides three versions of the moral law:
--- Act only so that one can will that the maxim of one's acts should become a universal law.
--- So act as to treat humanity as an end, never as a means only.
--- Act in such a way as would render a kingdom of ends possible.

Though arrived at in different ways these three versions express a single idea since all require that our actions be those which all rational beings could choose and accept as binding on themselves, namely that the rational choices of rational beings are to be respected.

Though the doctrine has been subjected to many well known criticisms, it has nevertheless been and remains very influential among philosophers and its conclusions are mirrored in many of the insights of popular morality where these do not depend on the precepts of tradition and religion. Deontologists such as Hare (1963), for example, see universaliability as the principle criterion of moral validity and sometimes give the impression that they would find separate and independent systems of moral rules acceptable provided only that they were internally consistent. Kant's requirement that in legislating morally, all interests should be discounted and only principle should be considered, is partly reflected in Rawls' (1973) proposal that an ideal system of justice might be arrived at by a group of individuals who must devise such a system in ignorance of their own position, and therefore of their own interests in that system. Rule utilitarians rely, as we saw, on the principle of universalisability in attempting to give an account of individual moral actions that appear to run counter to the requirement to maximise happiness. Even Bentham's requirement that, in summating happiness, each should count for one an none for more than one, clearly not itself justifiable in utilitarian terms, may seem to owe something to the idea that no-one may be seen purely as a means to the extent that his or her happiness may be written off as of less account than that of others. There is, too, a similarity between the way each of us sees him or herself as existing in our own right with concerns as important to ourselves as those of others are to them. The idea is also present in Colonel Rainborough's remark that the smallest he that is in England has a life to live as much as the greatest he (Clarke 1891)

At a popular level, a rebuke or objection may often be backed by the question 'What would happen if everyone did that?' or 'Suppose I did that to you?', by the injunction to do as one would be done by, the proverb that what is sauce for the goose is sauce for the gander, that you cannot give one person a pin while giving the other a needle and that treating rules as if they were only made for others is not on. Perhaps more striking is the fact that, in everyday discussion, particular indignation is reserved for those who 'use' others or 'make a convenience' of them. The question 'What about me? Am I to count for nothing?' expresses the same idea while the Russian expression 'Ya tozhe chelovjek' (I too am a human being) seems almost to have passed into the popular idiom directly from Kant's writings themselves. The notion that we should treat rational and therefore human beings as ends rather than purely as means may also seem to underlie the demand, nowadays widely accepted, that even though someone may have the power and even the undisputed right to do something, he or she should at least consult those who will be affected by it and hear any objections they may have.

In assessing the validity of Kant's argument, the first thing to note is that certain elements in it are very much the product of their time. Kant, like other moralists of the Enlightenment is, for example, impressed by the fact that the physical universe appears to be governed by inexorable laws and concludes from this that the moral universe must be so as well. Today, we no longer accept such simplistic parallelisms. Talk of the supposed 'laws' of the natural sciences is nowadays recognised to be a metaphor and we have no reason to suppose that they will necessarily be paralleled in the fields of human behaviour, history or morality.

From the need to explain how it is that the rational will, supposedly belonging to the world of ideas, is able to act upon the body which is part of the physical world, and therefore ought only to be subject to the laws of the physical universe, Kant escapes by recourse to a version of dualism which is partly his own and partly derived from ancient philosophical traditions. The physical actions of the body, Kant tells us, belong to the outward deceptive, empirical world of the senses whereas the will is part of the true noumenal self which is necessarily beyond the limits of human investigation. It is also from older philosophical traditions that Kant inherits the notion that anything that is to be important and truly valid philosophically must be derived a priori. It would be an understatement to say that he is highly disparaging of attempts to derive moral doctrines from knowledge of human nature or human affairs. Yet, as Hume (1748) shows, and Kant was certainly aware of Hume's work, conclusions for action can no more be derived from a priori argumentation than from physical facts alone. It also appears to be Kant's assumption, whether an effect of the general climate of his time or of his own personal background, that what he took to be required of secular moral argument was a single ultimate justification for a universal deontology that could be delivered with all the explicitness, authority and circumstance with which the prophet or preacher was able to pronounce upon the law of God.

A number of well known objections have been made to Kant's arguments and conclusions. Williams (Smart and Williams 1973) quotes Frankena's criticism that many things, like tying one's left shoe lace before one's right, could perfectly well be willed as universal laws but are not morally obligatory at all. From this it would appear that, even if Kant's argument can be used to forbid actions which cannot be made the object a universal law, it certainly cannot be used to render obligatory all of those which can. More serious is the problem of conflicting obligations, which may afflict any deontological doctrine. We cannot will that people should make false promises, but we also cannot will that they should allow harm to come to each other. But sometimes making a false promise may be the only means of preventing harm to someone. ('Promise to marry me or I'll kill your brother'.) Ingenious Kantians may be able to find a way out of such dilemmas by asking, in the present case for instance, whether a promise made under such conditions is properly described as a promise at all or by suggesting that we could perfectly well will that a universal law should read 'Only break a promise in order to prevent harm to someone'. But once we start to complicate the simplicity of the universal law, the possibilities of casuistry are extensive and it becomes a matter of contention which Orwellian adjustments to the simple law rational beings could reasonably permit themselves.

Williams (1985) makes the rather different objection, that Kantian rational beings would only seem to be committed by their rationality to respect their own humanity, not to that of others and certainly not to the whole panoply of obligations implied by the possibility of a kingdom of ends. Arguably, however, Williams, who is out to disparage all brands of moral theory, takes an unduly limited view of rationality in a being who, ex hypothesi, must respond to no human desires or commitments at all. Perhaps Williams' more telling criticism is that such a personally and socially detached individual could scarcely be capable of identity or of having any desires at all. Kant, of course, makes it clear that he is concerned only with the logic of the moral law, not with its application in the empirical world of human affairs.

Though we may be inclined to go along with Kant's conclusions that we should be consistent as between the things we do ourselves and those we demand of others, that we should respect the integrity and dignity of others and that we should collectively strive for something resembling a Kantian kingdom of ends, it is far from obvious that we do so on the strength of Kant's grandiose reasons. Rationality may set the conditions of debate: non-contradiction, the link between assumptions, fact, argument and conclusion, the avoidance of self interest, personal bias or appeal to emotion. But it is difficult to imagine rationality as the kind of substantive entity as Kant seems to conceive of it, with imposing qualities such as the ability to inspire awe or to command in such a way as to impel us to obey. Of course, all human beings possess dignity and deserve our respect, especially those that have a conception of their own position in the scheme of things and thought through rational purposes of their own. But this is not due to their role as potential 'legislators' in the kingdom of ends or anywhere else. Unlike Kant, we do not live in an age where legislators are thought to be ipso facto entitled to respect. Legislators may inspire fear, or sympathy for their near impossible task but if some of them have dignity and respect beyond that required by all human beings, this not on account of their role as legislators but because of their personal qualities as individuals. It is also the case that, in contrast to what seems to be implied by Kant's argument, our obligations are not limited to rational beings but to all that is to be regarded as 'other' in relation to ourselves, including human beings who are not yet, are no longer or never will be truly rational, to animals regarding which we seem to have an obligation, at least not to inflict unnecessary pain and in respect of, if not actually to, the physical environment.

We must also regard as problematic the notion that morality is only to be spelled out in terms of rules on the model of laws, edicts or biblical commandments. As will be argued more fully in later chapters, reasons to act may be of various kinds and the attempt to apply a single principle to all situations of decision or moral judgement is bound sometimes to lead to distortion, inhumanity or even the justification of evident wickedness. Human affairs are just too complicated to be conducted according to simple imperatives. Where matters of serious concern are at issue, many kinds of consideration may have relevance and in some cases no outcome may leave the agent totally immune from censure on one ground or another.

It is one of the ironies of Kantian ethics, which identifies moral freedom or autonomy as the pinnacle of moral achievement, that it appears to leave so little room for diversity or dissent, for the theory is explicitly and repeatedly predicated on the notion of rational beings engaged in rational conduct. Persons or conduct falling short of this rigorous norm lie outside the pale of moral justification. If it is irrational to respond differently in the absence of different givens, all rational beings would seem obliged to react to the same situation in the same way. Such indeed is a condition of the kingdom of ends in which that which one legislates for all, coincides with one's own will. For Kant, there seems to be no possibility of alternative rational perspectives and, in contrast to rights theory, there would appear to be no area of justified moral conduct reserved for private decision.

The defence that Kant is concerned with the underlying rationale of morality rather than its detailed working out in the uncertain empirical context of human life, raises a number of problems. Even if Kant' theory is coherent at a metaphysical level, there are, as we have seen, problems about arguing from a priori deductions about the features of rationality to action in the real world. It is also far from evident that all our reasons for action follow from or instantiate Kant's conclusions. No doubt, as in the case of Utilitarianism, lines of justification can, with a measure of ingenuity, be drawn between Kantian principle and any given course of action that seems morally justified but often the link between ground and action may seem more immediate and less ratiocinative than a Kantian account would seem to imply, a fact that would seem to render the metaphysical framework otiose.

None of this, however, is to imply that the moral educator may ignore the implications of Kant's ethical theory. Not only has it been culturally of great importance but the terms in which Kant's conclusions are expressed, particularly his prohibition upon treating humanity purely as a means, often provides emotive underpinning for many of our most stridently uttered moral criticisms. That someone, or a group of individuals, are being used as a means without due consideration for their own purposes and aspirations in public and professional as well as private life, is often regarded as the most damaging of all moral criticisms. With rather less justification, given the complexity of human affairs referred to above, we also tend to demand consistency, not only in conduct but in the possible implications of conduct, especially at the level of public policy.

Any account of Kantian ethical theory would no doubt be inaccessible to all but the ablest and intellectually most ambitious of school pupils. At all levels, however, it seems entirely appropriate to draw attention to the desirability of our conduct and our judgements of the conduct of others being consistent and reasonable, of considering the point of view, concerns and feelings of others and of striving for harmony with others who are prepared to do the same.

CHAPTER 8

VIRTUES

The accounts of morality we have considered so far take it for granted that moral goodness is a matter of conforming to certain rules: always do what will maximise happiness or well being, avoid infringing people's rights, act so as to treat other people as ends and not solely as means or in such a way that one could consistently wish others to do likewise and so on. The underlying assumptions of such views are that morality is about individual actions people choose to perform and that the business of choosing is essentially one of reflecting upon whether or not the action in question falls under one of the rules that we have so far considered. Though some people may have a greater tendency to follow their chosen rule than others, what is essentially at issue is not the character of the agent but the rightness of his or her action here and now. In principle, the approach envisages no absurdity in the idea of someone acting with impeccable morality one day and behaving like a scoundrel the next. This approach to morality is termed 'action based' rather than 'agent based'.

In the present chapter, we are concerned with an approach which focuses not upon particular actions but upon the character traits of those who perform them. People's characters are, of course, ultimately defined by the things they commonly do. Our approval of someone's character necessarily depends on whether or not we approve of the things they do or have done in the past. Nevertheless, many of our day-to-day moral judgements are about people, their characters and their individual character traits rather than particular actions. Concentrating our scrutiny upon character and character traits rather than actions may lead to insights that would otherwise be lost to us, not the least of these being the fact that it concentrates attention on the agent's motives rather than on the action itself. Did he or she do it out of generosity, pride or a spiteful desire to humiliate someone else? What sort of person are we dealing with here? This sort of approach, concentrating as it does on the character of the agent rather than on the details of individual actions, gives rise to educational reflections different from those provoked by giving attention to individual actions.

Much of the recent interest in so-called Virtue Ethics would appear to arise from the dissatisfaction and frustration felt with the action focused approaches we have considered earlier. Among other things, as we saw, Utilitarianism ultimately appears capable of justifying actions that, intuitively speaking, seem morally deplorable. Rights based approaches may seem harsh and litigious and the Kantian moral law may seem to fail to bridge the gap between the grounding reasons of rationality and the motivating reasons that can only be provided by the very inclinations which Kant himself rejects. Slote (1992) and Williams (1985) make much of the internal contradictions of Utilitarianism and its failure to take account of moral luck, of the logical gaps in the Kantian argument, of the universalism of both utilitarian and Kantian doctrines which do not explain the special duties we owe to those close to us. Anscombe, as early as 1958, points to what she sees as the absurdity of speaking of moral rules and moral laws in the modern secular world in which we are no longer able to acknowledge a divine law-giver and MacIntyre (1982) compares the state of contemporary ethical theory to what might be left of scientific knowledge after some catastrophe in which the underlying theories of Science had been lost. What has been lost, according to MacIntyre, is an understanding of the nature of virtue as represented by the philosophers of the ancient world, notably by Aristotle.

For Aristotle, a good person (Aristotle, of course, speaks only of a good man) is characterised by certain virtues or excellences that are the mean between two excesses. Courage, for example, falls between timidity and rashness, and generosity between extravagance and meanness. His list of virtues may be rather different from ours. We may set less store by physical courage or proper pride and he has little to say about charity towards the unfortunate or about humility. Significantly, however, Aristotle's virtues are not simply generalised descriptions of outward actions but reflect the inner motives and commitments of the individual concerned. Unlike the Kantian moral agent whose inclinations are irrelevant, Aristotle's virtuous person not only acts virtuously but is a lover of virtue. Significantly for the moral educator, though we become virtuous by performing virtuous acts, coercion is not a good strategy of moral education, for to become virtuous we must not only perform virtuous actions but must perform them out of a virtuous motivation. In addition to performing outwardly approved actions, young people must be brought to see the point and value of such conduct and act as they do out of a conviction that it is a right and admirable thing to do.

Thus simplistically stated, the notion of Virtue Ethics raises a number of questions, not all of which may be convincingly resolved. One of the most pressing of these is how we are to know which traits are to be considered virtues and perhaps even more importantly in terms of everyday debate, how exactly we are to know when the golden mean between the vices of deficiency and excess has been hit. Pincoffs' (1986) definition of virtues as dispositional characteristics that make someone the 'right' sort of person, the sort of person one would prefer, tells us little for it necessarily embraces all the positive qualities a human being may possess. His attempt to characterise the strictly moral virtues and vices, on the other hand, as 'forms of regard or lack of regard for the interests of others' (p. 89) and the opposite of moral virtues as 'taking unfair advantage of the other person . . . rejection of the other person, using him or denying consideration to him' comes perilously close to a Kantian position which, along with other 'standard' moral theories, it is Pincoffs' object to reject. Significant in Aristotle's answer to the question of the identity of the moral virtues and the location of the golden mean is the stress it places on the role of reason, though his particular reasoning may seem to rest on premises which we are no longer able simply to assume.

Those qualities are virtues, according to Aristotle, which lead to human flourishing, or human happiness or human well-being. For, as indicated by the variety of terms used by English translators to render it, the Greek term eudaimonia partakes of all these ideas. So what is the flourishing life for human beings? What would be a good example of such a life, a life lived by a good human being according to the virtues? If Aristotle's analogy between a good horse, which is strong and therefore good for what horses are meant to do and a good man, seems flawed to us, it must be borne in mind that Aristotle was able to rely upon consensus among his audience as to what actually did constitute a good life for Man, or at least a good life for a Greek. His much criticised teleological argument that the aim of human life was that of intellectual contemplation actually makes little significant contribution to his ideal of the citizen, who is courageous but not foolhardy, properly modest without being self-effacing, possessed of self-respect without arrogance, generous in contributing to the public weal without indecent extravagance, temperate without coldness and above all just. The ideal is that of a citizen actively and effectively participating in the life of the polis, rather than given to recluse-like speculation.

The picture is attractive, not to say edifying, but one which is, if to a lesser extent than some relativists might have us believe, one that is tied to a particular time, place and social group. It is, indeed, the central point of MacIntyre's *After Virtue,* that the nature of virtuous living and right conduct are not to be arrived at by universal abstract reasoning but are embodied in the values of particular societies and determined by its objective needs for self-preservation or practices (Medecine, Law, Science, Art) which contribute to the flourishing life of human beings and societies. It is also dependent on social roles. As MacIntyre puts it 'We enter upon a stage which we did not design and find ourselves part of an action that was not of our making' (MacIntyre 1982, p.199) Our role and the virtues that will be required of us depend on who we are, indeed what we are, whose child, father, servant or friend we are.

Such a conception of morality has obvious problems. It would appear to be both conservative and wide open to abuse. For all Aristotle's assertion of the importance of reason, the source of our virtues, at least on MacIntyre's interpretation, seems to be not reason but established tradition. Far from the critical young being able to arrive at their own values and conception of virtue by reflection, they are dependent on what is handed down to them. We not only enter a stage that is not of our making but have to listen to our elders as to how to perform our allocated role upon it. Needless to say, our list of virtues, especially those virtues we wish to see in others, will depend on our interests, those traits in others which seem likely to contribute to our own flourishing life. Taking our cue from Plato's *Meno* we might suppose that virtue in a wife requires her to be supportive of her husband, chaste obviously, affectionate but not too demanding and not given to asking awkward questions too insistently. Virtues in a servant will include obedience, respect, flexibility, diligence and zeal.

The notion of the golden mean between excess and deficiency is also far from unproblematic and Aristotle's account of it once again leads to conservatism. One man's courage is another's recklessness, one man's caution is another's cowardice and will certainly be so characterised by his opponents in debate. Where does the true mean lie? Recently there has been some political debate about attempts to shift the centre ground of politics to left or right and reference to the mean is a well recognised device of conservative rhetoric. 'Of course we wish to be caring employers. Far from us the wish to see workers or their families actually starve to death but . . .' The standard Aristotelian answer to the question of how the virtues are to be applied is that they should be exercised at the right time, in the right way, to the right degree and that in deciding how we should conduct ourselves we should ask ourselves what the virtuous person would do. On this view, the staple methodology and content of moral education would not be aimed at helping young people to come to a sensible and reasonable understanding about what they and others should do but pointing to the example of those whose conduct was recognised as virtuous and admirable, taking role models, perhaps, from real life, History or fictional tales. Such an answer chimes with our intuitive tendency in our moral dilemmas to seek the advice of the mature and experienced, rather than precocious youth but it is not clear in a rapidly changing world that reference to established or past models remains expedient. If the life-conditions of the present generation differ too radically from those of previous ones, it is understandable if the young take some convincing that the wisdom of established figures is any longer relevant to their own case. The stage on which we play out our roles may not be of our making but it is not obvious that those who have performed our roles before us have done so in a way that is appropriate to the particular conditions of our time. We shall shortly consider whether it is possible to draw generally defensible conclusions as to what constitutes a flourishing life for human beings or whether we are hopelessly subject to the necessities of historical determinism as society inexorably evolves through the gamut of political and religious ideologies or the arbitrary flux of fashion as one conception of the good or flourishing life, propounded by this guru or that, publicly succeeds another.

One of the strengths of Virtue Ethics is that it comes to the aid of the moral educator by providing something of an answer to the problem of moral motivation. Insofar as the publicly recognised list of virtues is necessary to the maintenance of a particular society, as in the case of the virtue of martial courage in a victorious heroic society, its point will be obvious. The values which the virtue reflects are already present in the society or, as it may be, in the worthwhile practice or professional activity in which it plays a part and to which the learner is already committed. If the virtues represent human excellences and are difficult to achieve, requiring judgement or strength of mind, they necessarily attract praise and justify self-esteem. In the context of a society or milieu to whose way of life the virtues are important, the growing child learns to value honesty, courage or self-respect as he or she learns his or her mother tongue (Taylor 1992). To possess these qualities just is to be a better person in the language and culture of that society. It is in one's best interests to have these qualities and it is in this sense that Plato (*Republic 1)* says that no-one knowingly does wrong, that no rational person would knowingly act against his or her most fundamental best interests. Seen in this light, the practice of a virtue such as honesty has a quite different feel from conformity to a moral rule forbidding untruthfulness, which may have little to do with pupils' conception of their own identity and actually seem to stand in the way of their best interests and even bring them into contempt, including self-contempt in a society or sub-culture in which material success and outsmarting others is all important.

Hursthouse (2001) argues that we can only appreciate the virtues of honesty, courage, charity or whatever if we are 'on the inside' of the values they represent and could not successfully argue for them from a neutral or objective position. This may be to rather overstate the case. She is no doubt right to say that we could not expect to convince a mafioso gangster or sharp-practising businessman but this is no test, for these characters suffer from the disadvantage of being already imprisoned inside another set of values. The lesson for the moral educator, insofar as the virtue ethicist's position is valid, would seem to be that it is impossible to make the liberal assumption that moral reasoning alone will enable students to arrive at valid moral conclusions independently. Appropriate value perceptions must first be communicated by the representatives of the adult society as part of the process of socialisation. It may also be necessary to 'release' young people from the inside of undesirable value systems by means of questioning and criticism or removal from the social context in which these systems prevail. This, however, need not lead us to the pessimistic conclusion that moral education is necessarily a matter of indoctrination or brain washing, for it is perfectly possible to pass on to our children in infancy, virtues that seem to us to contribute to a flourishing life for themselves and others without doing so in a way that precludes subsequent criticism, refinement or ultimately rejection (White 1970). Such a process is in no way ruled out by the traditional nature of Virtue Ethics for as writers such Oakeshott (1962) and MacIntyre (1982) have pointed out, traditions are not necessarily rigid or inflexible. The search for the flourishing life is unending but is constantly renewed from within. In theory, the search may lead wherever it leads. In traditions as in Biology there is no law of evolution. Only too radical or sudden a rejection of what has gone before is ruled out by our understanding of Virtue Ethics and the relation of a virtuous life to the established values of a particular society.

In the light of the above it might be supposed that Virtue Ethics raises the whole question of moral relativism, given the relationship between the virtues and particular ways of life. The question is whether certain ways of life and the virtues that support them can be unequivocally communicated to the young or whether we should, with exemplary political correctness, say that there are an infinity of different possible ways of life, each dependent on their peculiar virtues which may be described as equally flourishing or capable of flourishing according to whether their characteristic virtues are practised or not? Or are there objective criteria according to

which some ways of life may be pronounced flourishing and others not? The
question of logical priorities, whether society establishes the nature of moral
judgement or whether moral judgement may establish what is or is not a desirable
form of society, will receive further consideration in the next chapter. Here it is
proposed to consider what, if anything, can be said about the nature of human beings
that sets limits to the conditions under which they may be said to flourish and, more
particularly, whether there is any objective way in which some traits may be
designated virtues and their absence or shortcomings vices. Are there, as Plato
conceives it, traits which would both benefit any society and at the same time also
benefit their possessors and make them better qua human beings?

Our difficulty is that the proposition seems to presuppose some ideal pattern of
human life and human development against which such a judgement may be made,
but positing such a pattern simply restates our view of the virtues rather than
providing an objective template against which it may be tested. For Plato, this would
pose few logical problems. The wise man, the philosopher, would be able to directly
intuit the objective and unchanging ideal forms of the virtues just as he was able to
directly intuit the form of the good. Aristotle's attempt to define the ideal man is
equally unconvincing to the modern eye. For while sharpness and strength may be
the essential qualities of good knives and horses, no such simple quality appears to
define the essence of a good human being. Nevertheless, Aristotle does point to
wisdom, phronesis, as the ability to discriminate between better and worse and
notably between good and poor performance in the area of conduct. This may be part
of the answer, provided we can discover criteria beyond those of socially determined
intuition, according to which rational judgement can be made. In establishing these
we may, perhaps not surprisingly, be driven back on principles provided for us by
both consequentialist and deontological doctrines or, like MacIntyre, upon quasi
Marxist assumptions according to which the conditions of a flourishing life are in
part historically determined.

In an attempt to develop Aristotle's view that a good way of life is that which is
peculiarly good for human beings given their particular nature, Hursthouse (2001)
follows Foot in attempting a biological analogy, starting from the premise that the
term 'good' does not suddenly change its grammar when used in moral evaluation.
To pronounce something, particularly an organism, good is, she claims, to say that it
is a good specimen of its kind. For example, a good plant, one that is flourishing, is
one whose physical characteristics are such as to assure its individual survival and
the regeneration of its species. Similar comments may be made about a good
specimen in the animal world, except that behaviour as well as physical
characteristics will contribute to the successful survival of the individual and the
continuance of the species and its characteristic well-being. Evident pleasure in life
and absence of distress may be seen as additional markers. In social animals such as
bees and wolves, behaviour that contributes to the functioning of the group may also
be seen as characteristic of a good, non-defective specimen.

Hursthouse tentatively suggests that in addition to those physical aspects of
human excellence which we consider to fall under such categories as medicine or
health, our most commonly mentioned virtues: courage in circumstances of threat to

the group, charity, temperance, fidelity, truthfulness, care for the upbringing of the young, justice and so on may all be seen to contribute to the sociobiological ends of individual survival, continuance of the species and well-being. As far as it goes, this argument has some plausibility, though, as Hursthouse concedes, we may have to go in for a measure of special pleading for certain perfectly acceptable practices such as celibacy and single sex cohabitation not to be stigmatised. However, the argument does not go far enough. Individual survival is, of course, important and no doubt, as the environmentalists point out, the characteristically Aristotelian vices of greed and intemperance may actually threaten the continuance of the species. Fundamental as these are, however, they are relatively mundane human goals and provide a somewhat uninspiring rationale for the subtlety and range of human virtues that have been discussed over the centuries. Furthermore, the analogy between the physical excellences of natural organisms and the moral excellences of human beings is just that, an analogy, however evocative some may find it. We do, indeed, admire the excellence of physical attributes but the admiration we experience for moral qualities involving judgement, self-discipline and strength of character is of a different kind.

More, however, may be made of Hursthouse's comment that just as movement marks a significant step as we ascend the evolutionary scale from plants to animals, so rationality may mark a similarly significant step between the conduct of animals and human beings. Regrettably, like Aristotle, at least in the *Ethics*, she does little to explore the implications of rationality or unpick the characteristic well-being of human beings. With regard to rationality, Hursthouse points us in the right direction with her comment that animal behaviour is governed by nature and unreflective instinct; whereas that of human beings is at least in part the consequence of reflection, which may, in fact, countermand our instincts and inclinations. We employ our reason to change our conduct, and change it for the better. Milne (1968) distinguishes four levels of rationality: rationality at the levels of efficiency, prudence, wisdom and morality. We exercise rationality at the level of efficiency when we use a stick or spade to turn the soil instead of our bare hands and prudence when we set resources aside for foreseeable contingencies. Here, learning and understanding already play a part in our ability to improve our behaviour in response to rational decision. We exercise rationality at Milne's level of wisdom when we choose not only between means but between ends as when, for example, we choose between spending time with family and friends and working longer in the pursuit of wealth and ambition. Rational conduct at the level of morality, according to Milne, is chosen when we act with due regard for the consequences to others without arbitrarily (i.e. irrationally) discriminating in our own favour, even though rationality at the levels of efficiency, prudence and even wisdom may suggest that one should do so. In arriving at the conclusions of rationality at the levels of wisdom and morality, language will have played an even more important part than at the levels of efficiency and prudence, both as the medium by which the traditions in one's society have been communicated to one and in facilitating one's own reflections and discussions with others. Human beings are not only concerned to improve their own personal conduct at all four levels of rationality. At a political level, the use of language is important in debate as we strive to persuade others to, as we see it, exercise a greater degree of rationality at the levels of efficiency, prudence, wisdom and morality in such a way as to improve our human well-being by the way we arrange our affairs and employ and distribute our resources.

Human beings, then, characteristically employ rationality to improve their conduct in order to improve their well-being, including their well-being at the level of material satisfaction and self-sufficiency. It is also characteristic of human beings that, as the development of the Women's Movement has shown, comfortable survival and the mere continuation of the species is not sufficient for the well-being of many of them. In addition to the characteristic pursuit of change and improvement in conduct, human well-being also seems to require what might disparagingly be described as amusement but is perhaps more properly characterised as the disinterested pursuit or contemplation of skill or excellence. This may take place at various levels from popular pursuits and pastimes, athletic sports or Music, Art, Literature, Science, Philosophy, religious devotion, or whatever, some of these latter, be it noted, particularly engaging the mind.

The search for improvement through the application of rationality and interest in the pursuit or contemplation of skill or excellence would therefore seem to be, if not universal, at least fairly widespread characteristics of human life in society. It is not being claimed that these are necessarily defining characteristics of humankind. No doubt many others might be identified, such as the enjoyment of individual personal affections. Possibly settling on just these characteristics represents a selective reading of human cultural history or the undue influence of Western ideologies of progress. But if these are in any sense deep seated or significant features, they may enable us to reach some tentative criteria of human flourishing and the kinds of character trait by which it would be favoured.

Human beings would, no doubt, get a better and surely more flourishing life than many have at the moment if only rationality were universally applied at the levels of efficiency and prudence to provide the necessities of material well-being. A greater allocation of effort and resources at Milne's rationality at the level of wisdom might not come amiss either. But what is certain is that life would be immeasurably more flourishing for many if power and resources were distributed according to rationality at the level of morality, as expressed in the virtues of justice or, where gaps needed to be filled, the virtue of charity. Nor would life be rendered less flourishing by the exercise of such virtues as kindness, mutual respect or tolerance, such that no-one needed to walk in fear or practice hypocrisy rather than unfeigned sincerity or easy openness, where honesty inspired trust in commercial, political or personal relations, where temperance, reasonable diligence, good order and public spirit ensured that all and not merely a privileged elite had access to disinterested and exciting or stimulating activities. In view of the miseries, poverty, greed, hypocrisy, cruelty and oppression created by Western liberal societies, both within and outside their own territories, the criticism that the above is some kind of expression of a Western liberal perspective would obviously be absurd. It is, indeed, difficult to imagine any organised society in which life would not be enhanced or its miseries lessened by the virtues mentioned, though clearly their expression would vary from society to society and they would be more compatible with other values in some societies than elsewhere. What is obviously more contentious is whether we can say that since these virtues appear to chime with what are arguably near universal human needs, societies which encourage or at least do not inhibit their practice are in some sense preferable to those where the reverse is true.

Reflection upon the nature of virtue, or of particular virtues, desirable traits or virtuous character and their place in human life, gives us access to insights not available via thoughts about the rightness or otherwise of particular acts. One becomes aware of the way in which morality may inform all the actions and relationships of our daily lives and that moral judgement is not simply a facility to be employed when we are faced with difficult decisions. Honesty, candour, kindness, conscientiousness, moderation courage and the like, as well as the avoidance of their two corresponding vices of excess (deceit and pedantry, hypocrisy and indiscretion, meanness and profligacy, carelessness and neurotic scruple, fanaticism and insensitivity, rashness and timidity) are indeed the fruit of reason but a result of constant self-evaluation rather than conscious one-off debates about individual actions on the basis of higher order moral principles. They inform the way we are, the way we do things, the way we customarily interact with others.

Philosophical theories of Virtue Ethics have found practical expression in notions of character education. The term was widely used in the private sector of British education in the nineteenth and early twentieth centuries and again far more recently in America from the 1980s onwards. Despite obvious differences of context and emphasis, there are certain fundamental similarities in the two usages. In neither context has it been supposed that there was much problem about deciding what sorts of conduct were to be regarded as desirable, or the outcome of good character. Though in both contexts reasons were to be made explicit enough when they were not considered obvious, these were simple and to the point. There has been little room for speculative sophistication and even less for doubt and dissent. In both cases the virtues were essentially those which contributed to the public good at an obvious or immediate level and have been taken to be recognised unequivocally across society as a whole. Essentially, good character has been a matter of adhering to the recognised virtues with consistency, strength of mind and fortitude, when necessary in the face of difficulty or temptation. The British version particularly emphasised the link with identity and self-esteem. One's character was what one was and whatever one's other talents and achievements, determined the esteem in which one was held. A reputation for good character indicated that one could be relied upon to carry out one's duties or undertakings and see them through with persistence and fortitude.

Many of these connotations are also present when the term is currently used in the United States. Much concern with moral or values education in general and character education in particular has been a response to an outbreak of moral panic in America not unlike that in Britain described in Chapter 1. Lickona (1991) and many others have referred to the supposed deterioration of the social fabric, represented by the increase of such widely ranging phenomena as crime, divorce, vandalism, alcoholism, drug use, abortion, non-marital cohabitation, discourtesy, violence, petty dishonesty and welfare dependence. Tax and business fraud are also occasionally included. In addition to the standard virtues of truthfulness and honesty, trustworthiness and care for others, the socially approved virtues of character to be 'instilled' or 'inculcated' have included compliance, industry, cleanliness, orderliness, civic virtue, citizenship, chastity and patriotism. Values Clarification and Moral Development approaches to values education have been specifically rejected by the proponents of character education as well as anything that smacks of 'Relativism' or as in the case of Lockwood (1997) even, apparently, 'Multiculturalism'. Some writers (Schubert 1997, Lickona 1991, Purpel 1997) tend to use the term 'character education' fairly broadly to refer to moral or values education generally. Lockwood, by contrast, seeks a more explicit behavioural objectives oriented definition of the expression in terms of the 'shaping' of behaviour in the light of values producing socially approved conduct.

In contrast to some of the more conservative versions of support for the notion of character education, Lickona's (1991) highly influential *Education for Character* reads as an enlightened and largely practical guide in which the key virtues (or 'big ideas' as Lickona calls them) or the 'fourth and fifth Rules of respect and responsibility' are unpacked in terms of specific virtues or forms of desirable conduct. Respect, for Lickona, is characterised not as deference towards social superiors but respect for oneself, the rights and dignity of all persons and for the environment. This is referred to as the restraining side of morality while responsibility, the 'active side' includes taking care of oneself and others, fulfilling one's obligations, contributing to one's community, alleviating suffering and building a better world. Character education, Lickona argues, involves not only moral action but also the development of moral feeling (conscience, empathy, love for the good and humility) and moral knowledge, including knowing moral values, perspective taking, moral reasoning and decision making. The approach is distinctly teacher led. The learning of moral values, for example, unequivocally refers to coming to know and embrace the values held by the adult community rather than an understanding of values generated or identified by young people pupils themselves. However, the twelve strategies advocated by Lickona include the importance of the teacher's role as a care giver, the creation of a democratic classroom environment, the use of co-operative learning, the fostering of caring within and beyond the classroom, the creation of a positive moral culture and the involvement of the community in the classroom. If Lickona's list of strategies includes the explicit teaching of values through the curriculum and the practice of moral discipline, he makes it clear that the use of curriculum subjects and the cross-curricular programme involves the examination and discussion of ethical issues. The practice of moral discipline involves both the enforcement of rules and also the giving of reasons as a means of imparting the values behind the rules.

Despite the many elements of humane educational practice present in Lickona's work, one cannot but feel some anxiety, here as with other character educators, at his simplification of moral education and its goals, to the point where it becomes an intellectually comfortable transmission of the norms of socially acceptable and socially useful behaviour. One appreciates the need to work within the intellectual capacity of pupils of all abilities and the danger of encouraging that brand of relativism which allows pupils to feel that morality is no more than a matter of opinion and that one way of behaving is ultimately as good as any other. Nevertheless, the bland absence of any critical element, and the clear intention that values and behaviours offered should form a part of pupils' permanent repertoire, would appear to place the practice of character education on the edge of indoctrination. It is, after all, the mark of education in morality as in any other field, that learners should be left with a measure of uncertainty and angst about the adequacies of received opinion. Settled complacency is by no means inherent in the background doctrine of Virtue Ethics, given the progressive nature of moral traditions to which we have referred.

Valuable though the contributions of both a virtue approach and even character education may be to moral education, this cannot be the whole story. Though good character may carry us along happily through most of our day to day lives, there will also be times when we are challenged by actual decisions which confront us. Ought one to do this or that? One is offered a post (Let us suppose one works in a profession that brings considerable benefit to others) in another part of the country or abroad. One's decision will have consequences for oneself, one's spouse or partner at the time, one's family, one's present and future employers and clients, one's friends, one's dog. Virtues of loyalty, dedication, ambition to make something of one's life and care and consideration for others will no doubt all be elements in one's decision but cannot make one's decision for one. Typically one's virtues will pull in different directions; otherwise there would be no decision to make. It is one of the obvious criticisms to be made of Virtue Ethics that it provides no decision procedure in the case of conflict. To say, for example, that to possess the virtue of honesty is to know where, when and to what extent to speak the truth is to beg an all-important question. Up to what point is speaking the truth to count as having the virtue of honesty and at what point does it risk becoming the vice of indiscretion and disloyalty. To ask 'What would a virtuous person do in this situation? ' is not to resolve the problem but to restate it. In our relatively unhierarchical society, one can no longer point to eminent exemplars in justification for one's acts. One remains personally responsible for what one does. In cases of collective decision the right thing to do will normally be precisely that which is arrived at by debate conducted in terms of reasons, rather than by the assertion of conflicting virtues or reference to contrary moral exemplars. This said, it must be admitted that an absence of conclusive decision procedures, though particularly conspicuous in the case of Virtue Ethics, is a problem for much moral debate. Both consequentialist and deontological doctrines may produce irresolvable internal conflicts in particular cases as well, of course, as often conflicting with each other. It is for this reason that any attempt to teach some simple and readily identifiable difference between right and wrong represents such an absurdly inadequate characterisation of moral education.

Even, however, if Virtue Ethics, like other moral doctrines, fails to provide a comprehensive account of morality, it must undoubtedly play an important part in any satisfactory understanding of moral education. Quite clearly, honesty, reliability, courage, kindness and so on can be taught in an immediate and straightforward way by means of praise and blame. Distinguishing between good and bad everyday conduct is profoundly educational in the sense that it involves the developing identity of the learner, and the kind of person they want to grow up to be in a way that resolving fictional or even real life dilemmas does not. Insisting that someone should be honest or bringing home to them the despicable and inconsiderate nature of taking what does not belong to them may be accessible to pupils in a way that even relatively simple reasoning of a consequential or deontological kind may not be.

A further strength of a Virtue Ethics approach to moral education is that it is continuous with, indeed an element in, early socialisation. This, however, is also a pointer to one of its obvious dangers. Essentially, becoming committed to a particular virtue, holding it to be more or less important than other virtues, to be the supreme virtue or whatever, is a matter of socialisation and, despite Aristotle's references to the part of reason in virtue, it is far from evident what provision in a virtue approach would be made for critical consideration of the extent to which the virtues of honesty, courage, loyalty or patriotism and so on are appropriate in particular situations, let alone whether they are to be considered virtues at all. Indeed, many of the virtues someone might seek to 'inculcate' into the younger generation may be reinterpreted as Piagetian/Kohlbergian imperatives or prohibitions at, say, level three of their scales. Obviously enough, 'Do not lie' expresses the virtue of truthfulness, 'Do not steal', that of honesty, 'Share your things with the other children', that of kindness and so on. In an authoritarian adult-child situation this inculcatory pattern is probably the simplest and in the minds of some, perhaps, the only form of moral education to be considered. Insofar as the Piaget/Kohlberg account of moral development is in any way a valid reflection of the way things are, undue concentration on an unsophisticated virtue approach to moral education may result in rather inflexible adults who as parents (and teachers) may repeat the process with the next generation. What, in fact, seems to be the case is that the virtues and moral reasoning seem to deal with rather different aspects of morality. There are many things we expect people to do or avoid without too much agonising, though occasionally they may need to exercise a certain amount of determination or strength of mind in the face of temptation or pressure. There are also other issues, possibly of a more complex kind, which occur less often in everyday life but, nowadays at least, may occur sometimes in everybody's life, which are not to be resolved by the exercise of simple or traditional virtues but require to be thought through and perhaps subsequently justified to others in terms of the principles involved. Possibly, however, this process cannot even begin unless individuals first have a commitment to behaving well or virtuously as an essential part of their identity.

CHAPTER 9

COMMUNITARIANISM

Communitarian Ethics or Communitarianism is essentially a development of Virtue Ethics, sharing that doctrine's rejection of a view of morality as a matter of judging the rightness or otherwise of individual acts on the basis of universally valid higher order principles. Communitarian Ethics or Communitarianism may, however, be regarded as developing on two rather different levels. The former term is most frequently used for the philosophical version of this development represented by MacIntyre (1982) Taylor (1992), Walzer (1983) Sandel (1982) and others. Writers such as Etzioni (1988, 1993) and Bellah (1985) may be seen as representing a more popular, common sense advocacy of a particular but not unrelated attitude towards life in the United States, commonly referred to simply as Communitarianism. Like Virtue Ethics the philosophical brand of Communitarian Ethics is concerned with traits of character contributing to or constitutive of the flourishing life and ultimately derivable from the philosophers of ancient Greece. As we saw in the previous chapter, however, both Plato and Aristotle were concerned with a view of the flourishing life reflecting the essential nature of Man and, in Aristotle's case in particular, what were regarded as manifest and taken for granted human teleologies. For Aristotle, Man is a social and political animal and the flourishing life for human beings is therefore necessarily life in society. The nature of the flourishing life is determined by the nature of Man rather than by the nature of particular societies. In fact there is, for perfectly obvious historical reasons, little awareness on the part of Aristotle, either of the different forms the good life might take within a particular society or between different societies. His assumptions about the flourishing life and the virtues which support and constitute it, are essentially those of his own time, place and social group. The flourishing life as seen by the light of reason, can take but one form and requires a single set of virtues to support it. The fundamental assumptions and arrangements of the Greek way of life are more or less unquestioned.

The main target of communitarian criticism, however, is not Aristotle or modern virtue ethicists but the liberal notion that, as it is often expressed, the right is logically prior to the good. On the liberal understanding of things, moral judgements are to be made on the principle enunciated by Locke (1689) and repeated by many others in the liberal tradition, that all are entitled to equal freedom, subject only to the requirement not to interfere with the right of others to enjoy the same. All should be free to choose, pursue and amend their own conception of the good life for themselves without interference from others. In particular, government and government institutions, including state education, should not favour one version of the good life over others. There can, on this view, be no question of society pursuing any kind of collective good over and above the good of its individual members, other than the traditional ones of security and the establishment of the good order that all require to pursue their private ends. In Tönnies' terms (Tönnies 1887) society is essentially a Gesellschaft or association of private individuals who come together, each for their own purposes, rather than a Gemeinschaft or community of people united in pursuit of a common goal or common conception of the good life.

The debate between liberals and communitarians takes place largely at the level of political philosophy and two of the key communitarian philosophers mentioned above, Sandel and Walzer are explicit in directing their criticism at Rawls' (1971) *Theory of Justice,* while Rawls himself defends his theory (Rawls 1985) by pointing out that he is concerned with the political structure of the state rather than with the whole of morality. But the general liberal view that it is only right to interfere with or even express disapproval of others' life-style choices if they harm others is by no means limited to political discussion. Neither Macintyre nor Taylor explicitly address their criticisms to the work of Rawls at any length or write in such a way as to permit us to assume that their remarks only apply at a macro political level.

Historically, the liberal principle here being considered has been important initially as a criticism of religious persecution and later as a defence against religious and moral bigotry and personal oppression in social and family contexts. The claims that how one chooses to live one's life is one's own affair may also be seen as a protest by someone who feels they are being subjected to psychological coercion or criticised at a personal level. That we may not actively interfere with someone's way of life does not, however, mean that we are banned from forming the judgement that some ways of life are more admirable, worthwhile or inspiring than others. Ways of life remain a legitimate area of discussion and evaluation. The very notion of choosing one way of life rather than another or amending the way of life one is currently pursuing implies some notion of considered evaluation, even if we think that 'drifting into' rather than 'choosing' a way of life might sometimes be the more appropriate term. If we are to credit future citizens with any degree of rationality in deciding how they will live their lives, the attractions of different ways of life cannot be a no go area. One of the most obvious criticisms to be made of a purely liberal moral upbringing, if such a thing taken to extremes could be imagined, is precisely its negative quality. Unless the liberal ethic is itself conceived of as a positive way of life with its own positive commitments, it provides no guidance for those inducted into it and enables them to give no meaning to their lives.

Put in more sophisticated terms, the main criticism levelled by communitarian writers against liberalism, is that it misconceives the relationship between the self and its ends. Sandel points to the logical absurdity of rational deliberations on the part of a collection of shadowy, abstract selves, as yet unencumbered by commitments or value judgements either about how individuals should relate to each other or about how to live their own lives. This is Sandel's way of criticising Rawls' version of the original social contract in which rational beings, knowing nothing of their future lives or life choices but assuming that they will require maximum autonomy, opportunity and material resources, choose Rawls' version of the just liberal polity, in which all will have equal freedom and autonomy and material inequalities will be limited to those which benefit even the least fortunate. The underlying point is that it supposedly makes no sense to think of ways of life, values or whatever being chosen by the individual in vaccuo. Someone in such a situation would have no criteria according to which to choose anything. Choice under these circumstances, far from being a rational or judicious act could be no more than a spontaneous response to the desire of the moment. Even coherent desires, Sandel argues, are difficult to conceive of in this situation.

For communitarian writers, moral choice is quite different from the Humean notion of emotive preference and also from that of applying universal rules, consequential or deontological, to individual acts. Such a process is described by communitarians as moral atomism in which particular moral decisions have no connection with each other, form no pattern and cannot be the expression of an individual self having a particular identity. For communitarians, a meaningful self must possess an identity, which is something that cannot be possessed by the presocial or unencumbered self. For Taylor, our identity, our orientation in moral space, our sense of what is good, desirable, admirable, worthwhile or whatever, comes to us from the culture in which we grow up as we learn the language, using the term in its broadest sense, of our community. Without such orientation towards the good, Taylor claims, the very notion of human agency is not to be understood at all. To this extent our ends or goals are not personal to us as individuals at all but are shared. They are the ends of the various groups to which we belong, our country, our community, our family or our profession. For MacIntyre, the fundamental moral question is not 'What shall I do, here, now, on this occasion?' but 'Who am I?' for my commitments, the good for me, depends on who I am and the relationship in which I stand to others, to the history of my community and my role in that community. My own acts cannot be understood, do not make sense and cannot be judged apart from the practices in which I am engaged, the narrative of my life and the larger traditions in which these practices and this narrative are embedded.

If my identity and the good for me are essentially socially located, this may not be taken to mean that they are entirely socially determined and certainly not that I am, by accident of birth, thrown into a set of historically prescribed and immutable obligations and duties. The context of any incident in a narrative or tradition is set by what has gone before but the future is essentially unpredictable. Practices and traditions evolve in accordance with their broad teleologies. This may take place in the light of contact with other traditions, in the light of practical, moral or intellectual developments in the wider world. Flourishing communities will embody many practices and a number of traditions. The narrative of an indivdual life may embody more than one emphasis or develop in directions not apparent at earlier stages. MacIntyre has particularly harsh things to say about what he sees as the rigid Burkean conception of tradition that may be used to control and restrict future development and failure to adapt and grow may lead to a once dynamic tradition losing its vigour until it eventually dies or is absorbed into or superseded by others.

Though the virtues of a particular community or practice may be local and peculiar to that community or practice rather than to some supposed general human telos, it is, nevertheless, important if they are to be considered virtues, that they contribute to some defensible concept of human flourishing in the context of that community and the conditions in which it lives. If, however, the possibility of moral evaluation in universalistic terms is entirely dismissed, there is always the danger that the younger generation will be told 'These are the traditions of our community, our profession or your lineage and this you must do.' In addition to the danger of ossification leading to authoritarian imposition, there is also the danger of corruption and decay. Over time, estimable virtues and traditions may lose their meaning and become mere superstitions or even be applied perversely. One nineteenth century German writer (Droste-Hülshoff1842), for example, writes of a forest community in which the biblical injunction against theft has come to be taken not to apply to the stealing of timber, even when this takes place on a fairly large scale, while the prohibition against bearing false witness is interpreted to mean not bearing witness at all, that is, not reporting what one has seen to the authorities. For these reasons, despite their universalistic shortcomings, the critical possibilities of liberalism have to remain an important part of moral thinking and moral education. The possible dangers to individual human flourishing must also make us wary of Taylor's suggestion that, in a multi-cultural world, traditional communities may be justified in restricting the activities of their members in order to ensure the community's survival. The example Taylor gives is that Canadian Quebequois authorities should have the right to prevent francophone parents from educating their children through the medium of English. He, fortunately, does not suggest that francophone parents should be prevented from leaving the territory to seek an anglophone education for their children elsewhere but there are clearly dangers in the idea of protecting community traditions or the collective interests of the community by restricting access to other cultures or knowledge of alternative community values.

An important part of the value of a communitarian approach to morality has been the emphasis it has placed on the linking of values and desirable conduct to the web of particular obligations and expectations in which the individual's life is already embedded. The attack upon the liberals' supposed assumption of the priority of the self to its ends helpfully draws attention to the fact that choices must be based upon values and commitments immanent in the community to which agents see themselves as belonging in a way that is necessary to their sense of self. How one behaves is, after all, ultimately rooted in one's conception of one's identity.

The weakness of the argument is that it fails to take account of the vagueness and permeability of community boundaries and the relatively impermanent nature of human identity. In the modern world, values, examples of admirable conduct and representation of moral landmarks by which individuals orient themselves, may come from far and wide. Whether or not this is to be welcomed, and it is not clear why it should not be, it is certainly a fact of modern life. As for the individual's personal identity, this may sometimes develop as a smooth progressive narrative with twists and turns but maintaining an essential unity as MacIntyre envisages but often enough these twists and turns take the form of a fairly dramatic sloughing off of an old, perhaps restrictive, persona and the development of a new one as life enters a new phase in a new place or new situation. This may prove painful or even disorienting, or it may be liberating and fulfilling. Ideally, preparation for such a change would take the form of an anticipatory initiation into the new, often wider community. Though this may have the semblance of maintaining the unbroken narrative of the individual's life, it must nevertheless mark the abandonment of many of the constraints, values and expectations of the earlier community.

One possibility not considered in the discussion above is that of a reconciliation between liberal and communitarian positions. Rawls (1985) protests that in his A *Theory of Justice* he was not concerned to advocate a comprehensively liberal way of life but merely to set out the broad political framework of a state within which people pursue their own visions of the good. This is a plausible clarification of his earlier position. As such, however, it continues to maintain the priority of the right over the good. Pursuit of a particular conception of the good is only permissible if those pursuing other conceptions are not interfered with. For many groups this may be well and good but others, by the nature of the good to which they aspire, would be bound to see the structures of the liberal state as providing no more than a temporary truce under cover of which to seek tactical advantage wherever possible, while looking forward to the moment when it became possible to impose their vision upon the whole. Such groups might include religious fundamentalists who saw tolerance of heresy or unbelief as inexcusable weakness or backsliding, ethnic groups of a nationalistic temper who resented sharing the territory with traditional enemies, proponents of social elitism based on wealth and power perceived as merit or desert, or the more fervent advocates of social or environmentalist revolution.

A more intellectually viable approach to the possibility of reconciliation might be to abandon the liberals' claim to neutrality and, like Raz (1986) accept that liberalism, with its concern for human rights and the autonomous development of individuals, both separately and in communities, itself embodies a conception of the good and is itself a substantively valid way of life promoting human flourishing. Such a position is certainly defensible and has the added advantages that it legitimises government intervention in the interests of incontestable human flourishing of various kinds, which is what liberal governments are actually expected to do. It also avoids the embarrassment experienced by liberals when it is necessary to deal with oppressive or authoritarian communities within, or indeed oppressive regimes without, whose practices are patently inimical to human flourishing on any reasonable interpretation of the term.

The link between morality and identity is also important to the moral educator, in that it suggests a process of moral education distinctly different from that suggested by conceptions of morality based on general principles or the development of virtues appropriate to universal human teleologies. Though the intellectual presuppositions of critical appraisal remain significant, moral education is seen to require a development of the individual's view if him or herself as someone with certain commitments and who will necessarily behave in a certain way. This makes the process of moral education a more fundamentally formative and certainly more complex process than the mere development of certain intellectual capacities. Equally important is the link between morality and context. As educators have long realised, pupils come to us already involved in the values of home and their community or subculture, in which they continue to grow up as their school education progresses. It may therefore seem expedient, as well as morally appropriate, to critically build on elements of value pupils bring with them from their community, rather than ignoring or opposing them; a process more likely to produce rebels than converts. A communitarian view of moral development also underlines the importance of the school, both as a morally educative community in its own right and as part of the moral community to which the pupil belongs. If the school operates as a public success-oriented knowledge machine with little care for its less successful members, its values will be rejected by some and, even more worryingly, absorbed by others.

Finally the communitarian conception of morality lends support to approaches to moral and citizenship education suggested by the so-called Crick Report in Britain (Advisory Group on Citizenship 1998), as well as by others, aimed at community involvement. Such a proposal builds upon the well established practice in many schools of including social service of one form or another in their extra curricular programme. This practice confronts pupils with real, local moral and political issues in the adult community in which many of them will remain when they leave school. It both draws attention to the fact that many such issues may have practical solutions near at hand, while others can only be addressed at a political level. This process also brings pupils into contact with committed members of the local voluntary service community who may provide admirable and realistic role models, of a kind not always to be found among professional school staff.

What has been referred to as the popular version of Communitarianism stands to the philosophical version much as the Character Education movement referred to in the previous chapter stands to Virtue Ethics. Both versions of Communitarianism stress the link between community and morality. As we have seen, however, the philosophical version as represented by Macintyre, Taylor, Sandel, Walzer and others is concerned with the nature and foundations of morality and its link with the identity of individuals as it is formed by particular societies. The popular version largely initiated by Etzioni but clearly supported by many academics (see Etzioni 1998) is a social and quasi political movement seeking to reinvigorate the moral and social order and find some 'answers to all that troubles America these days.' (Etzioni 1998 p. xxxvii) In *The Spirit of Community* (Etzioni 1993) Etzioni invites readers to join him in his campaign and the quarterly journal *the Responsive Community: Rights and Responsibilities* was founded by Etzioni in pursuit of its aims. For Etzioni and his followers, the values to be promoted are those of community as such, as an antidote to what they see as the excessive individualism prevalent in the current social life of America. The focus is upon the particular ills of American society, and the loss of values, which communitarians regard as having been previously embodied in it. Etzioni describes Communitarianism as a 'third way' of thinking between collectivist or conservative authoritarianism on the one hand and moral chaos or market driven liberalism on the other. He claims figures in the German Social Democratic Party, not to mention Tony Blair, as adherents of his position. The main ideas of Etzioni's Communitarian Movement are succinctly summarised in the so called *Responsive Communitarian Platform: Rights and Responsibilities* (Etzioni 1998) signed by more than 50 American academics and other public figures. This statement draws attention to what is termed the social side of human nature, holding that the exclusive pursuit of private interests erodes the network of social environments on which we all depend. Communitarians are said to wish to activate the 'moral voice' achieving their aims through influence and education rather than legal enforcement. They therefore emphatically claim to be democratic rather than authoritarian or even majoritarian.

Throughout, the tone of the *Responsive Communitarian Platform* is that of common sense rather than philosophical rigour. Individual rights, it is said, should be balanced by responsibilities to the community. Etzioni claims to have been stimulated in his initial thoughts about Communitarianism by the fact that students were more inclined to insist on the right to trial by jury than to perform jury service themselves. His argument, however, depends, not so much on the logical point that rights logically entail duties, as on the belief that if social life is to be reasonably tolerable, decent citizens need to maintain a balance between what they expect from society and what they are prepared to give in return.

A similar common sense approach and convincing demonstration, if one were needed, that Etzioni is not a rigorous communitarian in the philosophical sense, is provided by the comment in the *Platform* that not all communities are good. Opportunistically drawing, not so much on the American Rights of Man tradition as upon Kantian ethics, Etzioni claims, and is no doubt supported by the *Platform's* fifty or so signatories, that racist and sexist communities, for example, are to be condemned. Communitarians, he holds, are to be judged by overriding criteria such as non-discrimination, which must be generalisable, justified in terms that are rationally accessible and draw upon a common definition of justice that meets the full range of legitimate needs and values. No rigorous explanation is provided as to precisely which needs and values are to be seen as legitimate and which are excessive, but the presumption must be that Etzioni's readers and the *Platform's* signatories and other responsible citizens of enlightened America will naturally have a good sense of what these are and will recognise them as they emerge in Etzioni's writings and those of others who share his views.

The *Platform* has a special section on what Etzioni sees as two key institutions of society, namely the family and schools. The family is held to be central to the moral upbringing, support and care of the next generation. The conservative position, which places all such family responsibilities upon women and demands tougher divorce laws, is roundly rejected. Both parents, Etzioni claims, are responsible for family matters which, it is suggested, should be regarded as more important than material or career achievement. With regard to schools, Etzioni stresses the importance of moral as well as intellectual education, transmitting what are said to be those values that all Americans share: the dignity of all persons, tolerance, abhorrence of discrimination, peaceful resolution of conflict rather than resort to violence, that truth is preferable to lying and a commitment to democracy. These values also include giving a fair days work for a fair days pay and saving for one's future rather than dependence on others to meet one's needs. There should, Etzioni believes, be more integration between school and work. Etzioni sees little place for moral reasoning. The values to be transmitted are those already present in the community, not others arrived at by a process of thought. Etzioni, like many of the character educators mentioned in the previous chapter, is highly critical of the Piaget/Kohlberg view of moral development and models of moral education based upon it.

On a wider front, it is urged that that everything possible should be done to support and create strong cohesive communities. He rejects the view that the market rather than community action should be solely responsible for meeting the needs of those unable to support themselves. The principle of subsidiarity, namely that matters should be dealt with at the most local practicable level is asserted, as well as the need for public-private co-operation in the provision of services. Civic duties are said to include keeping informed about social and political issues, participation in electoral and other political processes and the payment of taxes. Political reforms are urged to free politicians from dependence on their financial sponsors whose private interests may tend to take precedence over those of the community. A particular area in which rights of freedom should sometimes give way to the community interest is held to be that of public safety; reasonable searches and tests for health and sobriety are legitimate measures in the interests of public safety, as is the control of private gun ownership. The general view is expressed that humankind is best served by strongly moral democratic communities and that it would be well if the tendency towards these could ultimately be extended to humanity as a whole. The purpose of the *Platform* is said to be to assert what the Communitarian Movement sees as the responsibilities of parents, young people, neighbours and citizens. Some of these must be legal but most are moral. Like natural environments, social environments cannot be taken for granted and responsive communities must define and articulate what is expected of people. The *Platform* is said not to be a statement of fixed conclusions but a point of dialogue, and more and more Americans are invited to come forward and join together to form active communities that seek to reinvigorate the moral and social order.

There are certain undeniable superficial similarities between the two versions of Communitarianism. Apart from the use of the term itself, Etzioni and his followers do make passing references to Sandel, Taylor and MacIntyre, as well as to Aristotle. Both versions reject something that might be described as individualism but for the writers mentioned in the first part of this chapter the objection is a logical one, concerning the grounding of values and the nature of the individual. Their point is that values cannot be arrived at from the nature of rational beings per se or putative agreements that would be arrived at by presocial selves regarding the distribution of basic goods necessary to forms of flourishing life that individuals might choose for themselves, without reference to the social context. For those writers, the only source of values is the practices and community ways of life that support the best approach to a flourishing life in the circumstances in which people find themselves, be these the turbulent era of the Trojan War, the more settled fourth century Athens or the bourgeois life of the eighteenth century Scotland as presented by MacIntyre in *Whose Justice? Which Rationality?* (MacIntyre 1988).

By contrast, Etzioni's objection is to individualism as a substantive moral doctrine or way of life, because of its social and political consequences. To that extent he is ultimately a consequentialist but, as we have seen, with distinct deontological leanings in relation to the dignity of the individual. His concern is with moral reform in the direction of a certain kind of society that he, and those many readers and associates he successfully persuades, judge to be desirable. Such a society falls between the extremes of totalitarianism or the authoritarianism of the religious right and what he sees as the uncaring individual egoism towards which he sees modern America to be moving. The ideal of society which Etzioni envisages is attractive, sensible, pragmatic and not a little nostalgic. Families are caring but not unduly restrictive, schools are clear about their moral message but not authoritarian or indoctrinatory, privacy is generally to be respected but reasonable searches may be carried out in the public interest. Freedom of action is an ideal but private gun ownership is to be banned. Freedom of speech is to be protected but hate speech is to be institutionally discouraged. Society should affirm what is expected of its members but without Puritanism or oppression. Small wonder that Etzioni's ideas find support among sensible, enlightened, comfortably off people, though many will justifiably find it theoretically incoherent, not to say more than a trifle complacent. They may also find his explicit rejection of moral reasoning and criticism of established values as a significant element in the education of the young somewhat troubling. He takes his justifications where he finds them in support of a vision of the flourishing life supported by the virtues of neighbourliness, good parenting, responsible democratic citizenship and a proper but not excessive commitment to honest labour. If his position leaves everything to be desired as a rigorous ethical theory, one feels, and hopes, that neither he nor his fellow communitarians will be too troubled. As an expression of certain substantive moral recommendations, his proposals can scarcely be ignored by those involved in moral and citizenship education.

CHAPTER 10

CARING

The two most commonly quoted works expounding a so-called Ethic of Caring are Gilligan's *In a Different Voice* (Gilligan 1982) and Noddings' *Caring: a Feminine Approach to Ethics and Moral Education* (Noddings 1984) and it is convenient to discuss this view of morality and moral development largely in terms of these two works, with some reference to Noddings' more recent *Starting at Home* (Noddings 2002b). Both Gilligan and Noddings identify their position as a feminist one, though both deny holding either that all women see moral relations in terms of caring or that men are necessarily incapable of doing so.

The starting point of Gilligan's argument is dissatisfaction with studies such as those of Piaget and Kohlberg, which identify a capacity for recognising and applying the highly generalised principle of justice as the highest stage of moral development. Basing her comments on findings in three empirical studies of moral development and identity formation in adolescents and young adults, Gilligan concludes that women's experience is simply misunderstood and women's moral development underestimated or just left out of account when seen from a perspective that takes the development of males as the norm. In the light of such a perspective, she argues, the development of girls and women is necessarily seen as problematic, not to say retarded or deficient.

Gilligan quotes many studies from Freud, Piaget and Kohlberg to Levinson and Vaillant in which male development is taken as paradigmatic of personal and moral development, and the standard by which the development of women is to be measured. For Freud, the male child's fear of castration is taken to be essential to the full development of the superego and his rage at separation from the mother is the basis of all culture and civilisation. Boys' development requires separation and independence from the mother, while the continued relationship on the part of girls is seen as a relative failure to achieve such independence. In the case of boys, individualism and competitive aggression are restrained by the interiorisation of rules. Typically, in competitive games boys strive to win in accordance with the

83

rules, which are vociferously asserted whenever they are infringed. By contrast, according to Gilligan, girls see competitive situations in which someone is bound to lose as endangering relationships, and tend to avoid them. The preference for preserving relationships rather than asserting rules in an effort to win the game may all too readily be seen as a failure to progress beyond the desire to please as a way of regulating conduct.

As an example of the differing reactions of boys and girls to moral issues, Gilligan quotes Kohlberg's well known hypothetical dilemma of the husband who is obliged by the unreasonably high price demanded by the pharmacist to consider stealing the drugs needed to save the life of his sick wife. Gilligan's boy subject has little difficulty in giving a clear cut answer to the man's dilemma in terms of a hierarchy of moral rules. The boy considers that there is no problem, given that life is more important than property. The girl is less sure and is inclined to think that more details are required about the individual case, or that an alternative solution could be found which would ensure that no-one gets hurt. In the course of her study, Gilligan quotes the responses to this dilemma of a number of other, older female interviewees, all of whom interpret the dilemma as an issue of care or lack of it, rather than one of justice or rights. Such a concern, Gilligan suggests, does not indicate that women are 'stuck' at Kohlberg's level three of moral development, where the developing moral agent is principally concerned to please others rather than developing to stages four where socially sanctioned rules are consistently applied, or stages five or six where abstract concepts of justice are applied and critically considered. On the contrary, a response seeking to preserve caring relationships between all those involved, even if certain abstract moral rules are ignored or infringed, represents not a retardation of moral development but a distinct and separate but equally valid way of responding to moral issues. Succinctly put, the masculine approach to moral issues is typically characterised by a hierarchical ordering of moral principles while the feminine response is more appropriately represented by a network of relationships which all ought to be preserved as far as possible. In another hypothetical dilemma regarding the reporting of a minor classroom misdemeanour, the boy is again able to give a clear reply in terms of the principles involved. The girls, by contrast, can give no clear cut reply saying that their decision would depend on the particularities of the case and who would be most hurt. To the unsympathetic male interpreter this may be seen as a failure on the girl's part to subordinate emotional attachment to principled moral judgement.

In adolescence and adulthood, Gilligan argues, moral development and the development of personal identity continue to diverge in males and females. Young males may pass through a period in which all morality may be rejected before returning to a conventional moral stance or a post conventional one in which rules are reviewed in the light of principles. The mature personal and moral development of men is typically depicted in terms of increasing separation from family, individualisation and achievement. Attachments may assist this process but are subordinate to it and may sometimes need to be overcome and abandoned as obstacles in the way of further development. Ultimately, successful (male) adults on this view of things achieve a socially productive life and social leadership accompanied by relatively weak personal attachments.

Women appear to go through a rather different process in response to the vicissitudes of life. Much of Gilligan's data here is taken from studies of women contemplating abortion and reinterviewed a year later. For Gilligan's subjects relationships with parents, lovers, husbands and the unborn foetus are the constant theme. As in the case of men, however, the development of women goes through a process of recognisably marked stages:

--- A presocial stage in which self preservation and self interest predominate

--- A social or conventional stage in which moral issues are dichotomised in terms of selfishness and self-sacrifice. At this stage women may seek to avoid moral responsibility under the guise of self sacrifice and the desire to please.

--- A concern with caring and the preservation of caring relationships in which the self and self development are included among the candidates for care.

--- A stage at which morality is seen, not as an application of universalisable rules, but as recognition of the truth about relationships and actions, recognition that there may be no solution to some dilemmas in which no-one may be hurt. At this stage the individual takes responsibility for her own actions and her own life while striving to preserve relationships as far as possible.

It is Gilligan's argument that an ethic or care is at least as valid a basis upon which to conduct one's life as the male ethic based on justice. She acknowledges that the notion of rights, though unhelpful in resolving some moral crises, has been helpful to women in recognising that they too are proper candidates for care and in helping them to cast off the paralysing temptation to evade responsibility by accepting the morally less arduous and ultimately less caring option of self-sacrifice. It is her conclusion that a convergence of male and female lines of development in maturing may lead to a fuller understanding of human development and a richer, more complex appreciation of the moral life.

Gilligan, then, is centrally concerned with what she sees as the development of the feminine identity in its relation to others, which she posits as an alternative view of moral development to the masculine version offered by earlier developmental psychologists. Moral maturity is defined by Gilligan, not in terms of a commitment to a universalisable notion of justice, but of achieving caring relationships which are honest and in which the adult takes responsibility for her own actions and the management of those relationships. The contribution of Noddings is to posit a fairly developed theory of the caring relationship itself and what it entails, both for the person she refers to as the 'one-caring' and for the cared-for. Like Gilligan, she constantly points up the dichotomy between the masculine or father's conception of morality based on propositions and principles and that of the mother based on caring.

In contrast to traditional moral theory, Noddings starts from the assumption that what she terms the basic human reality is not our separation from each other but our relatedness. We long, she claims, for goodness and natural caring, a relationship which is intuitively perceived as good. Our impulse to be moral represents a desire to preserve that relationship. This desire is rooted in the memory everybody has of being cared for. These are our tenderest and most precious memories and through life we strive to preserve and enhance the growing store of our memories of caring and being cared for.

Noddings defines caring for someone as being committed to meeting the needs of the other, not in the sense of dutifully assuming the burden of care but as a result of a form of motivational displacement in which one apprehends the other's reality. One wants what the other wants and totally identifies with the other's point of view. The other's needs are expressed in terms of 'I must'. One does not manipulate or act on the basis of one's own preconceived notion of the good but is totally receptive to the other and his or her situation and perspective. One does, however, act in the light of one's own 'ethical ideal', one's own best conception of one's moral self. One's moral self is enhanced as one cares more deeply or casts the net of one's caring more widely but may be diminished if one allows oneself to abandon a caring relationship or restrict the range of one's caring. Unlike moral rules, caring does not prescribe particular actions. These will depend on the needs of the cared-for and the concrete details of his or her situation. It is for this reason that the feminine response to hypothetical moral dilemmas is so often to demand more information about the situation or the individuals involved. In the Ethics of Care there can be no question of universalisability since no two situations, the needs of no two cared-fors, the potential for response of no two persons caring can be sufficiently similar to make this possible. You who care would act thus, but I who also care, cannot. There is simply no more to be said.

This does not, Noddings claims, make the one who cares capricious or unreliable. On the contrary, it is the one who sets the rules, not to mention religious imperatives, above individual caring that cannot be relied upon to be 'there' for the cared-for. One is motivated not by rules but affection and regard. The formulation of rules may transform the situation into an abstract problem in which the all important needs of the cared-for or concrete details of the situation may be lost. All too often abstract rules do not support caring but serve to diminish the strength of the 'I must' or provide for exceptions to the obligation to care. One's rational powers are not diminished in caring but, in a manner analogous to that suggested by Hume (1748) when we respond emotively to a moral issue, are enrolled in the one-caring's engrossment in the needs of the cared-for.

For Noddings, the caring relation is essentially reciprocal, which is not to say symmetrical, and certainly not transactional. The caring relation only exists when the caring is apprehended by the cared-for; when the response of the one-caring is received by the cared-for as the expression of a caring attitude, an expression of the one-caring's 'I am here.' Children, and no doubt others are said to grow under the influence of caring and to respond in personal delight to the caring relation it represents. It is, Noddings says, natural for the one-caring to accept the gift of responsiveness by the cared-for but not to demand it. The cared-for remains free and a subject in the relationship, not an object to be manipulated for the one-caring's gratification. Nevertheless, the cared-for's response may serve to sustain and envigorate the one-caring, to preserve the relationship as a reciprocally caring one, preventing it from becoming a relationship based on 'cares and burdens' for the one-caring. That the caring relationship needs to be completed in the response of the cared-for differentiates the ethic of caring from that which Noddings terms 'agapism' or the ethic of universal love. We care first and foremost for those closest to us, for the proximate other, for the one who turns to us individually for help. Our ability to care is naturally subject to practical constraints. We cannot care for the whole world and Noddings says, shockingly, that we cannot care for starving children in Africa. She is scathingly dismissive of those who express what she terms 'caring about' those suffering in distant lands by means of charitable donations or political demonstrations, suggesting that those who express such concern should go there and do something about it themselves. She does, however, propose ways in which we can care for those outside our immediate circle through chains of personal connection or analogy with our relation to those closest to us. In her later work *Starting at Home* Noddings also expresses support for humane policies towards deviants, the homeless and other unfortunates outside the circle of our immediate acquaintance.

Noddings contrasts natural caring with what she terms ethical caring, as when we act in a caring way towards someone for whom we have no natural concern. How much one cares for someone depends not on how things turn out but how fully the one-caring 'receives' the other and his or her needs and wishes. The impulse to act on behalf of the other, which is derived from our desire to remain related, is innate and those who have a strong desire to be moral will not reject it. The desire to be moral is derived from the more fundamental natural desire to remain related and to reject it is to contribute wilfully to the diminution of one's ethical ideal. When one acts in a caring way for someone for whom one has natural affection, one acts to maintain an attitude to oneself as one-caring. Noddings describes ethical caring as a kind of premoral good which may develop into the real good of natural caring and give rise to a naturally caring relationship. Ethical caring springs from the ethical self, which is created by one's memories of one's best moments of caring and being cared for. Moral responses cannot be justified. They are not truths. They are derived, not from facts or principles but from a caring attitude. We are obligated by what is required to maintain and enhance caring. In acting morally we are not justified but fulfilled in our own life and that of others. In this sense Ethics is not about justified acts but about how we encounter the other morally.

Noddings' so-called ethical ideal is a product of the natural sympathy of human beings for each other and a longing to maintain, recapture or enhance our most caring and tender moments. We naturally seek to maintain ourselves as ones-caring. One's ethical ideal is diminished when one limits the range of those for whom one cares, either in self-defence, in the erroneous belief that others do not deserve to be cared for, or because of one's commitment to organisations, firms, political parties, churches or whatever. The ethical ideal is nurtured in the child by talk which accustoms the child to see situations from others' points of view, by shared caring activities and by encouraging positive self appraisal. It is important that the best possible motive be attributed to the child's actions. Joy in relatedness is said to encourage growth in the ethical ideal for we naturally wish to remain in contact with that which brings joy. Against Kant, Noddings claims that we are all responsible for contributing to the moral perfection of others by enhancing their vision of the ethical ideal, so that they will continue to meet others morally, that is, in a caring way. This, and not advancing through the stages of moral reasoning, is the aim of moral education. The aim of all institutions, Noddings claims, is the maintenance and enhancement of people's ethical ideal and this, rather than mastery of the so-called 'objective curriculum' is to be seen as the overriding educational priority. This process involves not only caring but responding appropriately, so as to create and maintain a caring relation when cared for by others.

What, then, are we to make of the Ethics of Care as an explanation of what it is to be moral and as a basis for teaching the young with regard to their conduct as individuals and as citizens? In the absence of empirical evidence to the contrary, it must be conceded that Gilligan's account of differences between the moral development of males and females is entirely plausible. Her demonstration of the way in which these differences have been construed as deficits in girls and women is also highly convincing. It is equally undeniable that caring is widely perceived as an admirable personal and even a moral quality. In the ancient world the figures of Creon, condemning his niece to death and Brutus doing the same to his sons, not to mention the God of the Old Testament demanding that Abraham choose between obedience and the life of his son are nowadays perceived as monsters, whatever the moral imperatives by which they were driven.

Defining the Ethics of Care as an essentially feminist theory furnishes it with a barrier of defensive rhetoric against the reservations of male writers who must necessarily feel some hesitation about entering what has been claimed as a feminine domain. From the point of view of those concerned to encourage gender equality in public and professional life, it must seem unwary to identify caring quite so specifically with the outlook of women and, at the same time, link it quite so distinctively with the private and domestic spheres. Though both writers are careful to deny holding the view that men are incapable of caring or women incapable of rational thought, these disclaimers risk being swamped by the general tenor of remarks such as that of Noddings, that the mother's care for her child is paradigmatic of the caring relationship and that concern with the objective school curriculum, or whatever, expresses the father's desire to take possession of the child. From the moral point of view and that of the moral educator, the aim is not to score points in the battle of the sexes but to establish that caring is a desirable moral attribute in both public and private life and should be equally encouraged and valued in both sexes.

Caring doctors, teachers, social workers, even managers, judges and police officers of both sexes are to be preferred to those who merely fulfil their strict professional obligations and walk away. It remains, however, to be seen how far an ethic or care would provide an adequate guide in the conduct of such people and how far it needs to be supplemented by other considerations. Even as a determinant of conduct at a private and domestic level it is not clear that caring alone will suffice. Noddings defines Ethics as a concern with how we meet or encounter the other, how we feel with regards to the other's needs, feel those needs as our own, and experience a displacement of our own needs towards the other. The other is an individual who, as Noddings puts it employing Buber's words, 'fills the firmament'. This would be fine if there were only one other being in the universe. The more completely we cared for each other in that situation, perhaps, the better, though Gilligan sees a balance between the caring for others and caring for self as a higher level of moral maturity than self sacrifice. Morally, however, the problem is that in caring for one individual who fills the firmament, one may be less than fair or just to others.

Noddings, as we saw, rejects justice as a criterion of moral choice but in claiming that we should care for all involved in any particular situation, she appears to be committed to something of the kind if our resources for caring are finite. In deciding how to act, are we committed to care equally for all involved? If so, where does the requirement for equality come from? We cannot derive it from the concept of caring itself. But if we are not to care for all equally, upon what ground does caring enable us to differentiate? That caring parents will devote themselves to meeting the needs of the moment would provide a verbal way out of the dilemma, but needs characteristically conflict. Were it not so, moral conduct would be a pleasant and satisfying pastime indeed. We could give ourselves up to the absolute care of each singular other as they successively filled our firmament and respond to their care for us like two perfect lovers on a desert island.

Conceivably, ideal parents in the 'best homes', as Noddings (2002) terms them, are able to care for their dependents equally, not on the principle of an equally divided finite resource but equally in the sense of absolutely in every case. In the real world moral problems are less readily resolved. Let us suppose that one is not an unencumbered one-caring with an infinite bounty of care to dispense upon the individuals in one's finite circle of care but someone involved in the public task of selecting someone for a coveted prize or position. One of the candidates is someone to whom one stands in a particular relation of care, either directly or through a chain of caring relationships. There is, however, no possibility of the relationship becoming public knowledge. Few readers will find the scenario too far fetched to be worthy of consideration. Someone guided by the 'masculine' principle of justice would at least think it right, whatever they eventually did in practice, to try to act impartially, possibly by removing themselves from the situation as an interested party. Even this, however, would be something of a betrayal if the cared-for were less than certain to be chosen as the successful candidate. One truly caring by contrast, her firmament filled by the needs of the cared-for would, presumably, reject the abstract principle of impartiality and do all in her power to meet the needs of the cared-for. It is true that Noddings (1984) does enter the reservation that one should strive to care for all the individuals involved in any situation of moral dilemma and that one may, in an extended sense, care by proxy for those for whom one cannot be said to care naturally. We may, however, equally suppose that the other competitors are entirely unknown to the agent and so distant socially and culturally that no notion of a reciprocal caring relation could be plausibly imagined. In this situation it is scarcely likely the other candidates would be treated fairly, especially if this endangered the caring relationship between the one-caring and the cared-for. It must be conceded, however, that this is only objectionable if we start by assuming what

Noddings specifically denies, that fairness is relevant to questions of moral conduct in the first place.

The shortcomings of an ethic of care in the domain of public life are even more apparent in relation to our duties of citizenship. It will be argued in Chapter 15, that in a democracy citizens are not only responsible for their own private conduct but insofar as they are able to influence public policy, partly responsible for that of their government also. With this in mind, it is difficult to accept that starving children and others in distant places such as Africa are, since we cannot entertain a reciprocal caring relation with them, beyond the pale of moral consideration. As such they may presumably be allowed to starve or, for that matter, be commercially exploited, colonised, bombed with napalm or whatever without compunction. One must, of course, take account of cultural differences that may allow writers in some countries to see things rather differently from the way they are seen in the rest of the world, but it is alarming to find such a view so bluntly expressed by one so influential in the moral education of future American citizens and voters. The gibe that idealistic young people and liberal politicians who are concerned with the fate of starving children in Africa should go there and care for them themselves would seem unspeakably callous, were it not for the fact that so many admirable young people from many Western countries devote part of their lives to doing just that.

In *Starting at Home* Noddings refers to her hard line limitations to the scope of one's caring, and therefore of one's moral commitment implied in her earlier work. It is not clear whether this is intended as a retreat from those views or simply a restatement of them. *Starting at Home* urges more humane government policy towards certain categories of unfortunates. The homeless, drug users and other deviants should, Noddings writes, be treated with the same quality of caring as that experienced in what she sees as 'the best homes', which appear to resemble the homes of liberal, reasonably affluent middle class couples in Noddings' own country. With this, of course, it is difficult to disagree but Noddings continues to repudiate any notion of generalisable justification. Her suggestion is that those in direct contact with the unfortunates concerned should respond to them in a spirit of natural or at least ethical caring and that others who are socially or in some other way connected with the carers through a chain of caring relationships will come to care, because those directly involved do so.

These links, it must be said, are bound to be somewhat tenuous and chancy. Many of the economically and politically most influential people in our society, who actually determine how the unfortunate are treated, may have no such links and may even go to some trouble to avoid them. They may see no advantage in associating with people caring for the unfortunate, regarding them perhaps as noisesome parasites on the body of the wealth-creating community. Those who take such a view may not be uncaring people as individuals, but may simply, in a spirit not entirely alien to Nodding's position, see their own immediate family as the proper objects of their caring. After that they may care for their more extended family, neighbours in their gated community, friends and colleagues. They may even deal in a generous and caring way with the particular unfortunate person who comes their way. But they may also quite consistently feel it their duty to oppose additional taxes, for it is disingenuous to pretend that caring conditions can be provided at no cost, to support more caring treatment for the unfortunate, if these reduce their ability to care at a personal level for those to whom they personally stand in a caring relation. This is an argument heard commonly enough in favour of conservative social policies. One's nobler ethical ideals may prevent one from suggesting that the homeless, drug users and other deviants do not deserve to be cared for. If others care for them, that is fine but, on Noddings' view, no-one is obliged to follow their example. Nor need one feel obliged to share the burden of such caring in any way, or support politicians or political parties that are inclined to sign up to such programmes.

One of the supposed virtues of an ethic of care is that it concentrates on our relations with those closest to us. Those are the people most dependent on us and most affected by our actions. In this, at least, it may be contrasted favourably with universalistic moral theories, which may sometimes seem to justify less generous treatment of those close to us for the sake of others who are less dependent on us or to whom, in fact, our individual actions may make little difference. Noddings explains that natural caring, which she sees as more genuinely moral than ethical caring, is given first and foremost to those to whom we stand in closest face to face relations, then to our wider family and our immediate community. Outside our face-to-face circle our inclination to care tends to diminish with distance, both geographical and cultural. We find it easiest to care for those who most resemble ourselves, those of our own country or our own culture. She does not say 'of our own race or our own class', which, though implied by her general position, would obviously be offensive. The principle of impartiality, the validity of which Noddings repeatedly denies, is, however, fundamental to morality in public life. Charges of nepotism, cronyism or undue consideration for lodge, fraternity or old school or regimental tie can these days no longer simply be shrugged off with the words 'Well, what would you have done?' It is not, of course, being argued that one cannot buy an ice cream for one's own child without buying one for every child in the world, merely that one cannot in good conscience and on the basis that one is only obliged to care for one's nearest and dearest, give support and acquiescence to a set of economic and political arrangements whose causal outcome is that some children are not only deprived of ice cream, but actually starve to death, however geographically or culturally distant from us they may be.

There are, in fact, perfectly good reasons, both consequential and deontological, for manifesting particular care towards those most dependent on us. Caring may also be seen as a virtue fundamental to a particularly valued and valuable way of life. It is the cement of communities and may even be a right (Wringe 1981) against those who have deliberately or negligently brought us into the world. To be morally educated is, indeed, to have acquired sufficient understanding and insight to be able to give caring its due place in our moral lives, but to do so alongside the many other considerations that should properly influence the way we behave.

The examples Noddings gives in denying the importance of moral considerations other than caring are less than convincing. She claims she would have no qualms about stealing to feed a hungry child, lying to avoid one's child being punished by school for being absent to benefit from an educationally more valuable experience, or hesitating to report the criminal next door who was a good family man and neighbour. Many of us, however, would say the same, but we could produce good traditional ethical reasons for doing so. Noddings' examples do not represent a conflict between caring and justice at all. We should, hopefully, feel less than comfortable about stealing from a hungry child if, for example, while we were on a rapid journey through one of the world's more impoverished tourist venues, someone to whom we stood in a reciprocal caring relation expressed a desperate desire for the meal a starving local child was about to consume. We should scarcely feel happy to lie to enable even someone close to us to carry out a major fraud, simply because the victims were unknown to us. Nor should we, hopefully, feel too easy about withholding information about a pair of child abusers and murderers among our neighbours, who posed no threat to our own particular caring circle because of their exclusive predilection for victims from nationally or culturally different locations, shipped in from overseas for the purpose.

We are here in the area of essentially contested concepts (Gallie 1955/6). Our argument is not essentially about which acts are or are not moral but about how the term 'moral' is to be applied. The criticisms made of Noddings above presuppose a concept of morality in which justice, fairness, truthfulness, commitment to the general good and trustworthiness in public affairs have a part to play. This is precisely what Noddings denies. On the one hand, morality is taken to be about what we ought to do and why. On the other, it is about how, in some sense of the expression, we are to meet the other morally. To claim that something is fair or right or a good thing to do is essentially to aim to secure the assent or at least the acquiescence of others and to provide reasons that are in principle universalisable, if also contestable. For Noddings, morality is defined by the caring relation, in which the individual other momentarily fills the firmament. In presence of such an experience there is no room for others and no possibility of reasons that can apply universally to beings outside the possible or imaginable circle of care.

Supporters of Noddings point of view may argue that since the difference between us is one of definition there is little more to be said. Men and women or rather 'men' and 'women' (for biological gender is held not to be decisive) inhabit different planets and if they use what seem to be the same words they do so with different meanings, as when someone uses the word 'air' to mean a melody or tune and is puzzled to learn that it is composed of one fifth oxygen and four fifths nitrogen. Such a denial of mutual comprehensibility must seem regrettable to those educators who would seek to promote understanding, co-operation and caring, as well as a concern for justice and humanity in future parents, colleagues and citizens of both sexes. Their regret must only be rendered the more poignant by the fact that they must find many of the comments of Gilligan and Noddings helpful, illuminating and undeniably enriching. In educational terms, an approach that ignored caring as an important aspect of moral life would be pitifully narrow and impoverished, if not incoherent. To be committed to justice, to the maximisation of happiness or the minimisation of suffering, to virtue, to a flourishing way of life in a moral community, to the sweeping away of the brutal denial of rights, is to care passionately about those things and to be warmed in one's heart if, like Noddings' plant growing through the mulch in spring, these things show promise of beginning to grow and thrive in the world.

What is of concern is the denial of any balancing interest in justification and universalisability and the implications of such a denial for moral judgement and action. Caring, as represented by Noddings if not by Gilligan, is something that happens to one, as destiny or fate or falling in love is sometimes thought of, rather than something one chooses because it is right, in a considered, sensitive and educated way. Whether one cares and for whom one cares, at least in the case of natural caring, is seen as something essentially non-cognitive and beyond one's control, partly dependent on the response of the cared-for. Ratiocination and judgement appear only to enter the picture at the level of means: how best to secure the good of the cared-for. None of this, however, is to deny either the educational or the moral value of caring in the way we treat others and if the so-called Ethics of Care seems deficient as an ethical theory, we can scarcely deny the psychological perceptiveness of both Gilligan and Noddings into the development of this quality which is such an indispensable element in the moral make-up of all human beings.

CHAPTER 11

MORALITY ONE OR MANY?

To date we have considered a highly diverse range of views as to what it is to be moral or to live a morally good life. Moving from the traditional view of morality as conformity to a set of consensually approved modes of conduct, which may or may not have the backing of divine authority, we have considered the view that morality is a matter of conforming to rules, not of traditional or divine origin but rules that could be arrived at by the exercise of reason. These may require actions that bring about certain results, such as maximising the happiness, good or well being of oneself and others, or those that accord with certain rational principles, or respect the dignity, interests and autonomy of others. Alternatively we have considered the view that morality consists, not in following certain rules at all, but in developing and manifesting certain excellences or qualities of character, which may be rooted either in a certain conception of the nature of human beings and their flourishing or in communities and the practices that contribute to human well-being. A third possibility is that the deepest and most important expression of morality is to be found, not in obedience to rules or qualities of character but in caring, particularly for those closest to us.

Changes of view regarding the nature of morality itself may be more or less directly linked to changes of fashion in moral education. If it is believed that the nature of good conduct is already known to the older generation or certain designated members of it, it will not be surprising if the standard mode of moral education is inculcatory: telling, preaching, the listing of rules for good or proper conduct, the explicit prohibition of things that must never be done under any circumstances. Proper conduct is all. Understanding is not at a premium. The question of why is not an issue. We must behave thus and not otherwise because we are so commanded on good authority. Since the command is clear and unambiguous, all are able to choose to obey or not and there can be no objection to ensuring greater conformity by backing up the command with sanctions or the threat of sanctions, human or divine. The threat of horrific sanctions to be dealt out by an all seeing God will no doubt be effective, so long as religious belief holds. At a secular level, confidence in moral

94

certainty and relatively uncomplicated notions of moral belief may justify the severity of sanctions and the use of the rod or tawse as instruments of correction.

The Enlightenment notion that the laws of morality are accessible to all through the exercise of reason, perhaps even the Protestant view that God speaks directly to the conscience of every individual, combined with a growing awareness of the possibly disreputable origins of traditional morality as a means of social reproduction, may readily be linked with fashions in moral education considered in Chapter 5, according to which young people were encouraged to build their own moral assumptions, independently of the views of the older generation or their supposed social betters. Morality remained a matter of injunctions and prohibitions, though derived not from authoritative commands but from supposedly rational principles. Authority, religious, social, generational, as a source of morality was suspect. Individuals were to arrive at the rules for themselves. The model for moral education became the philosophical seminar. But philosophical seminars are notoriously inconclusive and may leave some participants confused or believing that no conclusions are there to be reached. Established habits of behaviour may persist even when they have been shown to be intellectually indefensible. Intellectually, the lesson may be well learned but without the backing of authority and sanction such conclusions as are reached may not carry through in behaviour. Moral behaviour clearly involves more than correct moral belief, even when this can be achieved.

Links between Virtue Ethics and Communitarian Ethics and recent educational practice are less obvious but are claimed by some of the character educators discussed in Chapter 9. Insofar as a virtue or character trait is a disposition to behave in a certain way, there is sense in Aristotle's view that virtue is acquired by behaving virtuously. Habituation accords well with a virtue theory of Ethics as does the close monitoring of pupils' conduct and the ready use of rebuke or praise in a way that leaves little room for argument or ambiguity. That sort of conduct is not approved of, not considered acceptable in this community, not what we expect at this school. Someone who does that sort of thing is not, or is no longer, a gentleman or a lady. They are excluded from the group, beyond the pale. Membership of the group and its ways are celebrated, whether symbolised by the school tie or the socially integrated classroom. Virtue is determination in the face of temptation or adversity and self image and pride, as opposed to fear of sanctions in more traditional forms of moral education, are the emotions appealed to.

The view of morality as caring also implies particular educational approaches, some of them explicitly referred to by Noddings herself. If part of being moral is to care, learning to care is necessarily a key element in moral education, which may be achieved as children learn to care for animals, plants or even inanimate possessions. Making explicit the way in which parents and other adults care for children may also have a part to play in this process. Noddings' insight that the child's image of him or herself as a good, caring person needs to be protected and constantly extended is both highly perceptive and educationally invaluable.

What, then, are we to make of this diversity of views regarding the nature of morality and diversity of educational approaches that appear to spring from them? No doubt, further views and approaches will make their appearance in the future. We are therefore obliged to consider whether any one of the philosophical views of Ethics we have discussed is more valid than others and should be given a privileged hearing when educational practice is being debated (Wringe 2000). Moral philosophers have traditionally been quick to attack each other and declare that alternative views are incompatible with their own and therefore misguided, while moral educators have also not been slow to attack each others' methods.

The practice, indeed some might say the very definition, of Philosophy has seemed to require us to attempt to discover some overall criterion of desirable conduct and claim either that this supersedes all other considerations or that other considerations can be reduced to it. Within the tradition of moral reasoning, Utilitarianism is one obvious example of an attempt to find an overriding criterion. Universalism in versions from Kant's to Hare's is another. Each seeks to provide the 'one thing needful' (Arnold 1869) for justifying particular acts or classes of acts. Both doctrines suggest that there may appear to be conflicts of duty but that ultimately there can only be one true duty in any situation. Yet even in their own terms, both fail to demonstrate this. Utilitarianism does not tell us what we must do if the calculus of benefits and harms results in a dead heat (which the theory does not seem to rule out) or if, as is more likely, the preponderance of uncertain outcomes renders any such calculation unthinkable. Deontological doctrines of a Kantian kind may be equally inconclusive in situations of moral crisis, for it may always be debated which description applies to a particular situation and therefore under which principle it properly falls. Where two courses of action are available, there is no guarantee that one could desire the maxim of either, or indeed of any other outcome, to be universally followed. That conflicts of seemingly ultimate moral imperatives may conflict is the stuff of tragedy, as Nussbaum (1986) observes.

The possibilities of conflict within the doctrines of deontology and consequentialism are as nothing compared with those that arise between them. It can scarcely be right to use a person purely as a means for the sake of a small overall balance of felicity to others but it is equally difficult to deny that a small infringement of this rule may be justified for the sake of a major collective benefit. The complexities of our moral life undergo a further exponential increase once considerations of virtue or special care for those closest to us are taken seriously. Anscombe (1958) points to blatant conflicts between the demands of obligation and virtue, and virtues themselves may often conflict unless we adopt the dubious expedient of defining their limits in terms of each other.

Philosophers have frequently tried to deny the possibility of conflicts between duties (Hart 1998), between particular duties and an established regime of virtue and between the rights of some and the duties of others.That such conflicts should exist, however, is scarcely surprising for to suppose otherwise would be to presuppose some ultimate teleology to which all our actions were supposed to contribute or some grand design of God or nature in which the myriads of human actions were to fit together harmoniously as in some giant multi-dimensional jig-saw puzzle. Such is the presupposition of a human intellectual construct called 'rationality' rather than the product of our moral experience.

Those seeking a unitary account of morality, be they consequentialists, deontologists, virtue ethicists, communitarians or exponents of the Ethics of Care may have recourse to reductionism, arguing that other modes of desirable conduct are not so much subordinate to their own but really versions of it in disguise. Thus, deontologists may claim as their own the 'each to count for one' rule of Utilitarianism, interpret the virtues in terms of tendencies to meet various kinds of obligation to others, acknowledge and find a rule to justify the obligation to show particular care to those closest to one. Equally, the virtue ethicist may interpret the flourishing life as one in which happiness is maximised, obligations fulfilled, virtues practised, caring mutual relationships maintained and so on. As for virtues, almost any kind of desirable act may be said to conform to one virtue or another, for in a looser sense the virtues are simply a set of terms under which we describe an act when we wish to commend it.

In some cases the outcome of our moral deliberations may depend on which mode of evaluation we decide to employ, as much as on the features of the proposed courses of action themselves. Disputes between individuals frequently become vehement attempts by the protagonists to browbeat each other into accepting the mode of evaluation that favours their own cause, while for the individual attempting to reach a decision reasons for and against appear and recede in a kaleidoscopic 'now you see it, now you don't' succession, which various modes of evaluation seem to urge against each other but are unable to resolve. Such conflicts may be irreconcilable, not in the sense that the agent is ultimately unable to choose how to act but in the sense that whatever course of action is chosen must often seem to be both right and, more frequently, wrong depending on the choice of which perspective is taken at a given moment. This is no mere argument from enumeration and elimination. We have not simply reviewed known moral theories and shown that none of these qualifies as a master theory of moral evaluation, leaving open the possibility that some such theory might be discovered in the future. On the contrary, we have seen that different kinds of moral justification are perfectly persuasive in themselves but differ radically from each other in principle.

We have been warned by philosophers as historically far apart as Aristotle and Williams (1985) that we should not expect tidy and definitive solutions to moral questions and this warning is massively reinforced by postmodernist writers (Rorty 1989, Lyotard 1988, Baudrillard 1989) who, in their various ways, criticise the foundationalist assumptions upon which any contrary view might be premised. It is no longer possible to think of fundamental and reliable moral principles and impeccable procedures of moral reasoning which, if correctly followed, will enable us to identify incontrovertibly desirable courses of action. It is unsurprising that our moral determinations do not fit together in some pleasing pattern of coherence, for our moral evaluations are derived from no single source but arise in a number of quite different contexts. A commitment to various virtues may develop in separate and specific communities which have reasons for admiring this or that excellence of conduct. Our obligations are incurred in a variety of unconnected roles, sundry transactions, personal loyalties and other commitments. One may be engaged in collective debate about collective action in which the sole issue is one of immediate utility. Alternatively, the history, composition and social role structure of the group may render consistency and the following of impartial rules particularly important. One may be engaged in appraising the habitual conduct of another in terms of whether it is admirable or despicable in ways that are not first and foremost concerned with utility or the distribution of benefits and harms but with qualities of character and the predominating motives which determine their actions. One must act justly and impartially in one's public role but the demands of care in our more intimate relations are immediate and particular and the boundaries of the two spheres are always subject to contestation.

If moral education is to be adequate, the young must be prepared to handle these various demands on their moral life, but first they must recognise them for what they are, as capable of conflicts which do not necessarily represent the simple alternatives of right and wrong. The crucial lesson of moral education must be that to be involved in human life at all is to at least risk being involved in guilt and conduct which is less than admirable for much of the time. As Nussbaum so convincingly argues, the appropriate response is not to seek some overriding criterion that will enable us to reject one course of action as a mere prima facie obligation in order to pursue the other with self-righteous and self-congratulatory zeal. That is to fall victim to the dragon of absolutism, for more evils may spring from the bigotry of the morally self-assured than from the hesitations of the morally civilised who perceive that in the presence of moral conflict, the only appropriate attitude is humility and apology towards those who suffer as a result of our inability to perform all our duties when these are incompatible.

It follows from our talk of moral conflict that there can be no question of moral relativism, for if nothing is better or worse than anything else there can be no such conflict. It has nowhere been suggested in the arguments above that there is no difference between right and wrong, that for most of the time the difference is not plain enough to see or even that the difference cannot, or does not need to be, taught. On the contrary, it has been held that virtuous conduct is both to be admired for the qualities of judgement and self-control it demonstrates and often for the flourishing community life and desirable practices it promotes and constitutes. That an action contributes to the greater good of greater numbers of people in either private or, more especially, in public life is a reason for promoting it. Actions which treat others as if they were discardable means to the ends of others, ought truly to be deplored. It has nowhere been suggested that it is a matter of indifference whether or not we care for those around us. Indeed, in strongest contradiction to any notion of relativism, the moral life requires constant effort and the sharpest attention, becomes increasingly important as we grow older and our actions assume increasing significance, and is awesome in the humility it demands.

That the demands upon one who truly seeks to live a moral life may often conflict, obliges us to reconsider the place of the much maligned process of moral reasoning and its particular place in moral education, despite its apparent ineffectiveness in immediately ensuring socially acceptable behaviour in the young. We may, indeed, hope that where action is concerned, the future adults who are our pupils will behave well without too much hesitation or deliberation. Likewise we may hope that where need is evident, particularly in those closest to them or dependent on them, the response will be immediate and without reserve. To be morally educated, however, not only implies that one's actions will be judged moral but that one is capable of a measure of moral understanding, that one sees actions under a moral perspective.

However virtuous one's own conduct in promoting one's own flourishing life or that of one's community, one can scarcely claim to be morally educated unless one is able to stand back and review one's own actions and those of others in moral terms. Even publicly recognised virtues are necessarily subject to critical review by the morally educated individual. Like the virtues, one's caring actions and attitudes may also profit from reasoned review. Gilligan demonstrates that the growing balance and maturity in one's caring relations may be the result of a long, hard process of reflection and we may be hard put to it to reconcile the needs of two or more cared-fors when they conflict.

A further reason for the inadequacy of such predominantly non-cognitive conceptions of morality as Virtue Ethics and the Ethics of Care is that they focus unduly upon the personal moral development and private conduct of the individual in a way that is inadequate to life in the modern democratic world in which all are, to however limited an extent, potentially involved in public life. Hierarchies of unquestioned personal and positional authority are no longer accepted and moral conduct is no longer the private prerogative and responsibility of individuals. Frequently, the right course of action will be that which is arrived at after consultation and discussion. Virtue may indicate the course of action we should back but moral reasoning must be an essential part of collective decision making. Even when power and responsibility to act on discretion is conferred upon individuals (judges passing sentence, military commanders in the field, committee chairmen under certain circumstances), reasoned justification may have to be given, either at the time or subsequently. Decision makers can no longer get away with mounting their virtuous high horses and daring others to question their motives. In a democratic world it is the duty of active citizens (Wringe 1992) to subject not only their own actions to the scrutiny of moral reasoning but also that of others who claim to act in their name and with their consent. The aura of a generally virtuous reputation no longer guarantees the acceptability of particular acts or policies. In such a world, as will be argued more fully in Chapter 15, citizens are not only responsible for their own private conduct but for the collective actions of their communities or governments.

There is a further matter to be resolved regarding the notion of good or desirable conduct. To the modern mind, morality is seen as a constraint upon the actions of individuals in pursuit of their own aims, interests and desires (Wringe 1999). The commonsense perception that virtue and pleasure are necessarily in conflict is evidenced by the plethora of banal witticisms arising from the supposed ambiguity of the term 'the good life' which, in modern parlance connotes both virtuous abstinence and luxuriating far niente. To act virtuously is seen as turning away from the temptations of pleasure and foregoing part of one's well-being or even one's long term interests for the sake of others. For the Christian, the path of virtue is steep and thorny and in contrast to the broad and pleasant path to damnation, the gate of heaven is strait. For Kant there can be no overlap between virtue and self-interest, pleasure or inclination. In the case of those whose virtues reflect communitarian values or one-caring for a much loved cared-for, the constraint may be less consciously felt but even in Virtue Ethics and the Ethics of Care, the emphasis is upon the way in which what is required of the agent benefits the community or the cared-for rather than the agent him or herself. The modern moral educator is therefore faced with the task of either making morality seem pleasant or, perhaps more readily achieved, vice disagreeable. Hence the panoply of literature from mediaeval epics to Victorian moral tales and more recent expressions of popular culture in which virtue is consistently linked with attractive manly qualities of prowess in sport and fighting or, in women, the desirability and public honour attaching to chastity and obedience. If virtue is not always rewarded, vice at least is all but invariably punished, in the next world if not in this. Needless to say, such linkages carry little conviction with the street-wise young in the secular modern world.

To writers of the ancient world, by contrast, this conflict is less complete. For Plato (*Republic*) no-one knowingly does wrong, so that intellectual and moral education go hand in hand. The one who truly perceives the good is bound to pursue it. For Aristotle, (*Ethics*) all things, including human beings, naturally seek the good, virtue is pleasant and the just man feels pleasure in acting justly while Cicero, albeit somewhat unconvincingly claims (*De Officiis*) that Regulus, returning to Carthage to face torture and death rather than break his word, is actually happier than the sybarite whose life is entirely given over to pleasure. For these philosophers there was no clear distinction between morality and prudence. To live badly was not so much wicked in our modern understanding of the word, as foolish, the result of error or muddled thinking.

To moral educators there is obvious appeal in such a unified notion of the good life, not only in its potential to overcome the resistance to their teaching by young people, but also their own conscientious hesitations with regard to their role. If it can honestly be shown that it is in someone's interest to be virtuous, it makes the moral educator's activity rather more reputable than it might otherwise seem, for they would then truly be acting in their pupils' interests, contributing to their knowledge and enlightenment and long term best interests, rather than attempting to socialise them for the benefit of others.

We must therefore ask whether young people are, in fact, better off growing up to be moral or whether, in attempting to make them so, we risk sending them out into the battle of life with one hand tied behind their backs. If the only disadvantage to behaving badly were to lie in the risk of social and legal penalties that might ensue, parents who really cared for their children would not want them to learn to be moral but simply to avoid being caught. In trying to bring their children up to be good, are parents truly concerned for their children's well being or simply seeking to avoid the hassle that accompanies childish naughtiness or juvenile delinquency in the present and the danger of neglect and abuse in their old age? If we intuitively feel that the latter view is unduly cynical, we are bound to seek some account of how it is that when we encourage Johnny not to bully his little sister, gratuitously damage the furniture or take things that do not belong to him, this will not only be better for the sister and ourselves but also for Johnny, both now and when he is grown up.

In a relatively small, closed community in which one's conduct and way of life inevitably became general knowledge, it will not have been too difficult for Aristotle to convince his students that virtuous behaviour would lead to honour and that, in a society in which social and geographical mobility was limited, the advantages brought by honour were a valuable resource for oneself and one's family. We may have reservations about a conception of well being in which social approval played such an important part but, in perhaps a more indirect way than Aristotle supposed, well being is at least partly constituted by our relations with others and these are almost by definition inseparable from our moral conduct and moral attitudes.

In assuming that it is in someone's interests to live rightly, we do not have to assume that in the long run evil will out and that justice will prevail, for in many cases it certainly will not, especially if the ill-doing lies less in sanctionable breaches of specific codes than in, say, meanness of spirit, unkindness or personal oppression. Nor do we have to assume, like Griffin (1986) that the immoral life is necessarily crabbed and narrow. We may agree with White (1990) that it is perfectly possible to live an evil life on a grand scale and even think of a number of evil men and women who have done just that.

But this discussion assumes that well-being is merely a matter of getting one's way or at least achieving one's most rational long term desires by whatever means and is diminished whenever this is obstructed, whether by the actions of others or by one's own moral inhibitions. This so-called informed desire theory of well-being takes a Humean view of desires as arbitrary givens, problematic only insofar as they conflict with some other more all-embracing or, as White puts it, higher order desire. Yet it is far from obvious that our aspirations and purposes in life are of this arbitrary and unconsidered nature rather than the result of thoughtful on-going and maturing even if not necessarily explicit choice. We behave in what seems to us the most sensible way to live but it is difficult to see how choosing a life of wickedness could be the outcome of such judicious consideration. To live wickedly is not simply to defy petty rules capriciously imposed by religious or political authorities, it is to live or act in such a way as to harm others, either as individuals or as members of the community, or to prevent them from flourishing, so that by wronging someone one destroys the possibility of continued solidarity with them. The point is not that one risks being found out and rejected but that one destroys the consciousness of one's own solidarity with others and one's life is correspondingly impoverished. We can no longer honestly share their sorrows and joys and no longer unreservedly take pleasure or draw solace when they share ours.

We do not, like some eighteenth century philosophers, need to posit some universal emotion of sympathy to explain morality, though sympathy, like caring and the modest awareness that our actions are worthy, undeniably also enrich our lives. Nor are we simply making the mistake White attributes to MacIntyre, of taking our own life preferences for the good life for all. It is simply difficult to see how a life of total and thoroughgoing wickedness in the sense defined above can be regarded as a flourishing life in any sense, for a life of wickedness is a life of total isolation (Wringe and Kim 1997). For one living such a life, others exist only instrumentally. Friendship, trust and true intimacy are, in the nature of the case, impossible. One's true identity, as opposed to the bogus identity one presents to the world, is not validated by the responses of others nor is one's life given meaning by one's interaction with them. One no longer has significant others to whom one relates intersubjectively on a basis of mutual respect. One has relegated others to the level of the means to one's ends. That the tyrant has no friend is not a contingent observation but an analytic truth

White points to examples of such tyrants as Hitler and Stalin who have found ways of avoiding the immediate ill-consequences of their wickedness but, in fact, the example of celebrated tyrants is not convincing. Accounts of their lives and not just of their violent ends suggest that their power brought them little happiness and that they should be seen as objects, not of envy but of pity. Completely evil individuals whose every act isolates them from others are, of course, a limit case. For such an individual even shared undertakings of the kind envisaged by White in which egoism and altruism are seemingly reconciled, are only pursued in the fickle awareness that one may abandon them if one's private ends are more effectively pursued by other means or more personally desirable ends present themselves. Tyrants, racist mobsters, petty pilferers or whatever may care little for their victims and loss of community with them may be of small concern. If one is not an absolute or compulsive villain whose every act isolates one from others, the limited circle of one's confederates may provide some support and society. There may or may not be honour among thieves but such a range of relationships would be limited and limiting, only capable of co-existing with a limited vision of the human good and to that extent only protected by ignorance and therefore illusory. Given the finiteness of human life and the certainty of death, the more august the egoist's undertakings, the more pitiable such illusion must seem and the more valid and favourable the efforts of the moral educator must seem to the interests of an immature potential transgressor who, as a result of the educator's efforts, may be deterred from a life of selfish ill-doing.

Is it possible for the honest moral educator to be more positive, not only conveying the message that the benefits of bad behaviour are vain and illusory but that virtue can be rewarding. In a culturally unified and morally unsophisticated community in which honour was to be gained by courage in battle, striving for physical prowess through determined exercise and the practical virtues of honest toil, the educator's task in equating virtue with honour among the youthful peer group may not have been too difficult. In our own age, by contrast, to act according to a publicly accepted conception of virtue may seem to be at best tediously conforming, at worst to be pusillanimous, or a dupe. It is immorality, crime and ruthlessness rather than virtue that seem to demand the charismatic qualities of determination, courage and intelligence. The role models of modern youth are not most readily to be found among the courageous, skilful and honourable heroes of Homer but all too frequently in the worlds of promiscuity, outward glamour and the cultures of alcohol and drug use.

The young, however, are not impervious to the appeal of idealism. Attempts to 'tap into' this reservoir of good will to promote such useful ends as assisting old people or cleaning up the environment may seem exploitive and some expressions of youthful idealism, patriotic or religious, may seem misguided, if not the result of political manipulation. We need, however, feel less moral hesitation in our approval of youthful movements for political reform in some parts of the world or protests against nuclear weapons, destruction of the environment, cruelty to animals or abuses of human rights. Many young people do reject the comfortable middle class careers imagined for them by their parents and feel their lives to be more worthwhile in consequence. Bearing this in mind, repeated complaints from tired individuals that the present younger generation are in some sense morally less worthy than their forebears are blatantly absurd. While having due regard to the dangers of spiritual pride, the knowledge that one's life is dedicated to a worthwhile cause may be a reason for satisfaction and a positive self-image. One's life has purpose and meaning. While one is fully engaged with one's goal, one's awareness is heightened, one has challenges to respond to and problems to meet with determination and judgement. One's life has purpose and one's activity is experienced as unequivocally worthwhile.

It would, of course, be unconscionable, not to say counter-productive to attempt to use education to recruit the young for particular causes that seem important to us in the adult world. But there is no reason why, in the course of their education, young people's attention should not be drawn to some of the world's problems: poverty, conflict, oppression or the gross egotism of some of our commercial practices, or the fact that many, not all of them necessarily young, have derived great satisfaction from their attempts to alleviate them. This is not merely permissible but necessary if it is our aim to enable the young to meet the so-called 'responsibilities and opportunities of adult life' referred to in the British 1996 Education Act. The point, however, is that contributing to the solution of some of the world's problems is not so much an onerous responsibility but, for many, an opportunity, indeed one of a person's rights as a global citizen, to live a life which is fulfilling and worthwhile.

The main purpose of this chapter has been to bring to a conclusion two of the tasks set for ourselves in Chapter 1. We have rejected the relativist/nihilist view that morality is a mere chimera, a disreputable social construction whose aim is social control or comfortable social conformity. On that view the moral educator is no more than a charlatan or, if at all successful, an unwitting agent of indoctrination and oppression. It has, however, also been our task to combat the equally dangerous illusion that moral education is an essentially simple matter of inculcating certain modes of behaviour expressive of certain indubitable truths which, if not simple in themselves could be encapsulated in simple formulae, be these the injunctions of religion or tradition, the conclusions of certain philosophical doctrines, the practice of virtues supportive of taken for granted activities or the simple and misleading emotive response of caring for those closest to us. It has also been our aim to argue that, far from being a mere constraint upon individuals and their well being, commitment to the good may be in their most prudent long-term interests and a source of personal enrichment and satisfaction. From these discussions it has become clear that a varied but by no means necessarily confusing or unmanageable range of considerations have their contribution to make to our understanding and practice of the moral life and, therefore, to the moral education of the young.

CHAPTER 12

THE OUTCOMES OF MORAL EDUCATION

Our aim so far has been to show that moral education is something more serious and educationally more important than the mere prevention of anti-social acts and misdemeanours. This is not to say that such acts and misdemeanours do not need to be prevented or that the task of preventing them does not mostly fall to such traditional moral educators as parents and teachers. Minor acts of supposed naughtiness on the part of the young: thoughtless damage, refusal to obey safety rules, rudeness or inconsiderateness towards adults are pointless annoyances usually resulting from immaturity or incomplete social learning rather than moral shortcomings. The child simply does not understand that the book or wallpaper scribbled on cannot easily be replaced, that playing in the road is dangerous or that the noise made by banging the toy drum while his or her father is trying to negotiate a bank overdraft on the telephone, is annoying. The fact that he has 'been told a hundred times' may make no difference. The obvious remedies of constraint, distraction, removal of opportunity or sharp parental prohibition may have little to do with the child's moral development, however effective they may seem to be for the purposes of damage limitation or the securing of a tolerable life for adults.

The result of successful moral education is not simply that someone acts in a socially, or even in a morally acceptable way. It is also important that they do so for moral reasons. The central chapters of this book have been devoted to a detailed exploration of these reasons and the bodies of theory that affect the ways in which we attempt to distinguish desirable from undesirable conduct. All of the theories examined are shown to be persuasive in some regards and often overlap in the conduct they advocate or condemn but since they cannot be reduced to each other with regard to their ultimate rationale, they may differ in emphasis and may sometimes even conflict. Actions undertaken for utilitarian reasons may infringe people's rights, and recognising one person's rights may produce the lesser good in aggregate. Virtues may conflict with each other and to do only what one could will to become a universal law may both conflict with the undeniable values of one's community or virtues essential to practices that contribute to the flourishing life of individuals. We saw that recognition of such irresolvable conflicts does not amount to moral relativism since the reasons suggested by the theories we have considered may be perfectly valid in themselves and do not permit of the conclusion that anything goes. There are many good reasons but no single overarching rule. The discovery of right conduct is the fruit of wisdom, experience and conscientious reflection upon all the considerations that may have a bearing on what ought to be done.

It is important to distinguish between the goals of moral education and those of religion. We earlier acknowledged that many religious traditions embodied inestimable moral insights and injunctions and contact with or even participation in the life of a religious community may have a contribution to make to the moral education of some. We nevertheless rejected religious belief as a valid source of moral justification on a number of grounds. To act thus and not otherwise in response to a religious injunction, not to mention out of concern for transcendental rewards and sanctions, is not at all the same thing as to act morally, even where the outcome is identical. Few religions allow or require the faithful to act morally in pure accordance with their conscience without specifying fairly closely in doctrine or tradition what the virtuous conscience is expected to command. The range of thinkable actions is normally wider and the agony of choice therefore more perplexing for the sincere secular moral agent than for the religious believer. It will be obvious enough that some activities, particularly in the field of sexual relations, which are forbidden by many religions, nowadays seem morally unexceptionable to non-believers while the more extreme prohibitions and demands of some religions may even be morally obnoxious. The requirements of religious conduct are therefore susceptible of independent moral appraisal, which for the believer, however, may do nothing to detract from their force as imperious demands. The fact, however, that one is accepted as a member of a certain religious community, that others have expectations of one in consequence, that one's adherence or otherwise to the practices of one's avowed faith is of consequence to those close to one, may not be without genuine moral implications for one's conduct. The sensitive moral agent will also have regard for the religious commitments and susceptibilities of others.

That the moral agent acts thus and not otherwise on the basis of certain reasons, is not to say that these reasons are necessarily of a universalistic kind. It may simply be that this particular thing, at this particular time and place, seems a caring, honourable, admirable or worthwhile thing to do. The articulation of reasons is particularly important where a range of possible courses of action are available, not between acting well and acting badly but genuine moral choices where good and bad appear to be on both sides and various points of view or various ends and interests are to be considered. This is the kind of situation in which moral wisdom is required and learned. For moral wisdom lies not in the act or even the outcome of the act but in the reasons for which it was chosen. If we are prone to act in response to particular injunctions, however general, rather than in response to the particularities of the present situation, our action may not be quite right and cannot be relied upon to be quite right in the future, though others may be able to rely on us to act in a predictable way.

Wisdom comes with experience, because we have not only seen but reflected upon many analogous situations before, and one needs to have reflected in the right way. One needs to have reflected, not simply upon whether such and such an act breaches a particular religious commandment or moral rule, whether it infringes this or that person's rights, whether it exemplifies a particular vice or virtue, whether it fits with a certain narrative or tradition or whether it is the most caring thing to do, but upon each and any of the above, or any other consideration that may be relevant to the matter at issue, with the sole intention of determining the right thing to do. This is not to say that we have to pass all these considerations explicitly and consecutively under review. That way we should spend our lives in a state of Hamlet-like indecision. Often we need to act, or more likely give an opinion promptly or offer advice decisively. In such situations, as with Hamlet, indecisiveness itself is a moral fault. The person of moral wisdom, the experienced chooser of courses of action when something hangs on what action is taken or avoided, quickly identifies which are the key considerations and which may be given less importance on this occasion. We are here talking of the kind of person who has built upon a cognitively sound, diversified moral education in youth to autonomously develop his or her understanding of the moral issues that confront us individually and collectively in the adult world. Such a person will have led a positive, responsible life at whatever social level his or her life is played out.

There are a number of ways in which we can fall short of such a life. Like Hamlet, we may be all too ready to scan the issues involved to find reasons to avoid acting, remain hesitant, undecided, to wait for others or events to decide for us. Such individuals will always escape blame and, in public or professional life may be useful functionaries, but where collective decisions have to be made they have little to contribute. In private life their counsel is timid, indecisive and rarely sought. In matters of any importance, countervailing reasons will always be present, otherwise there would be no decision to be made. Right action at any level, from intimate personal or family relationships to affairs of state and world politics, may leave some disappointed, some angry, some actually wronged or deprived, and oneself subject to criticism and maybe some regrets. 'Yes, I know we promised to go to John and Mary's party but oughtn't I to go round and see Mother? She is worried sick about that gas bill.' 'Yes, of course, like everyone else I abhor the human rights abuses of that dictator but should we be so arrogant as to flout world opinion by using force to remove him?' Such is the nature of life in a world in which moral considerations are real enough, but in which there is no reason to expect them to fit compatibly together.

There are, of course, equal and opposite flaws to moral indecision. One of these is moral naivety. One is happy enough to be good and simply does not see the problems. The all-important intellectual nature of moral education has been neglected, has not been taken in or has not been seen to apply to the subject's own life. 'Be good sweet maid/fair swain and let who will be clever', as if one could be good, as opposed to innocent, without sometimes giving some coherent thought to one's actions or one's life. Another is moral rashness. One desires to be good right enough and, unlike the naïve person, one is acutely aware of the choices of good and evil in the world and of how much it matters that one is on the 'right side'. But whether because of the simplistic nature of one's moral education, because of one's lack of experience of having actually been involved in the making of moral judgements, especially with regard to action where the results of one's judgement or lack of it have become apparent, or simply because one has been in the habit of making one's decisions or judgements without thinking, or as it is sometimes disparagingly put, not 'agonising' about them afterwards, whatever moral education one might have had has not been developed and refined by reflection and self examination.

Even more dangerous is the morally single-minded individual who makes moral judgements in the light of a single principle. This may be the religious principle of obedience to religious commandment or scripture but it may equally be some such moral principle as the greatest happiness of the greatest number, the protection of particular rights, consistency, truth-telling, adherence to a particular virtue or tradition, obedience to legitimate authority or even caring for those closest to one. The danger of this approach is that, having identified one's overriding principle and having, at least in imagination, defended it against all comers to one's own satisfaction, one then feels able to make one's decisions by reference to this principle, come what may. One is insulated against remorse or self-doubt since other considerations do not weigh against one's chosen principle. Other considerations are simply misguided or irrelevant. To weigh a variety of considerations becomes proof of a lack of consistency or even duplicity. 'You never know where you are with him. He picks and chooses among his principles as it suits his convenience' is the accusation such a person might make of someone who urged him or her to take a variety of issues into account or found different kinds of consideration to be of greater weight in relation to different issues. Such a judgement would be unfair if, but only if, the person accused is, in fact, consistently concerned to discover the right course of action, whatever that may be and whatever moral theory, if any, it happens to instantiate. To abandon the search for the right course of action in favour of a settled principle is, as continental writers form Ibsen to Kafka have represented it, to sell out on the quest for right conduct in favour of a particular ideal or 'idol' (Shaw 1891). The argument is not that there are many principles and that one may simply pick and choose between them. There are right judgements, or at least some judgements that are better than others, but they cannot be recognised by the application of predetermined principles. Nor can they be asserted with absolute certainty or precision.

The greatest failure of moral education, however, is not represented by the morally single-minded, although some of the world's most ruthlessly perpetrated moral atrocities must be laid at their door. The most fundamental failure in moral education is represented by those for whom the desire to act rightly is simply not an issue. We are not here concerned with the great Machiavellian immoralists of history who simply rejected conventional morality in the pursuit of a particular goal but, rather, those who, while certainly concerned to keep their noses clean and stay out of trouble, have no particular interest in either their own or other people's good or right conduct. Their lives are simply unenriched by notions of the good, as others might be unenriched by notions of beauty or good taste. Whether such individuals exist outside the realms of the pathological or the minds of philosophers trying to draw up an all-inclusive list of categories is a further question. Nevertheless, it is at least possible to envisage individuals with no particular commitment to good conduct or the good life, blown hither and thither by the rhetoric of politicians or the expediencies of the moment. Actions are simply appraised in such terms as consistency with departmental policy, expediency, political correctness, liability to unfavourable interpretation or the likelihood of giving rise to complication later on. Whereas such considerations may properly guide us in the morally neutral matters of our daily lives, someone entirely dependent on them for the guidance of their conduct and who sees no further has been allowed to miss out on one of the central categories by which human beings appraise and relate to the world around them.

If such an appraisal is to be disciplined and consistent, the role of the cognitive is central. Among other things, the capacity for making moral judgements is part of one's intellectual education, for to be moral is not merely to act in accordance with morality, or even in accord with some pre-chosen moral principle, but to do whatever one does because it is, in whatever sense, and in this particular instance, the right thing to do. The more flexible and comprehensive one's understanding of what it may be for something to be right, the more successful and complete the intellectual aspect of one's moral education has been. This, of course, involves no highly abstract or generalised conception of morality as an ideal of perfection, but an appreciation of the of the full range of considerations that may come into play in the appraisal of a particular action or proposal.

To have received a successful moral education, as with all areas of education, implies that the individual should continue to advance autonomously in this field of understanding beyond the stage at which his or her education ceases to be the responsibility of others. Arguably, this is most likely to happen – some might say only likely to happen – if the individual is not only instructed but coached and encouraged to operate independently in this mode of thinking while in an educational environment. Here as in other areas of knowledge and understanding, reliance on simple formulae or the conclusions of others is inadequate in a changing and culturally developing world. To the foregoing, some may be inclined to object that the notion of moral reasons, and particularly the balancing of conflicting reasons, is beyond the capacity of many of our pupils, whose overriding need is for a set of simple rules that will serve them through life. Such a view might have some merit if such a set of rules were to be found but though the acts of theft, untruthfulness and violence, like the vices of sloth, lust and anger are normally to be condemned, the strength and consequences of our condemnation must be tempered by many considerations, even if we discount the rare occasions on which circumstances render them permissible or even morally required. To attempt to limit the moral education of some to the teaching of a few simple rules would be analogous to the view that mathematical education for the general populace should be reduced to the operations of addition, subtraction, multiplication and division or literary education to the learning of a few lines of Wordsworth, Browning and Shakespeare, on the grounds that the higher reaches of mathematical thinking or literary appreciation are beyond them.

The ability to think morally as well as simply act innocently is particularly important as young people mature into adult citizens for, as will shortly be argued, active citizens are not only required to act well in respect of their private conduct but, are, in a democracy, constantly called upon to judge the actions of others vastly beyond the private sphere, in situations that may be not only complex but novel. What has been said about morality and moral education ought to allay traditional fears that any serious approach to moral or more especially political education might amount to indoctrination. There have been many attempts to define indoctrination: attempting to teach a world view that is calculated to mislead, creating 'false consciousness' in support of the material and political interests of particular groups, teaching propositions in such a way as to make it impossible for learners later to be critical of what they have been told, teaching values as if they were facts and so on. None of these are implied by what has been said above. Indeed, quite the contrary. Of course there are those who are inclined to cry 'indoctrination' or 'propaganda' in response to any teaching, moral, political or sometimes even scientific, which seems subversive of their own, often highly inflexible and questionable beliefs, the holding and propagating of which the liberal is obliged to tolerate but not refrain from contradicting.

That we are able, however broadly, to specify the desired outcomes of moral education raises the contentious question of whether teachers should not make some attempt to monitor their progress towards achieving them (Wringe 2003). Such a proposal may be thought not only intrusive, raising the spectre of Orwell's 1984 or Bentham's panopticon but also, in principle, impossible. Neither of these objections is entirely valid. Since the Ages of Reformation and Enlightenment, received morality has had something of a bad press among those of a progressive disposition, tending to be regarded as an instrument of overbearing authority, if not of tyranny and oppression. Philosophical doubts about the possibility of providing ultimate justification for moral judgements have at times also led to these being regarded as arbitrary or a matter of personal or social prejudice. While accepting that the political authorities have a legitimate part to play in making and enforcing laws that protect the rights of individuals, the liberal view has been that conduct that does not actually infringe specific laws is an essentially private matter. Attempts to extend educational assessment into the area of moral development may seem to be in danger of confirming what some have always suspected, that education is essentially some form of social moulding or domination.

We need say little of hesitations clearly springing from misunderstandings about the nature of morality itself. Some norms may certainly vary according to time and place. Others may reflect power relations in a particular society or simply embody outmoded prejudices but, as we have seen, there are perfectly good reasons for wishing children to grow up understanding why they should be reasonably truthful, kind, responsible, not given to taking or spoiling other people's things, sufficiently independent not to be led astray and capable of reflecting in a mature and flexible way upon their own actions and those of others. As we also saw, these reasons are consistent with the long term interests of pupils themselves as well as those of others. A commitment to morality and the moral development of their pupils is, therefore, not something for even liberal teachers to feel ashamed of.

Further doubts about the propriety of assessing someone's moral development may arise because of our somewhat censorious view of failures to come up to ideals of moral perfection. Western religious traditions, with their notions of sin as disobedience to divine commands and the possibility of damnation, may have much to answer for here. Our moral judgements are frequently expressed in terms of infringements of moral rules or falling short of acceptable standards rather than constructively in terms of the development of positive moral qualities. Where education and not mere social control is the aim, however, it is the achievement of these moral qualities rather than the suppression of occasional misdemeanours that is the object of moral education and the outcome of satisfactory moral development: the growing habit of truthfulness about things, actions and events, self restraint, kindness and responsibility where impetuousness, greed and thoughtlessness would have been the more natural response, reflection and understanding in the place of condemnation or the blind following of rules. These are more relevant to moral development and educationally more worthy of note than isolated infringements. Yet these habits do not come naturally as we seem to assume when we take for granted that there is no comment to be made unless a specific rule or established norm is infringed.

In the adult world, we distinguish sharply between different kinds of reprehensible conduct. On the false assumption that moral development is irrevocably complete by the age of adulthood, some forms of deviancy are taken very seriously and lead the perpetrator to be labelled a liar or a thief or whatever for evermore. Other conduct we disapprove of may be allocated to a private domain of personal choice, which it is considered inappropriate to criticise. With the immature in an educational situation, this distinction between public infringements, which require public reproof or sanction and private shortcomings that good manners require us to pass over without comment does not apply. If we are serious about education, there are no private areas of conduct or opportunities to educate that we should ignore. Our progressive evaluations are not final as they are taken to be in the adult world. In the case of a morally developing individual, shortcomings and backslidings simply pinpoint more educating that needs to be done.

If we can see our pupils as engaged in a process of education and their progress as partly our responsibility, there is no reason why we should not comment, and record our comments for future reference on how well we and they are doing. Our explicit recognition of their positive development, their growing sense of responsibility, sensitivity, candour and concern for others, is not patronising as it would be in the case of a fellow adult. Even if we are less than impressed by the moral maturity shown by some of our pupils, there is no reason why this should be expressed in destructive or condemnatory terms, any more than it is nowadays customary to use such language in recording our assessment of a weak student's progress in Maths or English. Students may not relish being told that more is expected of them in terms of candour, industry, respect for others or tolerance, but it is perfectly proper to do this in an educational situation where the aim is their improvement, largely in their own interest. If one thinks these things about certain pupils it is morally obligatory as well as good educational practice to make clear to them the standard according to which their progress is being judged. As in every other area of education, the clear articulation of standards, occasional reminders of them and recognition of the learner's progress towards them may be a potent means of effecting improvement.

The notion that we cannot make a valid assessment of someone's conceptual development in the field of moral understanding is difficult to sustain. We may not accept the detailed accounts of Piaget and Kohlberg and would certainly wish to modify their conclusions in the light of the work of such writers as Noddings and, especially, Gilligan. It can, however, scarcely be denied that some such process of development takes place as the growing individual comes into contact with the expectations and appraisals of others, not to mention the positive and deliberate efforts of the school to advance their moral education. Insofar as the development of moral understanding is a form of conceptual development there are perfectly obvious analogies with conceptual development in the understanding of Science, History or Literature.

The day to day assessment of pupils' moral development need not involve the use of specially designed instruments like those used by developmental psychologists. It is perfectly possible for teachers to judge such development in the light of pupils' words and behaviour in the course of everyday school life and their comments in the classroom. There is no reason why opportunities for this kind of observation and appraisal of progress should not be built into classwork, as it is for the on-going assessment of progress in academic subjects themselves. One might hesitate to suggest the drawing up of a list of formal expectations on the model of the British National Curriculum Level Descriptions (Qualifications and Curriculum Authority 1999) but the work of teachers in this area would certainly be made easier by some form of standard professional guidance as to what to look out for as they attempt to note their pupils' developing moral perspectives.

The assessment of someone's understanding may be both objective and morally neutral, for understanding is not in itself a moral virtue and failure to understand is an intellectual, not a moral shortcoming. The assessment of attitudes and actions, by contrast, demands a number of caveats, though with due caution there is no reason why the assessment of moral development in terms of attitudes and conduct need be ruled out. Continuous and systematic attention to this task in the case of developing young people has both the moral and the professional advantage that our assessments remain up to date and are not the prejudicial residue of random and isolated incidents and observations in the past. Of course, we need to be cautious. We may be mistaken in our interpretation of certain observations and events as we may be in diagnosing the true extent of someone's mathematical understanding on the basis of a particular piece of work or classroom comment.

In the area of attitudes and conduct we cannot, as we do in other areas, assess progress by setting a series of formal tasks in which pupils either succeed or fail and, in a sense, we do not need to do so. For the young, as for us all, these tasks are set for us by the daily business of living, especially in an educational environment in which people are given a carefully controlled but progressively increasing amount of freedom and responsibility. Unlike development in most other areas, moral change may often seem to go from better to worse rather than vice versa. The biddable, co-operative ten-year-old may become a morose, aggressive, shifty adolescent and this may easily be mistaken for moral decline. For social, physical and psychological reasons, however, the growing individual is being faced with new challenges. As is sometimes the case in academic subjects at secondary level, the learning curve may have become too stiff and the learner is in danger of flunking out. Here, even more than elsewhere, there is a case for the careful observation, judgement, recording and communication of changes taking place in the pupil's understanding, attitudes, responses and conduct, so that prompt and appropriate pedagogic intervention can be made on the basis of good information. The monitoring, assessment and methodical recording of the pupil's moral development may indicate potential deteriorations to be forestalled, as well of course, as promising developments to be encouraged.

If we are truly concerned about our pupils' well being, we are obliged both to monitor their moral development and to devise ways of doing it as accurately and efficiently as possible. For if we are sincere in our intention to ensure that young people grow up to be good, honest, caring and responsible citizens we shall necessarily wish to ascertain how far we are being successful (cf. Flew 1976, 1979). If we are being less than maximally successful we shall wish to know this to be the case, in order to improve our practice, building more effectively on our successes or, as the case may be, intervening positively and promptly when things are going badly.This information is required by teachers and parents and all who are concerned with each pupil's education and well-being. Most of all, it is required by the pupils themselves if we believe that a clear definition of what is to be achieved and constant, especially positive, feedback about their success in achieving it is an essential prerequisite of individuals' taking responsibility for their own learning.

In today's world, if this were ever possible, someone's moral development cannot conceivably finish at the end of their formal schooling. In the more than half century of life that remain ahead of many school leavers in the Western world they will encounter a vast array of situations, opportunities, temptations and dilemmas which neither they nor their teachers could possibly have envisaged while they were in the sheltered context of a formal educational environment. The reasons for this are obvious enough. Many of our most acute moral dilemmas, responsibilities and temptations are specific to the condition of adult life and can scarcely be envisaged by those who have not reached that stage. This is but one particularly glaring instance of the general principle that moral issues cannot be well understood by those who are not involved in them. It is also the case that, in contrast to what happens in traditional societies, it is impossible to predict how the lives of many young people will turn out. They will certainly encounter many situations and dilemmas which neither they nor those who plan their education could have predicted. This is not only because their own lives, at an individual level, may turn out differently from the way they had expected but because the world itself and the issues facing all humanity are bound to change in unforeseeable ways. This is not only true in material terms of the dilemmas and problems of, for example, technological or medical advance but also because of developments in our moral understanding. Recent years have seen spectacular advances in our sensitivity and sense of justice towards the disadvantaged, those different from ourselves or living in different parts of the world. It is unlikely that development of the public understanding will stop there but we cannot know beforehand how things will change in the future. Nor can we be sure that all changes will be for the better. Changes in moral climate can go astray. The public may be misled by political demagogues, religious fanatics or trendy fashions and the need for criticism and judgement remains.

In addition to the personal responsibilities of adult life, we have referred above to the moral responsibilities of each generation of new adult citizens and engagement with these will no doubt make its own contribution to the development and moral reflections of those whose earlier moral education has been of the open, flexible and thoughtful kind we have advocated. It is, however, not obviously appropriate or socially desirable for individuals, post sixteen or at whatever age compulsory schooling comes to an end, to be left severely alone to sort out these complex and changing issues for themselves. There can, perhaps, be no sustained or co-ordinated government policy of moral education for those whose formal education is completed. Nor would it be tolerable for any group analogous to the Victorian social elite to take it upon themselves to effect the moral improvement of the humble poor. This, in any case, is scarcely the kind of moral education with which we are concerned.

The importance of continuing and lifelong education is, however, widely acknowledged and some anxiety has been expressed regarding the tendency of this to become purely concerned with technical and vocational skills. Lifelong education, to be worthy of the name, must necessarily include opportunities for personal and social development, of which moral development may seem to be an essential ingredient. We are, here, not concerned, any more than we usually are at school level, with explicit moral instruction. The mere drawing of attention to current issues and problems and considered discussion of these with a greater or lesser degree of discipline and rigour, is within the recognised traditions of adult and further education as well as being a valuable and certainly acceptable way of broadening moral perspectives in relation to the changing social and political situation. This kind of development may well take place in the context of vocational education of a liberal kind in the course, for example, of the professional development of those whose social mobility or increasing maturity takes them into positions of greater responsibility or influence on the lives of others.

In addition to formal institutions of continuing and lifelong education, there is no doubt also a significant role to be played in the personal and social, including the moral, education of the public at large by such bodies as political parties and trade unions, the arts and media, social agencies, charities and many other, not excluding religious, groups. Some of these may have particular moral axes to grind but, insofar as they express a genuine commitment to the good, all may, in an open, plural society in which alternative views are available, contribute to the perception of morality as a serious, worthwhile preoccupation, complex beyond the simplistic inculcation of traditional notions of right and wrong and an appropriate part of our the collective cultural life.

PART THREE

MORAL EDUCATION IN THE MODERN WORLD

CHAPTER 13

SEXUAL MORALITY

The topic of education in relation to sexual morality is one which prudent writers would probably prefer to avoid. To describe the topic as a minefield is both a banality and an understatement. One is bound either to provoke the contempt of liberal readers or the outrage of the more traditional or, by attempting to negotiate a neutral course between extremes, to end up by doing both. Any positive suggestions one may make as to how either young or mature people ought to behave in this area are in danger of seeming irresponsible to some or mawkish, out of touch or quite simply impertinent to others. Yet to omit the subject in a book of this kind would be an absurdity. For many, the word morality is synonymous with sexual morality. If one refers obliquely to a politician's 'immorality' it is commonly assumed one alludes to someone guilty of relatively harmless sexual hanky-panky with a member of their staff or a colleague, rather than to one whose policies blatantly favour the interests of his or her financial backers. Though the older generation may be in some doubt as to whether sex, violence or drugs are the most burning of moral issues as far as the young are concerned, it is probably sex that seems to the young to raise the most troubling questions, and upon which they feel most in need of advice. Unlike drugs and violence, sexual conduct is something with which virtually all young people will eventually be concerned.

I shall have relatively little to say about many of the issues raised in the fairly extensive literature of sex education in general: whether and at what stage sex education should be offered if at all in schools, whether it should be left to parents and religious authorities, how much information about various practices and malpractices should be imparted to children and at what age, and so on. Nor shall I enter into a particular critique of the British National Curriculum documents and other legislative and policy statements in relation to sex education except where these have bearing on values questions in relation to the education of the young. Archard (2000) and the special issue of the *Journal of Moral Education* (1997, Vol. 26, No. 3) provide good starting points for anyone interested in the general topic of sex education. It is, however, an orthodoxy of both public policy and academic writing about sex education that the discussion of values should form a part of sex education. The perspective taken below will be rather the reverse that moral education is the more fundamental category and that morality in respect of sexual conduct is a component of it. In essence, it will be suggested, there is no special kind of sexual morality as such but that sexual activity and sexual relations are part of human conduct and are largely subject to the same kind of moral considerations as other aspects of what human beings do and the way they live their lives. Discussions of sexual morality are, however, complicated by two factors, namely the somewhat prurient concern of religion with sexual matters and the phenomenon of falling in love. Hopefully, such a change of focus will be helpful in resolving some of the more vexed controversies by which sex education is surrounded.

It is also helpful to distinguish between the question of guiding, indeed controlling, the conduct of young people at the stage and in the circumstances in which they find themselves now, as pupils at school or as dependent children living in the parental home, and the more general issues of sexual morality as they inform life as a whole. In the past there have been extreme claims (Gamm 1970, Adams 1971, Ollendorff 1971) that children have a right to sexual experience and even to facilities and privacy in which to enjoy that experience and one may feel some sympathy with adolescents who are actually prevented by strict or anxious parents from associating at all with members of the opposite sex. However, parents are held responsible for the well-being and behaviour of their children living at home and would seem entitled to insist that they conduct themselves with what they, the parents, see as reasonable prudence, decorum and discretion while they are at home and materially dependent. This said, however, it is clear that not all parents are inclined to prevent their children from engaging in full sexual relationships. Schools, likewise, are justified in forbidding undue familiarity, not to mention more serious sexual activity between pupils while they are in school or engaged in activities for which the school is responsible. Quite apart from the school's reputation, which it is perfectly entitled to take steps to protect, such activity is disturbing and embarrassing and to that extent inconsiderate to others. There should therefore be no problem about insisting that there is a time and a place for everything and that that is neither here nor now. This, however, is more about immediate control than serious issues of sexual morality or long term moral development, though dealing sensitively with undue displays of affection between pupils may help to convey the message that one's relations with the opposite sex, involving both self-respect and respect for others, are too important to be carried on in an uncontrolled or undignified way.

Of more importance in the context of moral development are questions relating to sexual conduct at whatever stage of life as they affect both individuals and society. Among the most important of these are:

i.   When is it permissible for someone to engage in sexual activity at all?

ii.   How should people treat each other in relation to sexual conduct?

Discussion of these questions requires some reference to our earlier consideration of the relationship between morality and religion. In the present context, in which religion so frequently serves as a basis for injunctions, or rather prohibitions, relating to sexual conduct it is important to emphasise that a key distinction is not between secular morality and something that may be termed religious morality but between morality and religion tout court. As we saw, there are some who will deny this distinction on various grounds but for our present purposes it is helpful to distinguish between not doing something because the harm it causes outweighs and pleasure or benefit that may ensue, because it treats someone as a means to someone else's ends, or because to refrain would be in accord with a virtue that contributes to the flourishing life or is simply an expression of love and care and not doing it simply because one's religion forbids it. In the first case, whether something is permissible or not is open to debate and reasons on both sides of the question can be given and scrutinised, whereas in the second, no such process is possible. In this regard, religious and moral approaches to questions of conduct are entirely different.

For much of the time the distinction is of little practical importance. In the Judeo-Christian religion, and no doubt many others, murder, theft and the bearing of false witness are sins as well as usually being morally reprehensible. The field of sexual conduct, however, provides many instances where the overlap is less than complete. To give one somewhat hackneyed example: we may readily imagine a brutal, violent unloving husband given to bouts of drunkenness, but not so pathologically addicted as to need or deserve care, and to blatantly consorting with other women. The couple, we may suppose, have no children. In at least one branch of the Christian religion, the wife who leaves such a husband goes to live with another loving and considerate man, with or without the formality of divorce and remarriage, commits a sin and a mortal sin at that. From a moral as opposed to a religious point of view some might feel that the wife should not give up too easily but it is hard to find any convincing moral reason to blame her when she eventually leaves in search of a loving and fulfilled life elsewhere.

There are, of course many less dramatic ways in which the demands of religion and morality do not exactly overlap. Given that the requirements of religion are generally more stringent than those of morality this, especially from a public policy perspective, is usually unproblematic. Recognition of the clear distinction between the demands of morality and religion ought to be reassuring to those religious parents who are as concerned for their children's salvation as for their moral education. It is not obviously disrespectful or necessarily undermining of any faith to say 'Well, from a purely moral point of view, this would seem perfectly permissible but, of course, for those who like myself who are Christians, or whatever, (if this is the case) this is forbidden. This is the word of God and, morality or no morality, there can be no argument about it. Like Abraham, who is commanded to slaughter his own child, we must accept the will of God and resolve to obey.'

Though it is not for the moral educator to censure the sins defined by this or that religion, he or she needs to recognise that religion rather than morality may be the controlling influence in the lives of many of his pupils and their families. This in itself is no bar to continuing to promote pupils' purely moral understanding and it will be recalled that the British 1998 Education Act requires schools to develop the moral as well as the spiritual development of pupils in the school and of society. The situation nevertheless requires sensitivity and respect for the feelings and views of pupils and families. As far as overt behaviour is concerned, conflicts will rarely arise, even if at an intellectual level, some religious pupils may be inclined to deny the obligatory nature of moral conclusions that are not scriptural.

We can now consider issues of sexual morality in separation from the requirements of religion, in a manner credible to those who either have no religion or, while retaining some resonance of religious belief, are no longer strongly guided by it in their daily lives. Despite the fears of some religious believers, rejection of the religious imperative is far from authorising complete sexual licence. We may find it difficult, setting aside religious considerations, to justify the traditional position that, if you kissed someone of the opposite sex you had to marry them or that any kind of sexual activity from enthusiastic kissing and cuddling to actual intercourse before marriage is always wrong but even at a crudely prudential level there are reasons enough to encourage caution, discrimination and restraint. We may take as given the evils, both to individuals and to society of disasterously unwanted pregnancies and the sexual transmission of disease. In theory these may be avoided by means of contraception and safe sex, which are obviously minimum moral obligations in any encounter or relationship that is not expected to be reasonably long lasting. These events nevertheless clearly occur in many cases, and would not do so if people only had sexual intercourse in a stable and materially secure relationship, and were sexually faithful.

Simplistically stated, the extreme positions are, on the one hand, no sex or other intimate contacts before or outside marriage and no divorce and on the other, sex whenever two people feel like it, provided precautions are taken against the risks of spreading infection and bringing an unwanted child into the world. The first of these positions might be presented as the ideal in an educational context, while recognising that it is no more than an ideal, bearing little resemblance to reality, much as total truthfulness and probity are presented as ideals, even if they are rarely encountered in the real world. This, however, would be scarcely honest not to say totally irresponsible, in that it would provide no realistic guidance for the majority of young people and risk bringing the whole notion of sexual morality into contempt. Religious considerations aside, it is difficult to see much wrong with couples who are about to marry sleeping together or couples deciding to live and bring up a family together without actually marrying, while divorce or the break-up of a long-standing relationship often seems an event to be regarded as a sensible decision for all concerned, or a reason for sorrow and commiseration rather than disapproval. If there is nothing wrong with these actions, there is no justification for treating those involved in them as less morally worthy than others or suggesting to the young that they are so, especially as many pupils have parents or other relatives in such situations.

It might be thought that there was a slippery slope argument for insisting on no sex outside life long monogamous marriage and that once this line was breached it would be difficult to find a convincing place at which to draw another. This argument might have some validity if morality were something imposed from above for the purposes of controlling the populace to prevent what was seen as social chaos or disorder, and no doubt this is how morality is seen by some of the writers mentioned in Chapter 1. Establishing social order may be part of the function of morality as well as of law but neither morality nor law continue to be effective if they are seen to be without justification, serve no purpose or have come to be regarded as the oppressive remnants of outworn tradition, prejudice or a religion which is no longer taken seriously by many. This is precisely what has happened in the case of sexual morality and why such chaotic uncertainty reigns with respect to it.

So, are there any limits, subject to precautions against obviously undesirable consequences referred to above, why any two people who find each other tolerably likeable and attractive, should not have sexual intercourse whenever the opportunity arises? Sexual intercourse is, after all, usually a pleasant experience and young people are perfectly aware of the fact. As against this, and still remaining at a utilitarian level of discussion, there may be something to be said for the view that taking life as a whole, there may be more happiness to be gained from a single, faithful relationship, or at most a limited number of successive relationships of this kind, which could at the time confidently be regarded as permanent, which one could confidently expect one's partner to regard in the same way, and also rely on others to respect. If one thought that such a balance of happiness were likely to be the general experience, one might both moderate one's own conduct and reasonably counsel members of the younger generation to do the same, while also disapproving of conduct in others that threatened the relatively stable and well ordered society in which such relationships were possible. These must seem rather cool and far-sighted considerations for a young person, or anyone else for that matter, to set against the urge to enter into a sexual relationship here and now. This, however, may be as far as purely utilitarian considerations can take us in our attempts to find a reasonable basis for sexual conduct without recourse to religious prohibitions or taboos.

Morality, however, is not purely concerned with how one should conduct oneself in general but also how one should deal with particular others and this is nowhere more evident than in the area of sexual morality. Unless the other person involved is utterly hardened and insensitive, one's sexual activities and relationships are likely to have a profound and sometimes even devastating effect on the life of at least one other person. Sometimes, of course, more than one person will be affected if that other person (or oneself) is already involved in a relationship, or network of relationships with someone else as, for example, the parent of a family. The most pertinent question for the individual in this situation is therefore not 'Is what I am doing permissible or wrong according to this or that general moral consideration?' but 'What is going to be its effect on this or that particular other?'

Obviously relevant here are considerations discussed in Chapter 7. As was suggested there, all human beings, male and female, have rights, including the right not to be harmed or gratuitously used for another's purposes. From this it follows that the only legitimate sexual relationships are mutual ones, equally desired by both parties. Obviously ruled out are any sexual use of young children, of anyone too weak, young or inexperienced to be fully aware of the implications of what is going on or to resist, any form of deception or coercion. Coercion, of course, goes beyond the use of physical force. It used to be a feminist slogan that when a woman says 'No', no is always what is meant. Whether or not this is true is not our immediate concern but what can be said with confidence is that apparent acquiescence does not always properly indicate consent (Archard 1998). Literature is full of incidents of young women being coerced, or narrowly escaping coercion, into unwanted intercourse by oppressive employers, shop-keepers owed credit, landlords or predatory lords of the manor and no doubt such crassly coercive events have sometimes also happened in real life. Only slightly less obviously coercive are those situations in which an older, more experienced person takes advantage of a weaker, more dependent person's emotional involvement or even a school-age crush for the purposes of seduction. In such cases the victim's acquiescence or apparent positive initiative scarcely constitutes consent at a moral level. This is not intended to imply that all love affairs between individuals of unequal age, experience or status are necessarily exploitive. Princes may only marry kitchen girls in fairy stories but in the real world bosses may genuinely fall in love with their secretaries and teachers with their pupils and students. All of these may not necessarily live happily ever after, whether they actually marry or not, but many may continue to do so for just as long as couples who meet in other circumstances. What is important is not the status of the persons concerned but the genuine mutuality of their relationship.

Lamb (1997) complains of the divided nature of much sex education, which she sees as based on the assumption that boys need to be taught to moderate their demands while girls need to be taught to defend their chastity. This, Lamb argues, implies that only males are supposed to take the initiative in positively seeking a sexual relationship. One cannot but accept the thrust of this criticism and the notion of equality between men and women is one of the important values underlying any acceptable approach to sexual morality. Unlike some religious groups, enlightened men can no longer see women as only existing to provide men with sexual pleasure and women in some milieux may need to be dissuaded from seeing themselves in that light also. Possibly some parts of what has been said above have implied a model of sexual relations of the kind to which Lamb objects: of men as sexual coercers, oppressors and seducers and of women and girls as victims. Of course, the situation is not as one-sided as this may suggest. Women may also seduce, cajole or goad men into sexual relationships and sexual acts they may later regret. They may also use their sexual power to exploit and manipulate for material, social or political advantage, out of vanity, spite or, for that matter, out of a simple desire for sexual enjoyment. If I have suggested that it is often women rather than men who are the victims of sexual coercion it is because many unattached men, and not a few attached ones as well, would welcome and readily acquiesce in advances from any reasonably presentable member of the opposite sex so that the issue of men being coerced by women rarely arises. Possibly it is Lamb's point, to which there appears to be no obvious objection that women ought in all justice to feel free to respond positively with equal readiness.

Some readers will be critical of the fact that little, so far, has been said about love. Talk has been mainly about the desire for sexual pleasure and whether or not the relationship in which it is enjoyed is or is not equally desired by both parties. Yet it is the current orthodoxy that sexual relations are only really appropriate within what is described as a loving relationship. Those that have sex together are expected to love each other. 'We are in love' is regarded as a necessary and increasingly a sufficient justification for entering into a sexual relationship, whether marriage or otherwise. The idealised narrative is that of two young people of suitably assorted age and status meeting, being pleased or impressed by each others' appearance, coming to find they have sentiments or interests in common, taking pleasure in each others' company, falling in love and marrying, or something similar. Often enough, no doubt, that is what happens and when it does there is cause for celebration. If things were always thus life would certainly be simpler, and we should be deprived of much great art, literature and music. Besides being simpler, life would also be blander, often less painful but infinitely poorer. Great works of both comic and tragic literature and opera, not to mention much popular writing, concern those whose love encounters the barriers and taboos of class, race, age, religion or family division.

Thankfully, many of these barriers and taboos are now swept away, at least in the liberal West. Doctors are, however, still not supposed to give expression to their love for their patients or teachers for their pupils. We are not supposed to fall in love with close relatives or children or vulnerable people in categories referred to previously, with whom a sexual relationship risks being coercive or lacking in mutuality. Much that is said and written about sexual morality, including much of the content of the present chapter so far, may seem to assume that sexual relations are the exclusive domain of couples of opposite sexes and Reiss (1997) has some justification in finding this objectionable, though the reason may often be no more than the stylistic difficulty of finding more inclusive substitutes for such expressions as 'member of the opposite sex,' 'men and women' and so on. Be this as it may, it is clearly the case that some people fall in love with members of the same sex as themselves. Setting aside religious considerations, it is difficult to see any moral objection to such individuals giving expression to their love and living together in a loving and mutually caring relationship. This situation has caused difficulty for moral educators in Britain who, because of the infamous clause 28 of the 1993 *Local Government Act* may have felt unable to give some of their pupils the moral education, guidance and reassurance in which they, more perhaps than others, stand in need. It may also have inhibited some schools from dealing squarely and properly with the subjects of homophobia and homophobic bullying. To do this requires schools to establish clearly that, whatever the situation with regard to religious belief, morally speaking loving and affectionate relations and life partnerships between persons of the same sex are as valid as any others. To do less than this is to continue to categorise gay pupils as somehow deviant and less than equal.

The phenomenon of falling in love bears remarkable similarities to that of caring as developed by Noddings and discussed in Chapter 10. The person loved becomes the person closest to one, the person for whose sake one will do almost anything, regardless of other supposed moral obligations. It will be recalled that in Chapter 10 I challenged the view that caring should be an overriding consideration but conceded that it was certainly an important consideration among others. In the context of sexual morality it is appropriate to ask just what is justified by the fact that one is in love. The crossing of certain social and other barriers may no longer in itself present a moral problem though it may have profound effects on the relationships of those concerned with parents, friends and other members of their community. More morally challenging is the situation in which one or both of those who fall in love is already in a relationship with someone else, and this may include a relationship in which there are children. At very least, the new relationship will involve deception, even before any actual sexual relationship has begun. Eventually, whatever the outcome, at least one of those involved will feel betrayed. Vows, promises, implied undertakings will have been broken and much anguish and pain experienced. Often the rejected spouse or partner will not only have been emotionally damaged but their material circumstances and opportunities for happiness may be much reduced. They may suffer a lifelong sense of bitterness and feeling that they have been deeply wronged. If there is an official orthodoxy in regard to such situations, it is that infidelity is always wrong, and that people ought to avoid getting into such situations in the first place, that erring spouses should put temptation behind them, return to their husbands or wives and be forgiven. To outsiders this may seem the least disruptive outcome but may not be the best for those most closely involved, particularly the new lover who has been led on and rejected.

We cannot avoid a consideration of such issues in moral education on the grounds that they are beyond the experience of those at school, for ultimately they concern the permanence of marriage and its role in social life. At a more individual level we may reasonably predict that, on present form, about a third of our pupils are likely to become involved in such a situation in the course of their adult lives, even if not all divorces are the result of one of the partners forming an extra-marital relationship. Many adolescents, too, feel that issues of fidelity arise as soon as they form and declare affectionate relationships with others. Besides, morality and moral education are relevant not only as guides to our own conduct but in judging and coming to terms with the actions of others. Adolescents, in particular, may be deeply troubled as to how they should react to the divorce or separation of close relatives, including parents, the broken engagements of older friends or the ending of other less formal but possibly no less intense relationships among their peers. How should one feel about the actions of the person who has left the relationship, or comfort and support the person left? What should be one's attitude to the new partner? Is it disloyal to try to remain on good terms with both former partners? It is also unsatisfactory to offer as a reason for avoiding the issue of broken relationships, including marriages, that behaviour in this context is a purely private and personal matter and that it is inappropriate for outsiders to pass judgement. All actions by a moral agent are, in a sense, matters of personal decision regarding which no outsider can be in full possession of all the facts, or of total insight into all the agent's motives and sentiments. It is also true that no rules of a general kind can be given that govern moral issues of any complexity. We cannot say that infidelity or divorce are always wrong or, for example, that they are alright because everybody does it these days but we can reach reasoned judgements about both the conduct of others and our own intended actions. This, however, can only be done in the light of the circumstances of particular cases. How viable was the existing relationship? Who will be hurt and how badly? How dependent materially and emotionally upon the relationship was the rejected partner? Also, though not everyone is prepared to acknowledge the moral relevance of this aspect of the situation, to what extent will the new relationship enhance and enrich the lives of the couple involved?

People ought not to enter into affectionate or sexual relationships or abandon existing ones irresponsibly and if one lives and works, as most of us do, in environments in which both sexes are present, one ought, perhaps, to be on the alert for danger signs in one's thoughts and fantasies. As the most famous of Racine's tragic heroines observes to her cost, passion may enter the citadel of our hearts in all gentleness, but once established there, rules brutally and by force (Racine, 1677). If, in spite of someone's best intentions they become involved in a situation of the kind we have considered, their further conduct remains susceptible of moral approval or disapproval. One ought to conduct oneself with as much candour, consideration and kindness as possible. In judging the conduct of others one ought to bear in mind that one knows relatively little of the true story as it appears to those involved, to avoid rushing to judgement, to give the benefit of the doubt, help repair damaged relationships and restore trust and self-esteem.

Something must briefly be said about that other burning and highly controversial topic in the field of sexual morality, namely abortion, which is likely to be an issue for someone in most school classes at some time in their lives. As with divorce, opinion is sharply divided between members of some religious groups who regard its prohibition as unequivocal and the more nuanced approach of thoughtful moral judgement. Late abortions where positive steps have to be taken to prevent the baby/foetus (choice of terms begs all the moral questions) from being born alive, seem morally repugnant and little short of infanticide, which itself, however, has traditionally been more sympathetically regarded than full blown murder. At the other extreme, there would appear to be only a relatively fine distinction, though perhaps a distinction nonetheless, between a very early abortion and contraception, especially with modes of contraception such as the use of an intra-uterine device or morning after pill which may prevent an existing embryo from becoming implanted (and are actually regarded by some as a form of abortion). Arguably, an abortion which prevents a potential being who has actually been conceived from coming into existence is necessarily a matter of some account, even when this is overridden by other considerations. It may also be of significance that early miscarriages, which are not infrequent in the natural course of events, are often a cause of regret but are not usually viewed with the same sense of grief and loss that may accompany this event later on.

All this is a long way from the simple 'Thou shalt not ...' of the commandments and tact, discretion and, above all clarity of mind is necessary if it is to be communicated to the younger generation without either causing affront to reasonable parents or seeming censorious and out of touch to the young themselves. As in all areas of moral conduct there are no general or universal answers as to how free and responsible individuals should live their lives or what actions are permissible or desirable in particular cases. Given the personal and emotional consequences of sexual activities, however, these are a proper topic of serious, often agonised reflection and are so regarded by most people including, perhaps even especially, by the young. Public expressions of opinion and messages conveyed by the media in relation to sexual conduct are widely divergent, often extreme and not seldom confused and confusing. If schools are genuinely concerned to help the young to come to terms with the social and moral world in which they already find themselves, they cannot baulk what to many young people will seem some of the most immediate and urgent moral issues before them, both in the present and in their future lives. To merit the trust and respect of the younger generation, educators need to deal with these issues, not only with candour and wisdom but with a degree of sensitivity and understanding appropriate to such an important and deeply personal aspect of all our lives.

CHAPTER 14

FAMILIES AND FAMILY LIFE

In the previous chapter little was said about either communitarian or virtue perspectives on the personal relationships people form with each other, yet clearly both of these may have significant contributions to make to our judgements regarding conduct in this field. Appeals to tradition and community values are necessarily problematic at times of cultural diversity and rapid social change like our own and these problems are exacerbated when the very notions of tradition and the traditional are commonly taken as terms of rejection in the field of values and ways of doing things.

There nevertheless remains some social support for the traditional values of modesty, decency and restraint in relations between the sexes and the view that intimacy is something to be kept for the special person with whom one will spend one's adult life and have one's family. According to this tradition, young people, especially women, are required to remain more or less chaste until marriage. Courtship will be a decorous procedure, supervised and approved by both sets of parents. Proposal, acceptance and betrothal or engagement will be quasi formal events, formally celebrated with the buying and giving of a ring as a pledge of commitment. The marriage itself will take place in the family's place of worship and brings together both families. This is traditionally supposed to be he most wonderful day in the bride's life. Relatively affluent couples then depart on honeymoon soon, but not too soon, after the return from which the first child will be born to reproduce the tradition in his or her turn.

This is an attractive and inspiring narrative, obviously preferable to the possible alternative according to which the girl is coerced into early intercourse in squalid surroundings, becomes a teenage single mother or undergoes one or more abortions and has, in the course of a difficult life, a number of children by different fathers, none of whom stays around for long. Some of the children may be taken into care and all, lacking a stable home base, drift away and lose contact with each other and their mother. Realistically, the lives of some of our pupils will resemble the latter narrative more than the former. Those of others may fall somewhere between the two and contain elements of both.

It is, however, possible to speculate that we are currently witnessing the emergence of another tradition which is not merely a compromise between the two narratives considered above, or a debased version of the first, but a way of life positively, if unconsciously, chosen by young people, with its own rules and values. This, despite the fact that it may seem rather strange to speak of a tradition going back no more than one or, at most, two generations and which would earlier have been regarded as a series of irresponsible and morally reprehensible actions. According to this tradition, if so it can be called, young people will go through a number of sentimental, and in many cases sexual relationships, starting during the later stages of schooling. These will often take place with the connivance of parents. Partners may stay over at each others' homes, sometimes sharing a room with nothing being said. Responsible contraceptive measures will be taken, again with the connivance and advice of parents and in the occasional unfortunate event of pregnancy, this will usually be terminated promptly, responsibly and with relatively little agony.

Everyone recognises that these relationships are unlikely to be permanent. Parental mention of engagements, weddings, children or introductions to a wider circle of relatives are regarded as the most appalling solecisms. Partners are required to be 'cool' rather than 'heavy' or intense. The relationship is characterised by fidelity as long as it lasts. There is no question of simultaneous promiscuity, but jealousy and possessiveness are decidedly not on. When one of the partners decides to finish the relationship, and possibly enter into another, that is the end of the matter. The disappointed partner is expected, out of self-respect, to pretend that he or she is equally glad to be free of a relationship that had become tedious and burdensome. Such relationships normally come to an end when the partners go their separate ways in pursuit of continued education, training or employment but occasionally endure. Previous relationships will be avowed but not discussed in detail and not normally be the subject of recriminations.

It is a continuation of the above life pattern that eventually more permanent relationships may be formed, in which the couple move in together and may jointly buy a house and have children. Formal marriage may or may not take place at some stage and this is typically a quiet affair, attended only by close family and friends. Such partnerships or marriages may break up relatively amicably, both partners having retained their material independence and resources being divided with minimum litigation. Children typically remain in contact with both parents, though contact with fathers may sometimes be lost. Subsequent marriages or partnerships may produce further children and step and half siblings typically live on good terms and with each other and with step parents. Later life may produce further separations, remarriages and new relationships making possible in retirement and old age the pursuit of new interests or interests suppressed in earlier relationships.

Arguably, the above represents a commonly accepted way of doing things in our society and appropriate to our age when sexual relationships do not necessarily result in the birth of children, social and geographical mobility are common and women are perfectly capable of material independence. If this is so, a number of things follow. First, it must be candidly acknowledged as a basis for the moral education of the young in respect of family life. Families where divorce and remarriage have taken place should no longer be thought of as 'broken homes' or children from such families as the victims of tragedy, potentially troublesome and preconditioned to failure. Second, family life may be considered by some to be a kind of 'practice' contributing or even essential to human flourishing. In the older tradition considered at the beginning of this chapter, certain virtues may have been thought of as supportive of that practice: modesty, chastity, fidelity, discretion, industriousness, thrift, domesticity, submissiveness on the part of women and authority, protectiveness and good order on the part of fathers, and so on. The new situation, if it is to offer the possibility of a flourishing life, may demand some of the same virtues but a number of strikingly different ones as well. Primary among these will be such virtues as flexibility, restraint, reasonableness, sensitivity and, above all perhaps, understanding and emotional self-sufficiency. Life in the new situation is more complex than in the old. A greater range of moral dilemmas constantly presents itself, and a more profound range of moral understandings is required.

For most people, parenthood and family life are an important part of the challenges and opportunities of adult life for which schools are enjoined to prepare their pupils. Reference to the family and its importance occur in various British National Curriculum documents (National Curriculum Council 1990a, 1990b) though with pointedly little reference to the nature and form family life ought to take. Attitudes to the family have been highly ambivalent, not to say grossly ideological, during the last century, seeing it both as a source of warmth and support, but also of cruelty, abuse and oppression. Social changes referred to above have necessarily led to changing relationships within families and we may perhaps ask whether it continues to play the same essential role in the lives of individuals and in society as it once did.

In the discussion that follows it is proposed to understand a family as a small, non-transient group containing both children and adults, united by intimate and caring relationships and common material interests. The issues of value that divide the body politic, staff rooms and some families themselves in relation to the family include the permanence and exclusiveness of families as the locus of intimate relationships and shared material interests, the desirable or permissible combinations of individuals who may live together and form a family group, the appropriate relations of power, authority and responsibility existing between family members and the degree to which the state relates to these groups as groups rather than to the individuals within them as individuals. From the point of view of moral education the most important issue with regard to family life is the degree to which privileged recognition should be given to traditional patterns of family life and to which other patterns often associated with the changing nature of family relationships referred to above are to be discouraged or disparaged.

It is convenient to distinguish in what follows between family patterns which will be referred to as traditional/patriarchal, modern and deviant. These terms are employed for want of better and are intended to be descriptive, despite the evaluative overtones they may carry in everyday discussion.*Traditional families,* for our present purposes, consist of two people of opposite sexes, monogamously and permanently married, living with their offspring and supported by the parents' income, characteristically earned, or mostly earned, by the man's work. The woman's primary role is that of home-maker. *Patriarchal families* are an extreme form of this in which all power, rights and property are concentrated in the hands of the male family head, the situation existing in Britain until late in the nineteenth century and vividly described by Mill (1869) in *The Subjection of Women.* Typically, *modern families* are those in which two adults of opposite sexes are present in a relationship they currently regard as lasting for the foreseeable future. Some or all of the children may belong to one or other of the adults by another relationship. The adults may or may not have married. The group is economically independent. Either adult may be the main earner or their contribution to the household income and other household responsibilities may be balanced. Some modern families may contain only a single adult member. Though the term *deviant families* is here used descriptively, such groupings are widely disapproved of and may be officially proscribed or unrecognised. In such groups the adults may be of the same sex or more than two adults may live on intimate terms.

In considering our own and other people's attitudes to the traditional family and the assumptions that underpinned it, it is important to bear in mind that these related less to matters of sexual conduct than to other, more material imperatives. Prominent among these was the assumption that the material interests of the family were the priority concern of family members, that parents, or rather male heads of household had the power to control and were considered responsible for the conduct and well-being of other family members and that intervention in family affairs, notably by the state, was to be minimised.

If patterns of affectionate and intimate relations are important to defenders of the traditional family it is largely because of their bearing on the above imperatives. If the family is to be an exclusive self-contained unit whose interests are a prime concern of family members and for whose support and conduct the head of the family is to be held responsible, it is essential to be clear who is and who is not a member of the family. Both Richards (1980) and before her Hume (1739) cite this as the reason for the system of double standards which used to demand a greater degree of decorum from women than from men. Where property and status were inherited, the argument goes, there must be no equivocation as to the identity of the inheritor's father. A man's wife's honour must be beyond doubt. Male infidelities which entailed no substantial material responsibilities were more readily tolerated. In more recent times close relationships outside a marriage may dilute commitment to the family interest and may eventually divide its resources. Relationships not sanctioned by marriage blur the clear lines of role and responsibility, as do the various step-relationships, links with ex-spouses, ex-partners, currently stable partnerships not expected to be permanent, and so on. They are also subversive of parental power and authority. In the past, adults responsible for the behaviour and well-being of younger members of the household could normally insist on a show of deference and compliance even if in practice this may often have been negated by deceit. Where the young people concerned are no longer strictly one's own children, or where they receive moral and emotional support through a close relationship with someone outside the formal family structure, this is less easy to maintain.

The blurring of roles and responsibilities may also make necessary, and certainly makes easier, outside intervention in the affairs of the family. In a traditional situation, fathers were readily identifiable and could be held responsible for the conduct and support of their offspring. Husbands, who held the purse-strings, had been promised obedience at the marriage ceremony and were entitled to administer reasonable chastisement, could usually enforce seemly public behaviour from their wives. These latter, being often debarred from occupation outside the home (Mill, 1869) could be held responsible for the care and upbringing of children. Complementary parental roles were supposed to meet the needs of children in their entirety and the responsibility of mature adults for the well-being of their elderly parents could also be clearly ascribed. Whatever the sufferings and deprivations of individuals within families, traditional role relationships will, from society's point of view, have rendered unnecessary much of the current network of welfare provision, social workers, health visitors, family counsellors, juvenile policing and justice, intervention and care procedures, home helps and residential and day-care for the elderly. Prima facie the need for these is greater when relationships may be transient, may break up and re-form where more than one man or woman may be responsible for the parenting of particular children and where individuals may move on and lose touch with parents, children and former spouses and partners. Where relations between men, women and children are transient, and to a degree informal or ambiguous it is less easy to insist on their essential privacy or object to the intervention of social agencies.

Though some left-wing politicians may see rhetorical value in such slogans as 'providing more support for families' in advocating increased welfare provision, most politicians claiming to be 'in favour of the family' tend, especially in America (Zimmerman, 1992), to advocate more restrictive laws in relation to divorce, abortion, homosexuality and contraceptive advice for the young, less intervention in families' educational decisions, less education in controversial subjects ('These matters are best left to families') less intervention by welfare services and less day nurseries. That the advocates of limited government favour the strong traditional family is no surprise, given the way in which traditional families avoided the need for much welfare provision and minor regulatory activity on the part of government. Mothers come cheaper than social workers, fathers than policemen. Both, for all their lack of formal training, may deal with day to day situations more effectively, more sensitively more flexibly than professionals. There is less paperwork, less opportunity for formal complaint and less anxiety over procedural niceties.

The existence of families, especially traditional families, greatly simplifies the task of government. Families are intermediate groupings standing between the government and the individual. Traditional families avoid the need for government to deal separately with the infinite variety of individuals and individual relationships that exist in society. Where there are assumed to be only traditional families, government only has to consider responsible (male) adults, precisely the kind of people by whom and for whom legal, rational, democratic government was devised. In dealing with rational adults, government may, as Zimmerman points out, largely limit its concerns to regulation through laws, with sanctions attached. Responsible rational adults may choose to obey the laws, or disobey and incur the sanctions. Government does not have to concern itself with the young and immature, the old and feeble minded or for that matter, that half of the human race considered emotional and less than fully rational who might complicate the business of judgement by appeals to our pity. The well-being and conduct of such individuals is the responsibility of the family head who may, on occasion be brought to book for it.

The existence of more varied patterns of family relationships also complicates the task of government by requiring the regulation of sometimes contentious situations which, in the past, may not have existed, or may have gone unrecognised. Earlier governments may have seen little need to consider the needs and rights of unmarried fathers, or ex-wives bringing up children single-handed. More complex patterns of relationships may mean that many situations may need to be dealt with not by the application of a rule, but on an individual basis by social agencies, often by means of time-consuming consultation procedures. Traditional families also aid governments of some complexions by acting as a vehicle of continuity and a brake on social mobility and change. Where property and status are inherited according to set rules, intergenerational succession may take place with little conflict or disturbance. The socially stabilising effect of families is also apparent where it is the channel by which occupational knowledge is passed down, or when family connections are important for material success. Insofar as the family is a vehicle for the transmission of values this is necessarily a force for conservatism since it means that the most deeply rooted values of each generation will be the commonsense assumptions of the generation before. Family structure, by providing a model of natural hierarchy may also serve to consolidate the notion of unchanging positional authority.

Convenience, economy and simplicity of government may well suit those who desire nothing of government save that it let them alone and make few demands on their resources. The social effects of the traditional family outlined above are, however, a mixed blessing. The conserving effect of inheritance not only perpetuates and often amplifies injustice, but is socially inefficient. Too rapid social mobility may have its dangers, but its absence is wasteful of talent and leads to complacency. The passing on of occupational knowledge within the family may in itself be highly efficient and lead to great expertise and commitment. There have been impressive professional, political and commercial dynasties and it has been claimed, by a noted conservative, however, (Barzun, 1974) that any profession stands to be better practised when it has been carried on by members of the same family for two or more generations. The side effects of this process are nepotism and occupational stagnation.

Unsere Beleg-Nr. *Our Reference No.*	Datum *Date*	Kunden-Nr. *Customer No.*
0081008793	27.02.2007	2000507471

Bei Zahlungen/Rückfragen bitte angeben · *Please quote on payment or with queries*

DELIVERY NOTE

Rücksendungen, Bestellungen/Anfragen bitte an:
Returns, orders / inquiries please to:
Springer Distribution Center GmbH
Haberstraße 7
69126 Heidelberg
Germany

Verkehrs-/ BAG-Nr. 16091

V.A.T. Reg No.: DE 170864101

Springer
the language of science
Springer-Verlag GmbH

Books phone: +49 6221/345-4301
Email: SDC-bookorder@springer.com
Journals phone: +49 6221/345-4303
Email: subscriptions@springer.com
Fax: +49 6221/345-4229

Seite, *Page* 1 / 1

Produkt-Nr. *Product No.*	Titel, Bestelldatum, Bestellzeichen *Title, Order Date, Order Reference*	Auftragsart *Order Class*	Preisart *Price Class*	Betrag je Einheit *Net Unit Price*	Rabatt % *Discount*	Gesamtbetrag *Total*
	net weight 0,480 KG CIF Presse&Buch Int. Delivery by order: Springer Science&Business Media B.V Free Copies Dordrecht Van Godewijckstraat 30 3311 GX DORDRECHT NETHERLANDS					
978-1-4020-3708-5	Philosophy,Education Vol 14 Wringe,C.A.:Moral Eduation Bernadette Deelen 22.02.2007 1289012 000010 recommended price 64,00 GBP	Exhibition order				

MwSt *V.A.T.* Nettowarenwert *Net Value of Goods*	Nettoversandgebühr *Net Dir. Mail. Charges*	Nettoversandkosten *Net Carriage Charges*	Gesamt – Netto *Total Net Value*	MwSt. Betrag *Value Added Tax*	MwSt. % *V.A.T.*	Währung *Currency* EUR	Gesamtsumme *Grand Total*

Zahlungsweise / *Mode of Payment*

Menge
Quantity

1

1

Zahlungen bitt
Please remit pa
Deutsche Bank
IBAN: DE41 1007
Hypo Vereinsb
IBAN: DE73 6722
Dresdner Bank
IBAN:DE30 1008
Postbank, Berl
IBAN:DE73 1001 0

Allgemeine Lie

The style of social regulation that deals only with heads of families treats those families as if they were single individuals, or sovereign states whose members all have common interests. Their boundaries must not be infringed, nor their homes and castles invaded. The characteristically regulatory style of government to which this gives rise may not even suit all adult potential heads of families. That all such are rational, independent self-supporting individuals is one of the fictions of liberal democracy, as is shown by the prevalence of poverty and persistence of crime despite the most punitive judicial regimes. An even more significant shortcoming is the fact that relations below the level of the family in such a polity are essentially unregulated. The law that made the traditional family head 'master in his own house' made slaves of everyone else. Limited government may make men, or some men, free but it does little to protect the freedom of anyone else. In the traditional family, only family members are legitimate objects of love and it is to their interests alone that our efforts and resources are supposed to be directed. Young adult members are permitted to fall in love with someone outside the family, but only with a view to forming a new family of their own and the notion that falling in love may take precedence over the family's material interest is relatively recent.

If this rigid pattern has been replaced by one that is more flexible, it is because many people desire it. Whether this is to be attributed to the development of practical contraception, the increased economic independence of women or increased affluence generally is not our present concern. The fact is that some people have found that sex without the permanent commitment of marriage brings more joy than grief and that to leave one relationship and possibly enter another brings happiness or relief from misery. This is not to underestimate the misery caused by unintended extra-marital pregnancies or the hurt and anger usually felt when a marriage or long-standing relationship comes to an end, but actual long-term unhappiness or harm to either adults or children is hard to calculate or weigh against the brutalities, oppression or abuse so difficult to investigate or escape from in the closed, traditional families of the past.

Opponents of more flexible family structures make much of the supposed harm suffered by children when their parents separate or divorce. The view that such harm is suffered has achieved the status of taken-for-granted common sense in the explanation and justification or criminal or anti-social behaviour, or lack or educational progress on the part of less able school classes. Though both individual defenders and opponents of traditional family values often point to striking anecdotal examples supporting their point of view, supposed evidence that harm is caused by parental separation must, in principle, be inconclusive. Where a child whose parents are separated appears to be suffering it is impossible to know whether this is the result of the separation itself, or the effect of social disapproval or recrimination premised upon a commitment to traditional values or indeed of tensions existing within the household before the separation took place and which, but for the separation, would have continued and been exacerbated.

Close contact with adults of either sex may be important to a child's development but it is difficult to see why these necessarily have to be biological parents. Of greater moment than the blood bond would seem to be the psychological significance of whichever adults are present at key points in the young person's development. In any case the ethos of many modern families is precisely such that divorce and separation does not spell the end of one parent's relationship with his or her children, in sharp contrast to the situation in more traditional times when supposed guilty parties were usually forbidden access to their children. Traditionalists who complain most loudly about the harm inflicted on children by divorce usually have much less to say about the harmful effects of separation due to other causes as when fathers have to seek work in distant places, are sent to prison or are called to the colours in time of war. Little is said about the unsatisfactory development of the children of war widows.

Children may also need stability for the sake of their personal development. Responsible opponents of traditional family structures, however, do not advocate that children should be tossed hither and yon and this is in no sense the situation which the characteristic modern family represents. If some couples separate and re-form once or twice at significant points in the course of their own lives, this seems at least as likely to produce an emotionally satisfactory environment in which children may grow up as a traditional family held together by social convention, law or material necessity, from which close involvement with outsiders is excluded and in which values are unquestioned and unquestionable. The more flexible modern family has the advantage that neither partner can safely regard the other as a prisoner with no alternative but to tolerate whatever inconsiderateness, abuse or emotional neglect is handed out. From the point of view of the young person's emotional development and moral independence, family change, properly handled might even prove an advantage.

Nothing written above should be construed to deny that in many traditional families, couples may voluntarily stay together and successfully bring up their children in a loving, supportive and stimulating moral and emotional environment. The modern situation, however, provides greater opportunities for individual moral judgement than the old. When decisions to sleep together, live together or split up are taken by caring responsible people capable of weighing the interests of all concerned and responding sensitively, it is at least possible that the result will be a greater net sum of happiness, and less extreme misery for some individuals than when such matters were decided in the light of rigid rules whose function was as much the protection of material interests and relations of power as the preservation of human happiness. It is therefore questionable whether it is right to attempt to protect the traditional family either by means of law and economic manipulation or through any kind of tendentious educational programme. The modern family and the legal, political and moral climate in which it exists represents not moral decline but a moral context which is preferable to that which existed formerly in that relationships are freely negotiated and may be continually renegotiated. This may place extra demands on the resources of government and on the moral understanding, sensitivity and sheer moral goodness of individuals. Of necessity, therefore, the present generation of young people needs to explore as fully as possible the implications of a situation in which their own emotional and family lives and those of others around them may not follow the traditional pattern. Only with an understanding of such matters will they be in a position to draw the best from their own closest relationships and support and minimise the hurts experienced by others with whom they come into contact.

A similar plea for education and understanding must be entered on behalf of what we have called deviant families, given that at least some of our pupils are more likely to find happiness in such families than in any of the other options on offer. Mention of the possible existence of such families is usually a signal for outrage on the part of defenders of traditional family values and as we have seen, schools in Britain have not been allowed to suggest that such a way of life is a possible or viable alternative to the conventional one. Groups of more than two adults living on intimate terms are ipso facto objects of condemnation to defenders of traditional family values but it is difficult to see why additional censure should arise when such groups undertake the upbringing of their various children. Many children have grown up happily in households containing a number of adults and this is regarded as perfectly acceptable when relations are governed by traditional family or social structures, as when the additional adults are relatives, long-standing family friends or servants. It is not at all clear what difference is made when the adults relate to each other sexually. Conventional couples do not flaunt their sexual activity in front of the younger generation, and there is no reason why others should be expected to behave differently. Fear of the unknown is doubtless at the root of the public phobia with regard to people whose intimate lives are unconventional but if education is at all concerned with the elimination of bigotry, prejudice and irrational fear, the issue ought to be addressed in school as a standard part of pupils' learning about the range of personal relationships that human life offers and which provide fulfillment for some people.

Though family life in one form or another is bound to figure importantly in the future lives of many of our pupils, we ought at least to question the propriety of fostering the assumption that this is the only manner in which a flourishing human life may be lived. The condition of singledom is frequently marginalised. On the one hand unmarried men and women may be presented as exemplary individuals who have renounced the joys of marriage and family for the sake of their religion, art, scholarship, service or the care of an elderly parent. Alternatively, they may be regarded as having failed to find a mate and happiness through some shortcoming like shyness, inflexibility or misguided devotion to a lost love. The requirement of chastity meant that they were supposed to be excluded from important areas of human experience and understanding, and their marginalisation was completed by their partial rehabilitation in such peripheral family roles as devoted bachelor uncle or courtesy aunt. In considering whether as teachers we may legitimately regard and present the single life as a valid way of life in its own right and not one which is exceptional, be it heroic or deficitary, there are two principal issues to explore. First there are the potential political and social consequences of having significant numbers of unattached individuals at large in society. Second, there is the question of whether, in principle, a satisfactory human life is conceivable without family involvement.

As regards the first of these questions, Mount (1982,) sees the family and family concerns as a steadying influence and valuable sheet anchor against the dangers of a populace being swept along by the hysteria of totalitarian mass movements. We have already suggested that the conservative influence of family relationships is not always desirable and it is far from clear whether totalitarian movements benefit most from the enthusiasm of political activists or the apathy of those who are supposedly not interested in politics. Current increases in crime and violence are commonly attributed to a breakdown in family and community relations. If this is true, the reason may simply be that family life as we at present have it is, by its nature, no longer capable of engaging the young. In which case the answer is not to attempt to coerce the young back into the bosom of the family by suggesting that only family life can ultimately be satisfying and worthwhile. That way lie alienation and hopelessness. A more effective response may be to open up the possibilities of other aspirations and other ways of life with other satisfactions.

The question as to whether a life without family involvement can be regarded as a validly human one forces us to address the traditionally contentious issue of what is and what is not to count as a recognisably human life. To legislate that human beings are essentially familial animals and that family life is in some sense natural to humankind would be to beg rather than to answer that question. That the right to marry and found a family is regarded as a Human Right, (United Nations Organisation, 1948, Art.16) might seem to imply that that to be deprived of this right is to be condemned to a life that is in some way less than human. But, of course, the drafters of the *Universal Declaration of Human Rights* may have been mistaken, misled perhaps by the taken for granted assumptions of their day. Attempts to define human life in terms of the possession and exercise of intelligence (which would have let in the single life led intelligently) have long been recognised as unsatisfactory. More convincing, perhaps, might be the view that, if anything is distinctively human, it is the holding and pursuit of values and the role these play in giving purpose and meaning to our lives. If this is accepted, we are led to the question of whether family membership is essential for the acquisition of values.

A widely held view about the genesis of our ability to acquire values and commitments asserts that at least some of these must first be experienced as absolute in the small circle of the family or close community, even if particular value positions are later abandoned as a result of rational criticism. In essence, this is Burke's (1790) insight, or supposed insight, that no-one can feel love for the great battalions of humanity who is not first loyal to the small platoon of his local community. This, however, provides little support for the claim that the original small platoon must be a family in anything but a very extended sense. Many children do not begin their lives in a family, as such, though the first circle of the child's acquaintances is necessarily small. He or she will take their values and reference figures where they find them. Biological parenthood is irrelevant. We should expect the values prevailing in professional child rearing institutions to be liberal and humane, but from the point of view of this argument, the particular values are immaterial. Though such small groups of adults bringing up children may in some ways resemble families, membership of such groups need imply no life long affinity or commitment of the kind that binds us to parents or siblings. Some lasting friendships would no doubt be made in such circumstances but friendships are chosen and do not bind in the manner of family commitments.

Children are sometimes held to need parents to love them, to be entirely committed to them, to be turned to in times of trouble, anxiety or pain. Children certainly need someone to turn to at such times, but it is far from obvious that this must be a parent, unless the term 'parent' is interpreted so widely as to mean any adult who may be turned to. If the person turned to were less emotionally involved - which is not to say less concerned for the child's good - than natural parents are supposed to be, and less dependent on the particular child for the fulfillment of their own life, many damaging relationships of dependence might be avoided.

If the presence of an actual parent to be turned to in times of need were an absolute necessity of human life, humanity would be in some difficulty, for in the hard everyday world of empirical fact, many parents may be less than adequate in this regard, even where they are well intentioned and committed to their children's well-being, as they understand it. For many people, the all-loving, all accepting, all comforting parent may be no more than a mythical figure created by retrospective adult sentimentality. Indeed, only possessiveness and self-deception could lead us to suppose that we could fulfill this role continually in our children's lives. Children and young people may need someone to turn to who is adequate to meet the immediate need in the on-going rough and tumble of their lives. Bonds may be formed in consequence and sometimes these may persist, but in many cases they will be outgrown and forgotten, as life moves on.

Our main concern with the question of the single life as educators is at the point of entry into adulthood. There is a common-sense view that parents strive for success to give their children a better start in life than they themselves had and make sacrifices for the sake of the family without which, it is supposed, their lives would be empty and without point. Where work is remotely absorbing, however, 'for the sake of the family' may become the pretext rather than the motive for our striving, the explanation some people give their spouses for their long hours at the office or frequent journeys to exciting places. Even those with less stimulating occupations, both men and women, may find the companionship of the workplace more agreeable than the frustrations of home and the opportunity of overtime not entirely unwelcome. An adult life without family duties would not be totally devoid of point. Even those with families to labour for may be driven by other aspirations which, indeed, may sometimes conflict with the family interest. Goals and aspirations not instrumentally geared towards the family interest may provide satisfaction in their own right and might even play a more important part in the lives of many, were it not for the nagging feeling that it was time to be settling down to the real business of raising the next generation. A life without such concerns need not be in any way a selfish one. Being released from the obligation to maximise the family income might enable many people to undertake less lucrative and more altruistic as well as inherently more satisfying activities than at present. None of this, of course, is intended to deny that family life may also be a valid option in which many couples would continue to find satisfaction, as at present.

Though the single life may prove satisfactory in one's early adulthood and prime of life, it might not seem equally so in old age. There is also the consideration that when the young adult pursues a life without family involvement, this may be a cause of acute disappointment to his or her own parents. The present elderly generation, at least, appear to take pleasure in the presence of their descendants. Promising grandchildren may make the remembered hardships of a long life seem worthwhile. Some of those who have outlived their offspring or lost touch with them may seem pathetic to us and to themselves. They may complain that they no longer have anything or anyone to live for. Yet it is not clear whether this is because the absence of descendants is an essential lacuna in a truly human life, or the disappointment of a socially conditioned expectation. The instrumentalist illusion, that it is the product rather than the process of one's life that is valuable may also be to blame and if other elderly folk did not, or were not imagined to spend long, happy hours with their adoring grandchildren, the absence of one's own might not seem such a deprivation. In any case, the solution cannot be to deter the young from pursuing what to them seems the most satisfactory way of life. This would be a case of sacrificing one generation to another which, along with the recrimination that goes with it, is one of the abiding evils of the family system. Clearly the right and, in the end, only satisfactory solution is to enable all future citizens, those who opt for family life in adulthood as well as those who do not, to become culturally resourceful and capable of commitment to activities and pursuits unconnected with family interest and family relationships.

It might be asked whether human life is conceivable or tolerable without a sense of belonging. Allusion is sometimes made to the way in which those with no satisfying family life find substitutes in church, party, club or other institution. The term 'substitute', however, implies the unwarranted assumption that family affiliations have a reality and validity, which other forms of belonging do not. Providing membership of these other groupings is satisfying, there is no reason why we should regard it as inferior to that of those to which we are fortuitously linked by the blood-bond, with whose members we have ceased to have much in common and for whom we never had a great deal of liking. If we do have affection for our relatives or things in common with them, so much the better. But then the link is one of friendship, as with our other long-standing friends, superseding the arbitrary bond of kinship.

It might be thought that the value of kinship, like nationality or the religion into which one is born is precisely that it is given rather than chosen and provides a kind of non-negotiable reality, giving discipline and form to our lives. If we claim the freedom to choose everything, the argument might go, we are as if lost without a solid landmark in our lives. This is unconvincing. We cannot, perhaps, be free to choose or change all aspects of our lives simultaneously or reverse our commitments too readily without some damage to our sense of identity. But not to be committed permanently to a particular family is not the same as having no commitments at all. The commitments we have may be contingent and fortuitous or they may be consciously chosen. They may include deep personal affections between persons of the same or opposite sexes. They may be perceived as binding at the time but likely to be temporary in the long run, or they may be thought to be permanent, whether or not they turn out to be so in the end. All of these attachments and commitments may provide a sense of identity or belonging which an estranged or alienated family may not provide, and they need be no substitute for anything else. To live without specifically family commitments implies neither egotism nor anomie. A satisfactory human life involving values, purposes and commitments does not necessarily entail a society in which the family is the basic unit. The basic unit may be the individual whose linkages with others, however weak or strong, however stable or transient, are essentially undetermined and susceptible of renegotiation

The consequences of these conclusions for education are not inconsiderable. Most children will no doubt continue to be born and spend their early years in one form of family or another and it is not to be denied that family relationships are potentially a source of pleasure and satisfaction to many. But if children are to exercise autonomy in the ordering of their own lives, the ideological nature of much support for the traditional family and the injunctions and value judgements by which it is underpinned needs to be explicitly recognised and communicated. We should cease to speak apologetically about the more open, flexible nature of many modern families as if they were merely the result of moral decline and, on the contrary, assert their greater humanity, as well as drawing attention to the greater personal and moral demands they make on both individuals and society. We should also cease to accord family life and family affection the privileged place they have in the projected ideal future that is supposed to lie ahead of young people; instead we should recognise the value and richness which the individual life of diverse and transient commitments may hold for some.

CHAPTER 15

MORAL EDUCATION AND CITIZENSHIP

If we, however, provisionally, accept Aristotle's definition of citizens as those who share in ruling and being ruled, it will be clear that citizenship is already a moral relationship. It is therefore apposite to explore the nature and justification of that relationship and its implications for the moral education of future citizens. What is involved in being ruled? Are there other contributions beyond obedience to the law that citizens are bound to make to the group or 'polity' to which they belong? And what are citizens' responsibilities as those who share in 'ruling' as well as being ruled? Do the citizens of large modern democracies, in any meaningful sense, truly share in the ruling of those states, or is this just a piece of self-esteem boosting false consciousness to keep the populace happy while enabling those who really exercise power to continue to do so?

The moral relationship of genuine citizens to their polity is different from that of mere inhabitants of a particular geographical area or members of other kinds of political societies. Simply living in a particular place doubtless imposes certain general duties upon one: non-malfeasance towards those around one, honesty in one's dealings with them and perhaps even a certain benevolence and readiness to extend help in distress, but one has no responsibility for the way the community conducts itself or for the nature of its internal arrangements. The subjects of a monarchy or members of a theocratic or dictatorial regime certainly share in being ruled, or at least in being subject to government but are not expected to play a part in ruling. Unlike citizens, therefore, they have no responsibility for the way their country is run or for its conduct in the world at large. Much the same is true for the majority of those living in corporate or so-called 'people's democracies. Ruling is, or was, the prerogative of the governing party or elite who ruled in their populations' name and ostensibly in their true interest. The fact that people from Britain are officially referred to as 'British subjects' is, of course, one of our country's harmless historical relics of former times. In the terms of this chapter, British subjects are every bit as much citizens as the inhabitants of other modern democracies and certainly more so than the supposed citizens of corporate democracies.

Essential to the notion of citizenship is that of equality. All citizens are equally subject to the law and all are supposed to be equally entitled to share in the tasks and responsibilities of ruling the polity. Unlike the serfs of a feudal monarchy or the members of a corporate state, they do not belong to the polity or its rulers as possessions or resources. On the contrary, the polity belongs to them. It is their country they are living in. It is their laws and not laws imposed by someone else that they obey if they are good citizens. It is their prerogative to make, or at least sanction those laws and their responsibility, collectively at least, if those laws are ineffectual or unjust. Though the Enlightenment notion of an original social contract in which rational, free and equal individuals came together and agreed to be bound by their collective laws is no more than a myth, it nevertheless correctly represents the moral relationship of citizens in a liberal democracy to each other. In formal terms we are equals to whom the expression of dissent is both possible and permitted. The only restrictions the laws are supposed to impose upon us are those that prevent us from harming others and the only burdens are those that can be reasonably defended as being in the vital interests of all.

But can we take Aristotle's definition of citizenship as the basis for our discussion of the prerogatives and responsibilities of citizens in the modern world? In Aristotle's time citizenship was restricted to a select few, a minority of the population. Slaves, women and resident foreigners and those not citizens by descent, were excluded and might be put to death for attempting to interfere in state business. Citizens could be expected to make their way in to the forum, take part in discussion and eventually go along with what was agreed. Superficially, this bears little resemblance to the situation in the large liberal democracies of the modern world, so the question arises as to whether there is sufficient similarity for the model to serve as a basis for the discussion of the modern citizen's responsibilities and the education of future citizens that this would imply. Modern states are not only immeasurably vaster in territory and numbers than the polities of ancient Greece. Their affairs are infinitely more complex and their citizenship more inclusive. Athenian citizens were men of independent means, experienced in managing their own fairly extensive households, farms and other undertakings, used to exercising authority and the responsibilities that go with it. Except in matters of warfare and perhaps taxation, the impact of government upon the individual citizen was light and occasional. The notion that all who are subject to government should have a say in its conduct only emerges in the Age of Enlightenment, and then only by degrees. Various substantial categories of individuals were at first excluded from taking any part in politics by reason of their supposed incapacity to exercise their say rationally: the poor, those in service and, of course, all women who only achieved the vote, let alone the right to stand for election, very much later indeed. Though citizenship always carried with it certain rights and privileges over non-citizens, the notion that the state owes its citizens a comprehensive range of rights: political participation, legal protection and, especially, social and cultural benefits (education, health care, social security and financial support in old age) is also a characteristically modern notion. The most important difference of all between ancient democracies and those of our own age, however, is the fact that most modern citizens do not directly participate in government at all but only do so through their representatives. This means that some certainly have more access to influence on the conduct of government and have a greater share in ruling than others, though all are certainly aware that they are being ruled. To many, the periodic opportunity to take part in elections to decide between a highly restricted range of political options clearly seems too trivial a privilege to be worth exercising and the slogan, often seen scrawled on walls at election time, 'If voting changed anything they'd make it illegal' may express a common feeling of disempowerment. Such a perspective may understandably leave some people with the feeling that the laws they are called upon to obey are mere coercion imposed by others and certainly with little sense of responsibility for or interest in what government does.

Doubts about he so-called classical theory of representative democracy (that such a democracy is ruled by the people through its representatives) supported by empirical research indicating the often low level of political sophistication of many electors have led some (Schumpeter 1954, Dahl 1956) to propose the alternative view that ordinary citizens play little part in ruling at all. The actual ruling is supposedly done by various elites who, by one means or another, simply compete for power by obtaining a majority of the popular vote, having secured which they proceed to rule as seems best to themselves. Having no influence over what is actually done, citizens may, on this view, be supposed to have no responsibility for it either. This view has some plausibility. Elections are framed mainly in terms of choosing between individual candidates. Outcomes may hang on distorted image, appearance, personal style and self-presentation. Access to the media and financial support are also undeniably crucial. Despite possessing an air of cynical panache, however, the theory is ultimately incoherent and may be seen as an unduly hard-nosed characterisation of democracy influenced, no doubt, by the academic needs of empirical researchers in the field of Politics to maintain a supposedly value free definition of their subject. The theory also has the defect of depriving democracy of its moral justification. If voting were no more than a device for selecting rulers rather than, in some sense, the expression of popular will, there is no reason why we should prefer it to other, possibly more efficient and certainly less costly methods such as bidding for power by auction or the selection of rulers by a conclave of the great and the good, or even by the Greek practice of casting lots.

Allowance must undoubtedly be made for modern techniques of persuasion, the distortions of image management, the fickleness of electorates, the tendency of some voters to be influenced by irrelevances of appearance or rumours of candidates private lives or minor blunders and indiscretions blown out of all proportion by the media. Nevertheless, though electors formally choose between candidates as individuals, they are bound to do so in significant part on the basis of policies they may be expected to implement if elected. Government is therefore bound to remain sensitive to public opinion and the public may respond with considerable hostility to obvious examples of injustice, incompetence or, especially, self-interest or corruption. Governments also have ways of remaining in touch with public opinion by means of focus groups and sample polling, while the media are, despite the personal axes to grind of their proprietors, nevertheless bound in their own commercial or corporate interests to remain responsive to their audience or readership.

Politicians may appeal to the material interests of voters and to the values which alternative policies reflect. Though the detailed arguments for and against particular enactments may be beyond the ken of most voters and are, indeed, rarely placed before them, voters are, over time, able to make some assessment of the integrity and competence of governments and the tendency of a party's policies to left or to right, to the preservation of the status quo or to the promotion of radical change. Weighting and preferences between these considerations are moral judgements for which citizen electors are responsible and which politicians cannot ignore.

The objection that elections are relatively infrequent and that the individual voter counts for little is scarcely valid. There is more to democracy than casting one's vote at periodic elections. Political discussion is not limited to the run-up to elections and even those who are not vociferous on political matters often signal their opinions and thereby influence others by the way they respond to their comments. Not all decisions affecting the conduct of communities and the arrangements of their affairs are taken at the level of central government. It is characteristic of liberal democracies that many such are taken at local levels and may, in fact, run counter to central government policies. Here, of course, the influence of individuals will be greater and, in many cases, decisive. This applies not only to the actual institutions of local government. In a democracy, many institutions may be run on democratic or quasi-democratic lines according to which it is regarded as good practice to consult and take into account the views of those involved, even when the actual decisions are taken by others. The processes of democracy are therefore pervasive and on-going and the moral responses of citizens to policies may be effective in determining what is done. The citizens of a liberal democracy thus remain collectively influential upon, and to that extent responsible for the actions of their governments. Citizens of a democracy who supported or did not oppose the oppression or, to take an extreme case, the extermination of an ethnic or other minority, could scarcely claim not to share some responsibility for that policy and the same remains true when we support or condone lesser injustices on the part of governments.

Despite obvious differences between modern democracies and those of the ancient world, fundamental similarities remain. Freedom to criticise government is an essential feature of liberal democracy and may be better protected in modern states than in the ancient world, where the mood of powerful groups might turn ugly. All citizens formally have the same rights. None may be arbitrarily arrested, bidden to hold their tongue or prevented from coming and going as they wish by simple virtue of their status. Some may have more access to influence and power than others. Many are totally disempowered and de facto unable to exercise the rights they formally possess. These are imperfections in our democracy, fallings short of the ideal which there is a moral obligation to address. Part of the moral education of future citizens is both to draw attention to these imperfections and to provide those future citizens with the knowledge, skills and motivation that will progressively lead to their elimination.

One difference between modern and ancient polities, however, requires particular consideration and places particular moral, and to some extent intellectual, demands on modern citizens. Though there will certainly have been disagreements in ancient city states regarding particular strategies to be followed or measures to be taken, those states will have been culturally relatively homogeneous, since membership was most often by birth and based on the myth if not the reality of common ancestry. Among those qualified for citizenship, there may have been differences of wealth or occupation but no differences of race, class or gender, no special religious or moral sensitivities to avoid, no fundamental differences in conceptions of the good life. Issues of multiculturalism, pluralism and associated questions regarding the tolerance of difference will simply not have arisen.

In larger, non-democratic states of later times varying degrees of tolerance and persecution have existed but this seemed to pose no theoretical problem. Those whose beliefs and convictions and way of life differed from the mainstream simply had to suffer their rulers' edicts, like it or lump it, or go elsewhere. Liberal thinkers of the Enlightenment saw this problem largely in terms of religious dissent and saw no harm in individuals and groups privately believing and behaving as they saw fit, provided they did not act treasonably, subvert the good order of the state or interfere with others. The problem becomes more acute in an increasingly conscious democratic era, as dissenters become aware of their status as equal citizens entitled to their share in ruling. At an educational level, the problem is exacerbated insofar as the health of the democratic polity and the rights of its citizens are supposed to imply and require values, virtues and relationships which some groups may find offensive or even destructive of their way of life. Some religious groups have opposed extended education and participation in public affairs (Houlgate 1979). The right of young people to choose their own marriage partners or the practice of questioning and criticising authority and tradition are further cases in point. Certain groups may also wish to make illegal certain activities such as intimate relations between same sex couples, abortion, polygamy and the use of certain narcotics, which others regard as essentially private matters. There are also deep ideological differences over the degree to which community resources should be used to support and enrich the lives of those unable to provide for themselves.

A number of writers (Kymlicka 1999, Crittenden 1999, Callan 1997) have discussed educational issues that arise from this situation, drawing heavily on the later Rawls' distinction (Rawls 1985) between what he terms 'comprehensive' and 'political' liberalism. Comprehensive liberalism is described as a system of values or conception of the good life that celebrates equality, freedom, enquiry, participation in public affairs, dissent, difference and other related values that may permeate the whole of an individual's life, or that of a community. Political liberalism, by contrast, merely concerns the manner in which the polity's public affairs are conducted. All must have the opportunity to participate, all must agree to the procedural principles of civic justice by which differences are resolved. Debate must be in terms of 'public reason': that is, in terms of grounds that must be acceptable to all who see themselves as free and equal citizens but other matters are purely private or community concerns and no business of government.

There appears to be general agreement among the writers mentioned that all citizens need to understand and be committed to the assumptions of political liberalism and the need for tolerance, compliance with properly agreed actions and policies, including those to which they are opposed. These writers are, however, also agreed that to attempt to impose the values of comprehensive liberalism upon all groups of citizens in a democratic polity would be oppressive and contrary to the values of liberalism itself. There is also general agreement that there are many moral values: justice, truthfulness, the avoidance of harm to others, mutual help, self restraint, unselfishness, which are appropriate to the moral education of children from all cultural groups. At one level, of course, there is much truth in this. The claim nevertheless begs a number of important questions insofar as moral education concerns not only conduct but an understanding of morality and the fundamental difference between morality on the one hand and religious belief, authority and tradition on the other. Since the requirements of most traditional and religious belief systems are more stringent than those of secular liberal morality, conflicts between the two are relatively rare. Where, however, traditional practices: forced marriage, genital mutilation, female servitude, denial of medical intervention and deprivation of educational opportunity infringe the rights of free and equal citizens, these may properly be condemned and, indeed, prevented by state intervention. Democratic tolerance does not include tolerating the abuse of individual fellow citizens, even by their own families or communities.

The three writers mentioned above use Rawls' distinction between comprehensive and political liberalism in their discussion of whether all future citizens should attend common schools or whether there should be separate schools for pupils from homes where different belief systems prevail. It is not proposed to enter in detail into this particular debate, except to say that a policy of separation would deprive both mainstream and minority pupils of the experience of life in a plural community where tolerance is supported and difference respected. Quite apart from the dangers of such a policy to society as a whole, it would seem to do no service to pupils themselves, who are bound to grow up in a multicultural world. Whether such a deprivation amounts to an abuse which the state ought to intervene to prevent, is a further question. Needless to say, the state is under no obligation to permit schools or other institutions to exist, whose teaching or other activities threaten its own security or are detrimental to the good order which all citizens are equally entitled to enjoy.

Consideration has been given (Advisory Group on Citizenship 1998) to what, in a pluralistic democracy, should be done about controversial moral issues and the presentation and discussion of views that some groups find positively offensive and from which they would wish their children to be protected. There can be no moral or educational argument for teaching any moral beliefs, including those supportive of democracy, in a biased or indoctrinatory way, such that the learner is rendered incapable of scrutinising them critically, either in the present or in the future. This, however, is quite different from a situation in which teachers present such views positively to older pupils, explaining why they are held and even exemplifying them in their own conduct. Teachers who encourage pupils, even pupils from traditional minority groups, to question their statements or speak of a religious leader with reverence and respect are scarcely to be criticised. That certain beliefs are held in a plural society is both true and something all its members need to know, both in their own interest and in order that they may speak and act with what Kymlicka terms 'civility' in the presence of the holders of those beliefs.

That citizens are all to be regarded as joint possessors of the polity and all free and equal individuals who, however tacitly, are agreed in sharing in ruling and being ruled entails that, whatever empirical differences exist between them, all are to be considered morally equal. Modern citizens may be black or white, male or female, poor or rich, clever or less so, but all are entitled to the same respect as citizens. This does not mean that we may not admire strength, skill or beauty or despise sloth or ineptitude. Nor does it imply that employers and administrative superiors may not give proper instructions to their subordinates and expect them to be carried out, but there are no inferior classes of citizens, no natural subordinates who may be expected to show deference or self deprecation in the ordinary circumstances of everyday life. All may express their views or assert their entitlements in the idiom that is customary to them without gestures, words or turns of phrase indicative of subordination or apology. There has been much criticism of so-called political correctness, which requires us to avoid inappropriate reference to someone's colour, gender, age state of health, disability or other characteristic. Of course, there are absurdities to avoid, especially when these actually draw attention to the characteristic the speaker is ostensibly striving not to mention. Nevertheless, sensitivity to uses of language which, however unintentionally, may be experienced as denigratory, reflects a proper moral respect for the dignity of fellow citizens, as it does for the dignity of fellow human beings in general.

The reciprocal notion of the citizen who is at once someone who shares in ruling and being ruled requires particular consideration, given the way in which the linking of rights and responsibilities is so often used in the rhetoric directed at the young in respect of their conduct and the political claims they sometimes make. There has, in the past, existed a tradition of civics education, the burden of which was to din into the young the obligations of loyalty, service and obedience to the law in return for the democratic 'privileges' they enjoyed, and in virtue of the fact that the laws of the land were the result of democratic processes in which all had the opportunity to participate. Since there existed constitutional means of bringing about changes in the law, it was often added, violent or disruptive protest and demonstration was not permissible.

The argument is disingenuous while the underprivileged and the young have little real access to the levers of constitutional change and the majority may support the unjust treatment of minorities or be disinclined to oppose injustices by which they themselves are unaffected. For this reason, vociferous protest, including some measure of public inconvenience and minor civil disobedience are nowadays regarded as a legitimate part of the democratic scene, which may not be violently put down by the authorities. The main provisos are that injury to persons and damage to the property of uninvolved parties should be avoided and that the protest should be proportionate to the supposed evils against which they are directed. It is, however, perfectly proper to present and attempt to get future citizens to understand the nature of the democratic process, the need to consiliate interests and the appropriateness of so doing, the benefits we all receive from an orderly society, the reasonableness of going along with some laws we find irksome or disagree with. It also needs to be understood that the weapon of disruptive protest is a double-edged sword, which is also available to groups whose aims may be less than reputable. What is, perhaps, most important of all to understand is that, despite their shortcomings, democratic processes are a best attempt to involve all citizens in ensuring that laws are just and reasonable. If this is not understood, laws and other political arrangements risk being seen as the personal edicts of unpopular politicians young people see in the media which, like the commands of an oppressor, it is legitimate and right to disobey.

So much for the burdens and constraints of being ruled. But to share in ruling, insofar as ordinary citizens truly share in that activity, also carries responsibilities. The extent and nature of those responsibilities, however, requires some further definition. It was also suggested earlier that part of citizenship education consisted in acquiring the knowledge and skills that would enable citizens to undertake those responsibilities more effectively. Historically, the moral and political education of rulers has been taken seriously when these have been single individuals or small elites. Arguably, this should also be the case when citizens are required to rule themselves, particularly in the modern world where political wisdom or lack of it on the part of the population may have such important consequences for what politicians feel able to undertake.

If we agree that democracy is not just a system of government or a mere mechanism for selecting a set of rulers but a way of life embodying its own valued practices and procedures, we are bound to agree with Callan that political involvement is an essential virtue. Like Crittenden, we may accept that in our pluralist society some may not actively share democratic values as a central part of their belief system or way of life and we may even agree with Kymlicka that some, whose religious beliefs or private value systems seem to demand it, might be excused the burden of political involvement, despite the fact that they benefit from a tolerant political system maintained by the watchful involvement of others. To be confronted with the possibility of affecting the situation for better or worse, places the individual in a situation of moral choice so that even those who, for whatever reason, choose to take no active part in the political life of the community, are under a minimal obligation to follow the affairs of the day and form a judgement in regard to them, however rarely they feel impelled to give that judgement active expression.

We have referred to the existence of imperfections and even injustices in modern democracies. These include real and present infringements of people's rights which lead them to live lives that fall short of what equal citizens who accept the obligation to obey the law may reasonably expect. As such, a commitment to rectify such imperfections and injustices is a duty of perfect obligation upon the polity as a whole. The task requires attention hic et nunc. There are also other ways in which our polity falls short of perfection. Many of our social arrangements are not such as to maximise happiness or minimise misery as utilitarian considerations suggest should be the case. Others seem calculated neither to encourage the virtues nor to promote the flourishing life of individuals or of the community as a whole. Many of our social institutions, as Noddings (2002) points out, do not reflect caring attitudes and relations. Efforts to effect general improvements in the life of the polity and its citizens are duties of imperfect obligation. Such efforts are meritorious but we attract no blame if, in the general press of our commitments, we omit opportunities to perform them. The balance between such obligations and attending to one's own concerns and the pursuit of a virtuous life at the level of private conduct, must be considered largely a matter of personal choice. Some disinterested contribution to the common weal might, however, seem a desirable element in the morally good and personally satisfactory life and seem to provide one justification for the suggestion that citizenship education should contain an elements of community involvement. Where the polity's arrangements or policies involve positive injustices to individuals, however, the moral issue for citizens becomes more urgent.

Political activism and public protest, not to say violent revolution, have often appealed to the idealistic young, who may feel any lesser level of involvement to be morally compromising. Certainly, there are situations in some places where the victims of injustice could scarcely be worse off in the complete absence of civil order and in these situations attempts to bring about violent regime change may seem more than justified. Elsewhere, the disruption, inconvenience and harm caused by protest needs to be proportional to the harm it is supposed to rectify and consistent with the minimum and most effective means or bringing about the desired end, always bearing in mind that the purpose of the protest is to effect change and not to vent the spleen and frustrations of youth. All levels of activism within the law are, of course, legitimate and depend solely on the idealism and ambitions of the agent.

In many respects, a good citizen is simply a good person whose perspectives are sufficiently broad to take account of what is happening in the wider community or the polity as a whole. Good citizens will, for example, in both their private conduct and their responses to public life, have regard to the greatest good of the greatest number and will not regard their own interests as more weighty than those of others. They will certainly respect the rights of others, conduct themselves in ways that may be rationally defended and expect those entrusted with the government of the community or polity to do the same. Citizenship, including the citizenship of a culturally plural polity, is a way of life and the polity, if it is not to disintegrate, must see itself as a community, albeit a community on an enormous scale. Such a way of life cannot be maintained without the practice of the ordinary virtues of honesty, courage, unselfishness and justice, as well as the practices specific to the democratic polity whose members alone may be referred to as citizens. Citizens who do not care for each other as well as for the polity and its way of life are not good citizens. In addition to the obligations to which we are all subject as private individuals, the relationship of citizenship both confers upon us rights which are not enjoyed by those who do not live under democratic forms of polity and responsibilities in relation to which we view and acknowledge the way in which we are ruled, and the manner in which we participate in the ruling of our polity whose government is ultimately responsible to us for its conduct.

CHAPTER 16

AND GLOBAL CITIZENSHIP?

We also need to consider the moral obligations we have as citizens, not of a particular polity or state but as citizens of the world if, indeed, this expression can be regarded as a meaningful one (Wringe 1998). Do we have obligations due to the fact that we are in some sense 'citizens of the world' over and above the individual obligations we may have to the members of other polities whom we happen to encounter at home or abroad and, perhaps, certain collective undertakings we feel some general benevolent inclination to support? As for the expressions 'global citizenship' or 'world citizenship', do these have any real meaning or are they simply rhetorical devices used in support of international good causes or to justify bringing pressure to bear on particular countries who, for one reason or another, are making themselves internationally unpopular?

In approaching these questions, it is convenient to consider three ways in which individuals may be united in collectivities of various kinds. First there is the legal and political relationship between individuals and particular national polities, the national citizenship relation we considered in the previous chapter, according to which individuals share in the ruling and allegiance to the laws of their polity. This we may consider the paradigm case of citizenship to which any notion of world or global citizenship must exhibit certain plausible analogies if the term is to be meaningfully employed. A key feature of the national citizenship relation is the fact that, in addition to being normally obliged to obey their polity's laws and contribute to its defence and prosperity, citizens have certain important rights (Marshall 1950). Over and above their political rights to share in the ruling of the polity, they also have certain civil rights on the basis of equality with other citizens to the legal protection of freedom, security and property. More recently they have also been considered to have certain social and cultural rights to share in the country's material prosperity and cultural heritage. Narrowly conceived, the function of citizenship in the sense of legal and political affiliation is to distinguish clearly between those who are citizens and are therefore the state's concern and those who are not. To be denied or deprived of citizenship is to be denied access to some or all of the above rights.

Secondly, in addition to legal and political affiliation, individuals may be united by a sense of collective identity. A second part of Aristotle's definition of citizenship not discussed in detail in the previous chapter, refers to common origins and ancestry, common values and a shared way of life. Numerous more recent writers (Anderson 1992, Ignatieff 1994, Gellner 1998, Habermas 1991) have developed this theme under the head of 'nationality'. The relationship may include the sharing of a common language (Kymlicka 1999) common artefacts and common cultural icons as well as shared aspirations and a sense of common destiny. Though often coterminous with legal and political affiliation it is by no means always so. Members of the Scottish and Welsh nations share British legal and political citizenship with the English. Members of the Kurdish nation, insofar as they enjoy legal and political citizenship at all, may do so as citizens of Turkey, Iraq, or Iran. Political and legal citizenship of the former Yugoslavia embraced the separate nations of Serbs, Bosnians, Croats and others while former Soviet citizens in this sense belonged to many different nations.

Thirdly, individuals may be united as members of particular 'communities'. It should, however, be made clear that the term is not here being used with the affective connotations ascribed to it by the communitarian writers referred to in earlier chapters. In fact, many of those connotations are more apposite to the notion of collective identity described above. Here, the term is simply used to denote collectivities whose sense of belonging derives simply from living together or sharing common activities, interests and concerns in, for example, the pursuit of a common occupation. Communities may be based on geographical proximity but are not necessarily so. We may speak of the seafaring community, the diplomatic community, the academic community and so on, who may frequently come into contact with each other, may co-operate in certain undertakings, have significant common interests and be united by bonds of mutual sympathy, though they may share neither political and legal citizenship nor nationality.

We may contrast the above way in which individuals may relate to each other with a fourth way which it is convenient to refer to as the relationship of foreignness. This is the relationship in which we stand to those to whom we might consider we have no obligations of mutuality, or indeed any obligations at all other, perhaps, than the obligation not to be needlessly cruel or inhumane and who, similarly, can be expected to feel no obligations towards us. These individuals do not belong to our state, nation or community, but stand to us as in a state of nature, competitors in the war of all against all. Their fortunes are no concern of ours.

This is how the Greeks saw the barbarians who could be enslaved, killed, deceived or tricked if one could get away with it. It is no doubt also the way many citizens of the colonial powers saw the rest of the world: areas and populations to be colonised and exploited and with whom relations were ungoverned by any law save the will of the stronger. Possibly, it is the way directors and shareholders of some international companies might see their workforces around the world if they were to insist that commercial decisions must be made on grounds of profit and loss alone, mitigated only by considerations of public image and long-term interest. Our answer to the question of whether we can meaningfully speak of world or global citizenship depends on whether there is anyone to whom we can be said to stand in the relationship of foreignness today

It is tempting to limit use of the term 'citizenship' to the legal and political relationship between individuals and sovereign states, relegating notions like collective identity and community to less hard-nosed, more subjective modes of discourse (Gardner, 1990). This would be analytically tidy but would misrepresent our common understanding of what it is to be a citizen, not to say a good citizen. It also risks closing down fertile areas of speculation in the fields of political obligation and citizenship education. Far from being the only meaningful political relationship in which the individual stands to the collectivity, the relationship of legal and political citizenship is, in itself, a somewhat anaemic one. However great the coercive power of the traditional state it is, of itself, scarcely capable of holding the polity together, inspiring loyalty, co-ordinating aspirations or motivating collective endeavour. Arguably, the self-contained Hobbesian state, existing in a condition of nature in respect of other states, in which sovereignty was all or nothing, has been little more than a purely historical phenomenon (Mulgan 1997) arising in conditions under which rulers could most easily increase their wealth and power by centralisation within spaces of a certain dimension and conquest without. Those outside the territory were foreigners, objects of competition or exploitation as we have seen, who were to have no claim on the loyalty or sympathy of those within, while those within were to receive no support against their own government from other states who were forbidden to meddle in each others' internal affairs.

It is no longer possible to think of the way in which we, or our country, stand to those in other parts of the world in quite these terms and we are bound to consider ways in which other forms of polity have come to affect both our everyday lives and our moral obligations. Modern communications and rapid transport make trans-border links between individuals and groups easy and frequent, with the result that the boundaries of nation states are no longer the exclusive lines of political and moral division they once were. Our moral relationship to those outside those boundaries is no longer that of foreignness as it once may have been and conceptions of citizenship education and moral education which fail to take account of this fact are consequently deficient. Clearly, the world as a whole is in no sense itself a sovereign state and despite the imaginings of science fiction writers who suppose the future will be like the past only more so, we are not obliged to assume it will eventually become one, or that it is desirable that it should.

But is it perhaps possible to regard the world as a polity of a different, rather looser kind for whose conduct we have some responsibility, however tenuous, and people in other parts of the world as fellow citizens in such a polity? Are we to any degree under an obligation, as we are in the case of citizens in our own country, to strive to ensure that all people in the world have the right to political participation in the world's affairs, protection of their freedom, security and other important interests, and also access to a share in the benefits of the world's resources and cultural heritage? Would such an effort be either an impertinent encroachment on the sovereignty of other nation states, who may feel they are perfectly entitled to deny their inhabitants such advantages or, perhaps, an ideal so remote from reality that the terms world or global citizenship are no more than figures of speech and the commitments so vague that they cannot realistically be expected to enter the consciousness of practical people and need have no significant place in the moral education of the young?

In addressing these questions we must begin by acknowledging that the condition of many of the world's population does not remotely resemble citizenship in any recognisable form. At best they are the powerless subjects of their governments if they are not the slaves of the local tyrant or, in the case of women, of their menfolk. We might argue that such individuals are de jure fellow citizens with the same rights as everyone else and are simply oppressed de facto. This at least appears to be the message of various international declarations of the rights of this or that category of human beings, including the 1948 *Universal Declaration of Human Rights.* It might be argued that such an assumption implies the existence of some embryonic process, authority or power capable in principle of protecting people's rights, in short, the existence of some prototype form of world government. But we need not regard the world as a whole as some form of superstate with the United Nations Organisation as a rather weak federal super-government under which the nation states, not to mention individual citizens, are united. This is not at all the relationship in which the UNO stands to the governments of nation states. But as we suggested, the sovereign state or superstate is no longer the only conceivable form of polity. Nation states no longer stand to each other as in a condition of nature, in which the application of civil order stops short at state boundaries. It is no longer acceptable for merchant adventurers from powerful states to rampage about the world pillaging and colonising with the support of military force from the home country. Relations between states are increasingly those of interdependence and co-operation, whether at a governmental level or at the level of co-operation and trade between individuals and individual agencies. States are subject to international pressure and therefore indirectly to the pressure of international public opinion to conform to certain norms, both in the conduct of their external affairs and in the treatment of their own nationals, despite vociferous objections by some countries to international interference in their internal affairs.

It is true that we do not directly elect representatives to any kind of world authority on the basis of declared policies as we do at national level. Many governments are, however, constrained in their conduct of international affairs by public opinion at home. If this is in any way expressed through the ballot box or by other political means and if, in consequence, we are prevented from enjoying the benefits of our country's unjust actions abroad then, in however indirect a way, we may be said to have some share in ruling and being ruled at a global level. The same is true if our government supports international agreements limiting the production of greenhouse gasses and in consequence we have to pay more for our cars or electricity or if, as a result of international wild-life agreements which we support, we are prevented from feasting on the flesh of endangered species or fortifying ourselves from time to time with powdered rhino horn. The same applies to agreements, now or in the future, which may hopefully prevent us from profiting as customers or shareholders from the exploitation of workers in third world countries. As regards civil rights at a global level, Europeans do not enjoy unrestricted freedom of movement, rights of residence or freedom of association in countries outside their own continent. Nevertheless, countries wishing to benefit from international trade and co-operation are under pressure to ensure that people from foreign countries are at least properly protected in accordance with the law of the country they are visiting.

While millions die of starvation, preventable disease and exposure and lack the most elementary education, there can be no talk of de facto economic or social rights on a world scale. The view is widespread in the world at large, however, that this situation is unacceptable in the long run and aid programmes on a world scale organised through governments receive tacit support from the public in affluent countries, even if these programmes are meagre and often arranged so as to benefit the material interests of providing countries. Foreign policy, including policy relating to aid and overseas development and ethical overseas trade may form part of political parties' platforms in many countries and are to that extent part of the moral responsibility of citizens.

In would thus seem that we are both obliged to accept certain constraints upon our interests as a result of international political processes and have a responsibility to attempt to influence what happens to fellow human beings in other countries through the influence and control we have in relation to our own politicians. In addition to this, admittedly attenuated role we have as legal and political citizens of the world, can it be argued that we have ties with the inhabitants of distant places analogous to those bonds of group identity we are supposed to have with the fellow citizens of our own nation? This is made more problematic by the fact that such group loyalties often consist precisely in cherishing differences between ourselves and those of other groups. Nevertheless, pride in humanity, human history, human achievement are not entirely unfamiliar notions, for there has been much to admire and identify with in terms of courage, intellect and creativity at many periods and in many places.

As regards community, ease of travel and revolutions in communication make it impossible to ignore events in even the most distant parts of the world or regard those living there and their fortunes as no concern of ours. We hear news of their lives, learn of their celebrations, see photographs of their cities or live television showing the effects on them of disaster and war. We also have a number of pressing common global interests. Despite talk of economic competition all, in fact, have an interest in global prosperity, in the avoidance of conflict in the form of war or terrorism, in abolishing ill-health and the spread of disease. We all have to fear the disastrous effects of exponential population growth, irreversible damage to the environment and massive and uncontrollable population movements in pursuit of material well-being. As inhabitants of the same world we are in many respects all in the same boat in which we sink or swim together.

So far it has been suggested that there are sufficient analogies between our citizenship of our nation state and our relationship to the world at large for the notion of world or global citizenship to be meaningful, not merely as an aspiration but as an incipient if attenuated reality. The world, it has been suggested, has some semblance of an organised polity whose inhabitants may be regarded as, in some sense, world citizens possessing de jure if not de facto, and certain rights. There are certain norms of political participation, legal treatment, welfare, access to education and opportunity, which not only receive widespread approval but are also explicitly enshrined in documents endorsed by a majority of state governments. The influence, albeit indirect, which citizens in many countries have on world affairs may seem to imply obligations to use that influence positively and with due moral consideration. This obligation of world citizenship is supported by notions of the common identity and common aspirations of humanity and a sense of humanity's common interest, even if these notions are, perhaps, not universally shared, and the world citizenship rights they imply not universally implemented.

In the most fundamental ways, the principles of moral judgement in relation to our citizenship of the world are necessarily the same as those that apply at a national level and are, indeed, those of morality in general. Desirable actions and policies are those that bring more well-being than misery and respect the rights and dignity of individuals. Principles that clash and require balance and integrity in their weighting at the level of personal conduct will certainly do so when the vital interests of thousands are affected. Insofar as the world has become a single community in which we may come into contact with members of various different local and national groups and undertake activities that directly or indirectly impact on the lives of such individuals, it has become necessary to develop certain special virtues appropriate to this situation. These may include courtesy and patience in understanding points of view that may express very different cultural assumptions from one's own and, perhaps, a certain fastidiousness in the choice of political and commercial regimes with which one is prepared to collaborate, for tolerance and understanding need not be uncritical. A communitarian conception of morality suggests that we owe most to those closest to us but restraint in pursuing, or demanding that our political representatives pursue, the sectional interests of our own local or national group is a virtue contributing to the flourishing life of the world community. We can, perhaps, as Noddings claims, directly care only for those we confront directly but, whatever our justification, we may still wish to see public policy in respect of fellow citizens of the world as well as of our own nation state, embody the values of caring, acceptance and tolerance. That such commitments as those mentioned above require support as principles of public policy, as well as being expressions of private virtue, needs to be communicated as part of the moral education of young people in the modern world.

Though the principles of virtuous private conduct and those of good citizenship may be the same and virtuous private conduct is an important part of good citizenship, it does not exhaust the duties of the good citizen. The term 'active citizenship' has been used to denote the practice of volunteering to carry out socially useful chores in the gaps left by public provision. This is no doubt particularly necessary at a global level, given that there are, in so many places, so many contingencies to meet for which there is no organised public provision and little possibility of anything of the kind materialising rapidly. Though most may not feel called upon or able to undertake community involvement abroad, morality is a matter of attitude as well as of action and those who are active in performance of the good may only be able to be so with the support and approval of others. Active citizenship also involves taking an active and critical interest in the affairs of one's polis (Wringe 1992), in this case of the world. One is linked to what is done in the world, especially to what is done by one's own government, through the ballot box but also, and perhaps even more importantly if less directly, by one's informal contribution to the formation of collective public opinion by which the agendas at issue at the ballot box are determined.

As in all aspects of moral education, an important part is played by factual information. In the past, a key lesson in the teaching of elementary Ethics concerned the importance of supporting moral conclusions with ethical as well as factual premises. The point was to counter the so-called naturalistic fallacy of arguing directly from facts to moral imperatives without considering one's underlying assumptions of value. Such assumptions are, of course, essential to moral judgement and discussion of them has occupied the major part of this book. Equally, however, we cannot make explicit moral judgements about what should be done, what actions or policies should receive our approval or support, without a factual knowledge of the circumstances to which they relate, in this case the material and political situation of the world's various inhabitants, their way of life, circumstances, needs and resources. In grandiose terms, members of the younger generation cannot each be expected to contribute their miniscule share in the management of the world's affairs without knowing what is going on there. Young people also need to know what is being done by governments, international agencies and voluntary organisations. It does the cause of effective world citizenship no good if some newspapers, politicians and saloon-bar loudmouths go unchallenged in the view that poverty, disease and strife are part of the unchangeable natural order of things, that international assemblies are useless talking shops, and that international agencies are an ineffectual waste of money that could be more usefully spent at home.

In the area of world citizenship, as in all areas or moral endeavour, there will no doubt be some, a few, who will respond with enthusiasm, become actively involved and find fulfilment in dedicated pursuit of the good. But such dedication is not for everyone. What is also important is that many should see the point of such activity and nourish it in others with their encouragement and support. As in all areas of education, the dispelling of aggressive ignorance is important alongside the establishment of positive truth. To refute the denigration of worthy activity and, even if only by one's silent refusal to afford it validation, to undermine support for misguided or malevolent opinion is already to make a small contribution to the progress of the good.

CHAPTER 17

MORAL EDUCATION IN PRACTICE

Having considered in some detail both the scope and content of moral education and what it is to be morally educated, we might be tempted to say that the manner in which moral education is to be achieved is a matter for empirical rather than philosophical enquiry or simply one of personal or professional experience. Different children, different groups of children, children in different personal and social circumstances, we might feel, need to be dealt with differently and only individual experience and individual insight can enable educators, be they parents, teachers or youth workers, to sum up individual learners and the situation in which they find themselves. Neither philosophical deduction nor, indeed, empirical generalisation can identify the child for whom moral considerations are not yet an issue or the one committed to a notion of good conduct that is uncritical and one-sided. A similar point may be made about groups of pupils or other learners. In some school classes there may be a strong sense of doing what is sensible in the interests of all, of justice and fair play, but not much sign of caring for those who lose out in life, while the members other groups may respond with care and concern for each others' joys and sorrows but not have much awareness or commitment to the rights, interests and reasonable expectations of those outside the group. Does one attempt to build outwards from the strengths of the pupils one has, or begin by tackling what one sees as weaknesses and shortcomings? This will depend on the educator's judicious assessment, not only of the learners concerned but of his or her own strengths and weaknesses and what McLaughlin and Halstead (1999) term pedagogic phronesis.

Formal empirical enquiries into the effectiveness of moral education need to be framed with some care. Those that attempt to correlate inputs or structural conditions with behavioural outcomes may mislead or simply be beside the point, given the centrality of reasons for conduct rather than observable conduct itself in the evaluation of moral development. On the other hand, a difficulty with more individualised, interpretive enquiries is that young people are bound to see researchers as adults whose approval they may seek or against whom they may

159

wish to protect their private thoughts. If skilfully constructed and sensitively carried out, however, such enquiries may be helpful in bringing to the attention of educators the range of moral attitudes among both learners and moral educators themselves. Though the professional experience of teachers and other groups involved in various ways in the task of moral education and the accumulating wisdom or parents and other carers may lead to the development of strategies for coping on a day to day basis with the task of moral education, there nevertheless remain a number of general points to be made about the practice of moral education in the light of our understanding of this task as we have developed it in the foregoing chapters.

Some writers (Pritchard 1996, Kymlicka 1999) have felt it appropriate to touch upon the issue of whether it is appropriate for maintained schools to concern themselves with moral education at all. This question seems to have been principally of interest to writers in the United States where the cultural and especially the religious rights of communities have been a matter of particular concern. The issue is whether a programme of moral education carried out in publicly maintained schools amounts to a programme of indoctrination infringing the rights of parents to bring up their children according to their own moral and religious traditions. As we have suggested, this concern may be partly met by distinguishing clearly between the behavioural requirements of morality and those of religion and recognising the validity of both for those who believe. It is nevertheless easy to understand the anxieties of those who wish their children to grow up to behave according to religious requirements, that their offspring may be led astray by the less restrictive requirements of rational secular morality. In the process of moral education, schools at least need to recognise and even explicitly acknowledge that what may be perfectly acceptable in purely moral terms is, nevertheless, a sin in some religions and therefore to many pupils in the school and to their parents.

This concern of some parents cannot, however, be a reason for totally excluding moral education from schools, and the writers who raise this issue mainly appear to do so in order to dismiss it. Pritchard notes that some eighty per cent of American parents are in favour of schools undertaking some form of moral education, though he admits that the portmanteau term moral education may cover a multitude of meanings. In Britain there has been little public or parental protest against the affirmation in the 1988 Education Act of the longstanding tradition that moral education is an integral part of the function of schools. To this extent, we must suppose that these parents assume that the work schools undertake in this area is continuous with the moral upbringing they would wish to provide at home.

Both Kymlicka and Crittenden (1999) draw attention to the overlapping requirements of what we may describe as reasonable morality and those of most commonly practised religions. They also point out that most school pupils of whatever community background will later interact with the wider community and need to behave in a way that will not only be morally acceptable but also enable them to achieve a measure of social acceptance in that community. They will also need to understand and to some extent accommodate the values and moral assumptions of conscientious and well intentioned members of the wider society, which may be in some regards less restrictive than their own. Children are not the property of either their parents or their community and have the right to develop those virtues and other qualities of character that will lead to their being approved of in the wider community of their peers. They are also entitled to what Feinberg (1980) terms 'an open future' in the sense of being in a position to make their own rational assessment of the life they are to lead, even though they may ultimately be drawn to that embraced by their parents and others in their community. Development of the capacity for considered choice is not indoctrination but the antidote to indoctrination, which neither parents nor communities are entitled to practise at the expense of the younger generation. Schools also have a duty to society at large as well as to parents. This is not to concede that rationality and rational morality are just another ideology which it suits mainstream society to inculcate into its citizens. A younger generation committed to the application of rational judgement may be highly critical of mainstream society and the values it currently embraces. Such, indeed will be part of the aim of any well conceived programme of moral education in a society whose moral perfection is as yet incomplete!

Schools can in principle not opt out of the task of moral education. All institutions must embody both rules and values if they are not to descend into chaos and those who spend a formative part of their lives in those institutions, unless they are irremediably alienated, are bound to absorb some of those values, be they good or bad. It is just possible to conceive of a school attempting to inculcate certain bodies of knowledge and skill in a sterile and morally antiseptic way, keeping order where necessary by coercion and fear, but such an institution would scarcely be morally neutral. The message conveyed by such a school where teachers withheld any intimation, let alone promotion, of their own views regarding kindness, the avoidance of violence and cruelty, honesty, co-operation and mutual respect would be the morally devastating one that such considerations were of no account to those we are expected to emulate in our adult lives.

As with many valid educational methodologies, there is a strong presumption of congruence between ends and means of moral education: the link between teaching and learning to be good is not contingent. Aristotle's dictum that we become virtuous by performing virtuous acts is, however, all too easily misinterpreted as advocating a training or habituation model of moral education. On such a view one learns courage by facing threatening situations, fortitude by being made to endure hardship, truthfulness by being made to acknowledge untrue statements and tidiness by putting away one's things before going to bed. Though this may produce morally acceptable and reliable members of the adult community and satisfy many advocates of more effective moral education in schools, it is scarcely likely to lead to more moral responsibility, moral autonomy, moral courage or moral wisdom or, necessarily, more flourishing lives for the individuals concerned. Debating whether simply instilling the habits of good behaviour truly constitutes moral education or whether this is merely socialisation or training may seem to be to engage in the game of definitions for its own sake, for teachers, parents and others charged with the task of bringing up the young must sometimes engage in all three. It is, however, helpful to identify moral education as something peculiarly appropriate to moral beings or those on the way to becoming so. To develop as a moral being, we have suggested, is to become someone who not only chooses to do what is right but chooses to do so because it is right. Baby's moral education only begins when he can be persuaded to stop trying to poke Kitty's eye out with a spoon because it is unkind to Kitty, or to stop pulling Daddy's hair because it hurts Daddy. To drink up his milk 'like a good boy' indicates moral progress while doing so in response to the threat of some minor sanction does not.

It is sometimes supposed there is an issue about whether there should be specific periods or specific activities set aside for the purpose of moral education in schools or whether we should, in some way, use other subjects as a medium for moral education. More vaguely still, it may be suggested that we should simply expect values to be absorbed from the whole school environment. Quite clearly these are not exclusive alternatives and there is a strong case for making the best possible use of all these approaches. There is no reason why we should neglect any opportunity to educate morally, intellectually or in any other way. Schools certainly need to embody the values they wish to transmit and no doubt the most important of these will be publicly celebrated in school mottos, prospectuses, mission statements, public addresses on speech days and the like. These are all helpful in making values explicit, though a sense of style and judgement is necessary if they are not to seem smug, complacent or so blatantly at variance with actual practice in the school as to engender cynicism rather than commitment. The goals of moral education are, no doubt, best achieved when young people grow up in a moral community, where what is done is done because, for one reason or another, it is right. Communities exist in which a range of different reasons for doing things may predominate: pride, vanity, family or local prestige, hostility to certain outsiders, ease and pleasure, commercial profit or whatever. In themselves these motives may not necessarily be inconsistent with acting morally or even, other things being equal, with acting for moral reasons. In a community where the predominant driving motive is financial profit, individuals may be fiercely righteous, even in their commercial dealings. So also may educational institutions strongly committed to the pursuit of knowledge and the development of human skills and capacities. Danger only arises when those learning to be moral or otherwise perceive, as adolescents are quick to perceive, that moral reasons play a secondary role to reasons of a less worthy kind and may, in fact, sometimes be given in pursuit of less worthy goals. The conclusion all too readily drawn in such circumstances is that moral reasons are always used in this way.

Reasons for action may, however, be genuinely mixed. This is a common literary theme, particularly in the genres of comedy and satire. Such literary treatments may perform the morally educative function of setting us on our guard against self-deception or the deception of others, but it is wrong to assume that publicly given reasons are always insincere. The uncritical assumption that they must always be so is one of the more morally corrosive habits of mind and speech that, without stifling healthy scepticism where it is merited, moral educators may need to pick up on and correct. Some sincere nineteenth century philanthropists may have felt it expedient to argue before their shareholders that it was in their companies' commercial interests to treat their workers more humanely while idealistic politicians may defend their contributions to overseas development by maintaining for the sake of their more hard nosed supporters that they are in the long-term national interest.

The importance, from the point of view of moral education, of acting rightly because it is right makes it clear that any programme of moral education that neglects the cognitive and the question of specifically moral motivation, does so at the risk of not being a programme of moral education at all but one of socialisation into conformity. The young person therefore needs to grow up in a community that not only behaves morally but one in which moral reasons are articulated, however cursorily and infrequently this may be done. This poses something of a problem. In the everyday life of adults, those who justify their actions too often tend to be unpopular, if not actually suspect. They may seem to be either setting themselves up as paragons or trying to coerce us into co-operating in their projects. It is important, however, that those parents, teachers and others whose role is an educative one should not be too inhibited by such thoughts. They are, after all, supposed to be guiding and even where necessary controlling the actions of the young. Besides, if reasons are given, this needs to be done not so much by way of justification – that way hypocrisy is learned - but simply as explanation. In such a situation, a young person might learn to do what requires courage, endurance or some personal inconvenience because older people they like, admire or identify with seem to do it naturally because there are reasons for doing it. 'This will make a lot of difference to old Tom and it won't really take us long' ' Others depend on our doing it and would do the same for us', 'It's only fair to Mrs. Jones', ' We care about people, our town, the environment, don't we?', ' Doing it will be an achievement.', ' This is something to take a pride in doing.', From this it necessarily follows that if the older generation is to be successful in morally educating the young it must begin by reforming itself. We cannot expect young people to learn kindness and caring where the weak are bullied and abused, tolerance and respect where role models are destructive and censorious, truthfulness where school mission statements, while avoiding literal falsehood, are couched in terms calculated to impress rather than enlighten and guide, or justice where privileged and underprivileged alike are bound to perceive that neither material advantages or life chances are distributed fairly.

Schools are likely to be more powerful as agents of moral education if they are experienced by their pupils as communities of which they themselves are members, rather than as somewhere you have to go each morning and stay there until three-thirty, or somewhere you go with the instrumental aim of eventually obtaining certain educational qualifications. If teachers are to be morally significant figures in the lives of pupils they need to be experienced as part of the 'we', older and, of course, more influential members of that community, rather than purely as figures of authority or objects of hostility, alien figures who dispense the instruction one goes there to get, who are there to keep order or actively persecute one or one's friends as the case may be. How successful a school is in turning itself into a community rather than an institution will depend on many things: interpersonal relations between staff, between staff and pupils, the accessibility of the school and its facilities so that pupils come to see it as 'theirs', the richness of out of school activities and the number and success of whole school social events in which pupils, parents and staff take part.

Insofar as teachers are significant figures in the lives of pupils, their own conduct is likely, for good or for ill, to be influential. This is not an argument for the old-fashioned view that teachers should be persons of irreproachable private lives. More important is the way teachers interact with their pupils and the way they are seen by pupils to do their job. Children are not the shrewd judges of character they are sometimes said to be. Arrogant bullies are often thought to be 'strict but fair' by those who are lucky enough not to be victimised by them and those who are conscientious and kindly may be thought of as weak unless they sometimes go out of their way to use the word 'must' and mean it. They are nevertheless capable of deciding which of their teachers are conscientious, care enough about them to prepare proper lessons, do not waste their time and show sufficient respect to hand back work promptly and decently marked. They also know which are lazy, ill-organised, self-opinionated or wretchedly mean-minded.

The importance of growing up in a community in which values are explicitly articulated obliges us to touch once again upon the complex relationship between religion and moral education. Whilst distinguishing between morality and religion as a source of values and noting that the requirements of the two may not exactly coincide, we also acknowledged that many religious traditions embody codes of value and conduct which demand our approval, not to say in many cases our extreme admiration. Religious observance, sermons, the words of hymns, prayers and blessings offer some of the few occasions in modern life where virtues may be articulated and celebrated without awkwardness or embarrassment, while the public offering of explicit guidance remains part of the approved role of ministers of religion and a privilege we no longer accord to other authority figures such as employers, politicians, royalty or other members of the traditional upper classes.

It would be unconscionable, not to say offensive to sincere believers, for the secular world to be seen to use religion for its own educational purposes, like the free-thinking squire who thought that regular church attendance was a useful means of keeping the peasantry in their places. Nevertheless, the manner in which religions embody and explicitly celebrate independently justifiable moral values provides one reason for retaining the study of religion and the opportunity for non-sectarian religious observance in schools. Needless to say, this needs to be of a strictly non-evangelising character and, with due sensitivity towards religiously committed pupils and communities, critical distinctions need to be drawn between those many values which are independently justifiable and those which, along with other articles of belief, are simply part of a particular religion. It remains, of course, possible that however critically the study of religions and religious observance is undertaken in an educational context it may result in some pupils finding meaning in one or other of the great religions whose values and beliefs are considered. Such a pupil may eventually come to embrace that religion in its entirety, including those articles of faith and those injunctions and prohibitions which seem to the non-believer not to stand up to critical scrutiny. This possibility may seem troubling to some. Others may think that educators in a democratic society, in which autonomy and the individual choice of a meaningful life are valued, should not view such a possibility with too much anxiety.

We have suggested that the morally educated person both knows what it was to be moral and is committed to the ideal of moral conduct in the sense not merely of behaving according to a set of socially approved rules, but of striving to do what is right even when to do so seems to conflict with some of those rules. We saw that to see the point of moral conduct was in itself in a sense to approve of it and be committed to it. It might be thought that one difference between moral education and other aspects of the educational curriculum resides in the fact that while other subjects are largely technical, being primarily concerned with knowledge and skills, moral education is more importantly a matter of motivation and behaviour. It is not only important, it is sometimes said, that children should know what is the right thing to do but should both be committed to doing it and actually do it in practice. As we saw in our opening chapter, there are many who see no problem in determining what ought to be done and regard the whole task of moral education as one of ensuring conformity to what are seen as established and simple moral norms. If there is a distinction to be drawn between moral and other aspects of education, it is one of degree rather than of essentials. Much has already been said about the importance of the cognitive aspect of moral education but it is equally a mistake to dismiss the motivational and performative aspects of other educational areas. We should think little of the aesthetic education of someone who, though knowledgeable about the various arts, showed no interest in them or was unconcerned about his or her own personal appearance, surroundings or possessions, or of the historical education of someone who did not care about the past or his or her society's heritage and traditions.

We should not minimise the crucial importance of motivation in the process of moral education, or the dilemmas it poses. Direct instruction is not always well regarded these days and, by itself, is inadequate as an educational strategy. It is, nevertheless the most basic and obvious way both of transmitting information and belief and of influencing behaviour. 'Such and such is the case.' 'These are the reasons for believing that such and such is the case.' 'Please do so and so.' 'You really ought to do so and so.' Without making too many sweeping assumptions about human nature or relying too heavily Milgram's (1974) findings, it can be said that, both as children and as adults, we are often inclined to go along with the wishes of others and are glad to receive their approval. Praise and blame are powerful motivators and at various stages in their lives children are pleased to be thought of as 'big', 'clever', 'nice' or 'good' boys and girls and are pleased to be included in the community of those who are approved and admired. Teachers' guiding and controlling discourse offers numerous opportunities for explicit reference to values, both in acknowledging kind, thoughtful, considerate or responsible actions on the part of children and in the issuing of rebukes which must inevitably happen from time to time in every classroom. 'Stop that. No-one talks in *my* lessons. Do it again and you'll regret it. Is that understood?' and 'Don't do that, please, Michael. Susan wants to get on with her work. If you do it again you'll be behind at break, which would be a pity when you were so helpful to Peter when he spilt his paint.' Both ways of phrasing the rebuke may achieve, or fail to achieve, the desired result and it should not be assumed that the second will necessarily be less effective. But the moral message conveyed by each is somewhat different.

There are obvious caveats to be observed with regard to the use of praise and blame in moral education. Teachers, parents and others should not be coy about saying what they consider good or bad or in expressing approval or disapproval but it is important that young people should eventually be weaned off dependence on the approval of others. In many cases this will occur all too readily in adolescence when young people seek independence and come to see the older generation as naïve and out of touch. At this point, though it remains important to continue to guide, the terms of approval need to be more carefully chosen and more subtly expressed. Where undue dependence on approval appears to persist, it may be necessary to nudge some young people in the direction of criticism. 'Yes, I know so and so is keen for you to do such and such, but do you think he is right?'

Beyond the immediate family and school, the case has been made (Advisory Group on Citizenship 1998) for quasi-formal community involvement on the part of young people as part of a programme of citizenship education and social service units have long been part of the extra-curricular offering of many schools. Not a great deal has been said about the actual educational rationale for such activities. The services such units provide are no doubt welcome to their recipients and to the community generally when members of the school visit people in hospital, help old folk tidy their gardens or give their time in cleaning up the local environment. The so-called Crick Report merely speaks in a somewhat circular fashion of 'pupils learning about and becoming involved in the life and concerns of their communities, including learning through community involvement and service to the community' (Advisory Group on Citizenship 1998 p. 40)

Insofar as these are to be educative experiences as opposed to merely useful ways of occupying young people's time, it is because of their group nature. These are essentially social activities and young people are involved together in doing something, which both they and others recognise as worthwhile and to that extent satisfying. Younger members of the group become committed through following the example of those who are older and school pupils come into contact with obviously worthy and admirable adult members of the community prepared to give their own time and effort for no apparent material gain to themselves. The notion of disinterested activity in pursuit of a worthwhile end, of doing something because it is a good thing to do, becomes a real and meaningful possibility in a way that no amount of purely verbal exhortation can achieve.

This is no mere example of virtue being acquired through the performance of virtuous actions. If virtue is acquired in such circumstances, it is being caught rather than taught through the performance of worthwhile actions in the company and emulation of others. The activity is validated by the approval and participation of others like oneself, those one aspires to resemble, those by whose approval one sets some store. If it is important, from the point of view of moral education, that young people should learn not only to act well but to do so because it is the right thing to do, appropriate reasons for community involvement or voluntary activity need, however tacitly, to be both recognised and acknowledged in the group. School heads who sell these activities as a good thing to be able to include in one's curriculum vitae or university applications risk jeopardising their morally educative value if it is done in too hardnosed a way. We referred earlier to the possible compatibility of generous and self-interested motives. The ability to harness the two together without either agonising too grievously or falling too complacently into self-deception may also be an important part of moral education. If certain activities things are useful for inclusion in one's curriculum vitae or university applications it is because they are in themselves worthy, and no harm is done if this point is made explicit to pupils.

Expressions of moral approval and disapproval may not always be sufficient to influence the behaviour of children and young people in the desired direction, and this must necessarily lead us to a discussion of the issue of sanctions and punishment in an educational context and the part they have to play in moral education. During several stages of their development, children clearly wish not only to please but also to be approved of. Praise, reinforcement of the child's self-image as a good boy or girl and the gentlest of chiding or expressions of disappointment are motivation enough. At others, these seem totally ineffective. During the tantrum stage of toddlerhood, physical containment may seem the only option. One can scarcely speak of punishment here and the voice of reason only seems to fan the flames of fury. The firmness of containment at this stage is sometimes seen as contributing to moral development by establishing firm boundaries but an alternative interpretation is to regard moral education as simply having been put on hold until the stage is past. Something similar may be said with regard to the period of adolescence when certain 13-14 year old classes are described by experienced teachers as needing a firm hand and may seem unresponsive to anything but stern authority and the certainty of immediate sanctions.

What is important here is that parents, educators and those involved in the process of correction and reform should not, at any of these stages including the earliest, feel guilty about the use of sanctions or constraint. There is, of course, an obligation to ensure that these are used at a level of severity that is the minimum at which they are unmistakeably effective. Anything less may only harden resistance and prolong the undesirable behaviour. The intention must be to bring about an improvement in the learner's behaviour, insofar as this is possible, rather than simply to prevent the educator or his or her institution from losing face. It goes without saying that if moral education and reform are our concern, reasonable steps need to be taken to help the individual to see why his or her actions are unacceptable, rather than simply ensure conformity under threat of more severe sanctions in future. Sometimes, however, through no fault of our own, we may be unsuccessful in this endeavour. There are no doubt mature offenders upon whom, for whatever reason, moral considerations have no purchase and who may see moral reasoning as no more than a rhetorical device, which only the gullible take seriously. There are also those who are calculating and ruthless but succeed in never actually falling foul of the law. These are in no sense on the path to becoming moral beings capable of responding to moral constraint or, even appreciating the meaning of right and wrong. We cannot win all battles though we should, perhaps, not give up trying too readily. The point at which we may reasonably do so is itself a moral issue, but both the adult world and civilised society are perfectly justified in taking reasonable steps to protect themselves and their own tolerable lives against those who may find themselves temporarily or permanently outside them.

The view that traditionally reward and punishment have been the instruments of moral education is scarcely even half the truth, for little is said of the use of pleasure as opposed to pain in the history of moral education. The ferocious punishments meted out to Roman slaves or the eighteenth century poor may or may not have achieved social control but will have effected little moral education in the community at large. Happily the infliction of physical pain as a means of correcting the conduct of children seems to be on the way out in civilised countries. Behavioural psychologists have seemed to demonstrate that the use of positive reinforcement is more effective than punishment in the shaping of behaviour, as it is logically bound to be where moral initiative rather than mere conformity is required. It is, however, a solecism to equate either reward or punishment with mere positive or negative reinforcement in the behavioural sense. Such deliberate behaviour shaping in respect of potentially rational beings is scarcely conscionable and can no more be regarded as part of moral education than 'sleep learning' (if such a process were possible) could be regarded as part of education in other fields. Even punishment used as a threat to deter is a long way from the Skinnerian notion of negative reinforcement, for it assumes that the recipient of the threat consciously generalises the nature of the forbidden act and makes a deliberate judgement whether or not to do it. To be educationally effective, rather than simply inculcating submission to the will of the stronger, the threat of punishment has to be coupled with an understanding and acceptance of the wrongness of what is forbidden. From an educational perspective, the point of punishment is not so much the infliction of displeasure upon the offender as the unambiguous expression of disapproval by a respected authority and the ignominy of having had such a mark of censure inflicted upon one. This necessarily assumes that the punishing authority is respected by the offender and others in his or her social group and that the offender has reason to want to be approved of by the punisher. The offender must come to see him or herself as someone who has fallen short of a standard to which he or she aspires and has been brought back into line, not as a heroic martyr resisting an arbitrary and vindictive oppressor with the support and approval of his or her peers.

The appropriate severity of sanctions also raises a number of dilemmas. In the world of adult criminals who are assumed to choose to do wrong, the severity of punishments may need to be significant so that the risk of being caught at least outweighs the benefit of the crime to the offender. The punishment of crimes against individuals also needs to inflict a sanction proportionate to the harm suffered by the victim, so that justice seems to favour the victim rather than the criminal. Somewhat different considerations apply in an educational context if we consider that most childish or adolescent misdemeanours are the result of thoughtlessness or impulse rather than the deliberate calculation of advantage. The point of the punishment is to bring home the seriousness both of what has been done and the disapproval of the educator. It does matter, and is not just a hilarious bit of fun, if a teacher's lessons are constantly disrupted. It does matter if people fool around with dangerous power tools in the metalwork room or damage expensive equipment by using them without proper supervision or failing to follow proper procedures. It does matter and should be a cause of shame if younger or more vulnerable children are bullied or treated unkindly. Adults may sometimes point these things out over and over again without avail until some form of significant sanction is employed to make the point that their rebukes are something more than empty words.

Sometimes more serious misdemeanours may happen in schools: deliberate and malicious damage, systematic theft, severe acts of violence leading to injury, the use and distribution of drugs. Dealing with such events only remains within the educator's competence for as long as there remains some possibility that the perpetrator's future conduct may be improved by the use of sanctions and other resources available to the school. Where serious material harm results from a pupil's actions it may, in any case, be necessary to involve authorities outside the school. Similar comments obviously apply when a pupil's behaviour, though less serious in its consequences, is in other ways problematic and does not seem to respond to the normal resources and procedures available to the educator. The role of educators differs from that of both policemen and psychologists, though they may sometimes be called upon to co-operate with and seek the co-operation of both.

We referred earlier to the ways in which other school subjects and activities may contribute to moral education. Various philosophers of education (Arnold 1989 and 1997, Butcher and Schneider 1988, Carr 1979, Meakin 1981, Wright 1987, Drewe 2001) have written about the potential contribution of Physical Education and Sport to this goal, and this, along with promoting health and fitness, has traditionally been given as a reason for their inclusion in the curriculum. Suggested moral benefits have included the development of 'character' by learning to show determination in rigorous training to improve performance, facing the physical hardship and risk of knocks and bruises in some sports, notions of fair play within an agreed set of rules, a readiness to exert oneself or sacrifice one's own opportunities to shine for the sake of the team, the opportunity to show generosity towards opponents in appreciating and applauding their achievements in both victory and defeat and the ability to combine intense competition within the game with decent social relations off the field.

These possibilities are not to be denied, though it is all too easy to be naïve in our attempts to find educational justification for including Physical Education and Sport in the curriculum. Competitive games are not always played in a morally edifying spirit. Happily, some professional sports have recently seen the importance of cleaning up their act and some star performers have shown responsibility in recognising their influence as role models for the young. Even at school and youth levels, however, the desire to win at all costs, or for one's team to win if one is a coach, may sometimes exert a more powerful influence upon attitudes and behaviour than the ideals of sportsmanship, fair play and respect for opponents. Achievement in sport may lead to arrogance, machismo or locker room bullying. Generosity and appreciation are not always shown towards the efforts and achievements of the physically ungifted and the importance of excelling, which is inherent in the nature of so many sports, necessarily brings with it the dangers of exclusiveness and elitism. As with many opportunities for moral education and moral development, teachers need to do more than simply institute a promising activity and expect the educational results to occur of their own accord. If moral development is part of the justification of Physical Education and Sport in the curriculum, it must be explicitly recognised as an aim of the subject, for the achievement of which teachers must see themselves as responsible, along with, but in many ways educationally more important than success in promoting achievement and excellent performance in the sports themselves.

The extent to which some other school subjects should serve as vehicles of moral education has not been entirely uncontroversial. Some purists may feel that the inherent standards of their subject are compromised or diluted if they are used for this or any other wider educational purpose and this may even be seen as indoctrinatory. Of course, there have been the unfortunate examples of Lysenko and his politically motivated attempts to prove that acquired characteristics may be inherited and Nazi pseudo–scientific theories of racial characteristics, not to mention the nineteenth century use of History teaching in many countries to inspire patriotism or, more recently, to demonstrate the superiority of democratic government. We must necessarily be on our guard, for to corrupt the rigour of academic disciplines is an insidious form of dishonesty and scarcely an appropriate mode of moral education. The making of valid moral judgements implies a prior effort to gain an accurate view of the situation being judged and this in itself is an important moral lesson. Moral judgements must not only be based on sound reasoning and valid moral premises. A point less frequently made is that their other premises, their factual ones, must be sound also and intellectual rigour may be essential to ensuring that this is so. Intellectual rigour is a fastidious moral virtue and sophisticated form of honesty and if morality is to count as anything more than opinion or ideology, its conclusions must be susceptible of rigorous support. This is not to suppose that rigorous argument in morality follows the same rules as rigorous argument in Science or Mathematics. One of the grosser errors that those with no education in moral reasoning often commit is to demand that it should do so or abandon its claim to intellectual respectability. But the underlying demand for honesty in reasoning is common to both. One cannot cheat on the laws of Arithmetic or change them by stamping one's foot or throwing a tantrum. This is an important moral lesson and many fallacious moral arguments trade on a refusal to take proper account of numbers. All disciplines have their characteristic areas of rigour and their characteristic temptations. One does not massage one's results in the physical and social sciences, quote literary texts with misleading disregard for context or apply value loaded descriptors to the personalities and events of History to suit one's ideological prejudices.

The facts of Science may have moral implications. To draw attention to these may not itself be Science but it is certainly a proper part of scientific education, for it is to give such facts part of their due significance in human life. When vice in literary works is punished and virtue rewarded this is morally satisfying, but it would be crass to treat such works as if they were simply improving tales. Quite frequently it is the reverse that happens but the moral point of view is rarely absent from such works. We are usually left in no doubt as to which characters we should detest and despise and which we should identify with. We would rather be the virtuous hero and heroine who are doomed than their odious persecutor who triumphs over them. The amiable rogue may have moral qualities which, in human terms, seem more important than the mere respectability of his or her oppressors or victims. It is one of the characteristics of many literary works to bring out the subtlety required in our judgement of character, actions and situations in a manner which entirely accords with the goals of moral education. To bring out these subtleties does not subvert the proper aims of literary studies: to fail to do so is to neglect an important aspect of them.

Similar comments apply in the case of History. Unlike Literature, neither its personalities nor its events have been created with a moral perspective in mind and one of the tasks of academic historians may be to rid our perception of them of any such aura. This, however, is not to deny that there have existed genuinely estimable men and women, as well as villains traitors and tyrants, noble achievements and acts of mercy as well as treacheries, cruelties and mindless acts of slaughter. These quite properly evoke admiration or contempt. Insofar as this is true, History teaching may, without abandoning its essential integrity, evoke idealism and admiration for achievement, as well as humility in face of its transience. Whatever the claims of moral objectivity upon the academic historian, it can scarcely be the aim of school History teaching to entirely extinguish such responses in order that such personalities and events should entirely leave them cold.

It is, finally, difficult to think of good reasons why some quite specific portion of curricular time should not be set aside for purposes of moral education. I do not take seriously or propose to address the objection that the curriculum is already so over-crowded as to make this impossible. The kind of person someone grows up to be is ultimately more important than the various skills and items of academic knowledge he or she may also possess. If this is true at an individual level, it is also true socially. It is difficult to doubt that a society of morally aware and morally sensitive individuals is likely to make possible a greater degree of human flourishing than one whose members are merely well informed and highly skilled.

Nor is it obvious that such a society would be less prosperous economically or, certainly, that such prosperity would be less justly distributed. Moral education, as we have argued, necessarily includes important aspects of citizenship and sex education and someone's personal and social development is also part of their moral character. Given that our moral judgements must take due account of facts about the world, moral education will also need to make reference to current events and information mainly dealt with by other subject areas. Overridingly, however, an understanding of and commitment to what are valid reasons for action are essential to morally aware citizens in their private and their social and public conduct and in their response to the conduct of others. Various teaching and learning strategies will naturally be used during the time dedicated to moral education and the level of lesson objectives will necessarily be appropriate to the age, capacities and existing knowledge of the learners concerned. Moral education is too serious a matter to be left to the whims and fancies of individual teachers to be added on as an appendage to other subjects or dealt with at odd moments in form periods after registration. It is an area in which acknowledged bodies of content and argument exist and in which it is perfectly possible to put together a programme of balanced coverage capable of being delivered in an expert and professional way, by appropriately qualified teachers.

For a number of reasons, discussion is likely to figure prominently among the teaching strategies employed by those involved in the regular teaching of moral education. Though such discussions may bear some resemblance to some of the 1970s experimental work referred to in Chapter 5, they are likely to be conducted in a rather different spirit and on the basis of rather different assumptions, given the now commonly accepted reservations noted in that chapter and in some cases more fully developed in later ones. We are nowadays less confident of Piaget's and Kohlberg's stage related picture of moral development, taking place spontaneously in response to stimulus materials and more or less unguided discussion. We are now less ready to accept that grasp of higher order rational concepts such as justice represents the pinnacle of such development. The reaching of sound moral conclusions no longer seems to us purely a matter of pitting one higher order principle against another. Though as doubtful as ever of the absolute validity of certain traditional moral injunctions and prohibitions, we no longer think that individuals should reach their own moral conclusions and live according to them, irrespective of the feelings and moral assumptions of others. Going along with the accepted customs and practices of society, provided they are not the cause of suffering or injustice, no longer seems the act of moral cowardice and enslavement it once did. To be critical is no longer to challenge everything put to us by a member of the older generation and we no longer assume that individuals are bound to reach sound conclusions in morality, or indeed anything else, except by building on the achievements of others. In particular, we no longer suppose that the goals of moral education are achieved simply by reaching sound intellectual conclusions.

Nevertheless, discussion remains, as it has always been, a key feature of progressive teaching and learning, particularly in the fields of moral, literary or aesthetic judgement where there are no chains of irrefutable argument or bodies of authoritative record or tangible evidence to be transmitted. There is no reason for teachers to disguise their own point of view or attempt to play the neutral chairman. Besides being arrogant and supercilious, this deprives learners of one, hopefully valuable, perspective. The teacher has, after all, lived longer and probably seen more than most pupils and has presumably given some thought to the issues being discussed. Those hoping to succeed in their role as moral educators will necessarily seek to lead their pupils to what seem to be morally reputable conclusions rather than attempting to inculcate such conclusions by force of authority. They will also appreciate that recourse to coercion, moral browbeating, factual misrepresentation and other devices of indoctrination, even if apparently successful in achieving persuasion, are in fact contrary to the aims of moral education. Successful moral education is less about instruction than engagement. Discussion is an essentially social activity in which not only shared views but also group commitments are generated.

Insofar as moral education is, in part, cognitive and conceptual, these aspects need to be developed and sometimes this may require direct teacher intervention and explanation, but without interaction there is no feedback. The teacher does not know what is understood, far less what is believed, except by the crude and relatively inaccurate methods of teacher controlled question and answer or more formal modes of assessment. In moral, as in other kinds of education, critical understanding cannot be achieved if the learner does not have the chance to both try out and rehearse his or her understanding of what has been learned and be coached in the modes of criticism appropriate to the kinds of discussion taking place. Some of the *Schools Council Humanities Curriculum Project's* recommendations with regard to the conduct of discussion remain as valid as they have ever been in civilised educational circles. Everyone needs to be encouraged to participate, and reason rather than rhetoric or abuse has to prevail. The suggestion that consensus needs to be avoided seems less valid. The tone needs to be that of seeking a common understanding rather than of an adversarial war of all against all, for it is the point of morality that we can reach commonly acceptable agreements as to what ought to be done or how life ought to be lived, while recognising that there remain questions between us upon which judgement may be reserved (Gert 1998).

In addition to developing the conceptual apparatus of moral reflection and commitment to supporting the implementation of morally acceptable conclusions, discussion may have a further important role to play in moral education. Ours is, or aspires to be, a society of equals both politically and in domestic life. The nature of modern work increasingly requires consultation with colleagues rather than the independent performance of our allotted role and the consultation of subordinates increasingly comes to be seen as good management practice. Consultation in the workplace no doubt most frequently concerns such practical questions as the best way to complete a certain task but, especially in the public services and caring professions, discussion may also touch upon the rightness or otherwise of what is being done or the moral acceptability of the demands being made of individuals. This is all part of the valued moral climate of our society, one of our valued traditions, albeit perhaps, a fairly recently established one, which it is part of the task of moral education to support and preserve. The skills of moral debate, identifying relevant issues, the avoidance of browbeating, recognition of the rights and point of view of others, the reasonable weighing of conflicting considerations, all need to be learned and this may possibly be best achieved under the tutelage of a skilled and committed teacher.

Notwithstanding the importance of discussion in the pedagogy of moral education, there will be, as in other subjects, certain aspects that are best introduced by means of direct teacher input or presentation. With older and relatively able groups, this may perfectly well include the explanation of various kinds of moral justification and the differences between them as well as presentation of factual information about current situations and events that have moral implications. These are genuinely of interest to many children as they grow up, and passionately so to many adolescents. They are also issues on which one-sided, extreme and ill-informed views may be embraced, simply for want of reasoned discussion and criticism. Straightforward didactic moral instruction and, indeed, preaching have traditionally been part of this process and, despite the obvious shortcomings of teaching as telling as an educational process when employed alone, it is an absurd prejudice that we can learn nothing of value by simply being told it and the direct presentation of a point of view at least has this to be said morally in its favour, that it is explicit and up for scrutiny in a way that ideas delivered by other approaches may not be. Needless to say, any such presentation would normally be followed by discussion and opportunities for debate in a way quite foreign to more authoritarian styles of moral instruction in the past. To be of genuine value to either society or the younger generation, the programme of moral education needs to ensure that pupils have at a suitable level, some notion of our society's principle moral perspectives: the general good, rights and social contract, respect for persons, the celebration of certain virtues and values, and caring. At the same time it needs to address such general issues as mindless relativism and cynicism as well as equally mindless and inflexible absolutism, the relationship between morality and religion and the way in which, in many cases requiring moral judgement, the appeal to principles, though helpful, may not resolve the issue without careful scrutiny of the particular situation.

It will, hopefully, not appear from the above remarks that what is being suggested bears any resemblance to the authoritarian and inculcatory approaches to moral education suggested by some of the writers referred to in Chapter 1. We have travelled a long way from that position in the course of this book. Morality is, indeed, a serious and sometimes demanding guide to conduct but it is not to be trivialised by being reduced to a set of narrow formulae to be dictated to the supposedly ignorant and uncomprehending or used by members one generation to protect their comfortable lives and world view from disturbance by the adventurous and occasionally wayward explorations of the next. Moral reflection opens up a universe of possibilities for understanding the way we are and the way things might be. The overriding goal of moral education must be to make this universe accessible to the young as they eventually surpass us in the continuing quest to discover the good life for human beings and the manner in which human life may best be lived.

BIBLIOGRAPHY

Adams, P. (1971) 'The infant, the family and society'. In P. Adams et al. *Children's Rights* , London: Elek Books.

Advisory Group on Citizenship (1998) *Education for Citizenship and the Teaching of Democracy in Schools,* London: Department for Education and Employment/Qualifications and Curriculum Authority.

Anderson, B. (1983) *Imagined Communities,* London:Verso.

Anderson, D. (1992) 'Domestic Economy: improvidence, and irresponsibility in the low income home'. In D. Anderson, *The Loss of Virtue: Moral Confusion and Social Disorder in Britain and America,* London: Social Affairs Unit.

Anscombe, E. (1958) 'Modern Moral Philosophy', *Philosophy,* 33, pp. 159-73.

Archard, D. (1998) *Sexual Consent,* Oxford and Boulder Colorado: Westview Press.

Archard, D. (2000) *Sex Education,* London: Philosophy of Education Society of Great Britain.

Arnold, M. (1869) *Culture and Anarchy*, Cambridge: Cambridge University Press, 1932.

Arnold, P. (1989) 'Competitive sport, winning and education', *Journal of Moral Education,* 18, pp. 15-25.

Arnold, P. (1997) *Sport, Ethics and Education*, London: Cassell.

Ayer, A.J. (1967) *Language Truth and Logic,* London: Gollancz.

Bailey, C. (1975) 'Neutrality and rationality in teaching'. In D. Bridges and P. Scrimshaw (Eds) *Values and Authority in Schools,* London: Hodder and Stoughton.

Barrow, R. (1991) *Utilitarianism, a Contemporary Statement,* Vermont: Elgar.

Barzun, J. (1959) *The House of Intellect* London: Secker and Warburg.

Baudrillard, J. (1989) *Selected Writings,* ed. M. Poster, Cambridge: Cambridge University Press.

Bellah, R. (1985) *Habits of the Heart: Individualism and Commitment in American Life,* Berkeley: California University Press.

Bentham, J. (1789) *An Introduction to the Principles of Morals and Legislation,* London: Dent, 1910.

Berger, B. (1993)'The bourgeois family and modern society'. In J. Davies (Ed.) *The Family: Is It Just Another Life-Style Choice?* London: Institute of Economic Affairs.

Blake N. (1997) 'Spirituality, anti-intellectualism and the end of civilisation as we know it'. In R. Smith and P. Standish (Eds) *Teaching Right and Wrong,* Stoke-on-Trent: Trentham Books.

Bond, E.J. (1983) *Reason and Value,* Cambridge: Cambridge University Press.

Bourdieu, P. and Passeron, J-C. (1970) *La Réproduction,* trans. R. Nice as *Reproduction in Education, Society and Culture,* London and Beverley Hills: Sage, 1977.

Bradley, F.H. (1927) *Ethical Studies,* Oxford: Oxford University Press.

Bruner, J. (1963) *The Process of Education,* Cambridge MA: Harvard University Press.

Burke, E. (1790) *Reflections on the Revolution in France,* Ed. T.D. Mahoney, New York: Bobbs Merrill.

Burke, E. (1790) *Reflections on the Revolution in France,* Harmondsworth: Penguin, 1970.

Butcher, R. and Schneider, A. (1988) 'Fair play as respect for the game', *Journal of Philsophy of Sport,* 25, pp. 1-22.

Callan, E. (1997) *Creating Citizens: Political Education and Liberal Democracy,* Oxford: Clarendon Press.

Carr, D. (1979) 'Aims of Physical Education' *Physical Education Review,* 2, pp. 91-100.

Carr, D. (1991*) Educating the Virtues,* London: Routledge.

Chandler, D. (2002) *From Kosovo to Kabul: Human Rights and International Intervention,* London: Pluto.

Clarke, Sir W. (1891) The Clarke Papers, ed. C.H Firth, Vol. 1, *Camden Society Publications,* London: The Camden Society.

Crittenden, B. (1999) ' Moral education in a pluralist democracy'. In J.M. Halstead and T.H. McLaughlin (Eds) *Education in Morality,* London: Routledge

Dahl, R. (1956) *A Preface to Democratic Theory,* Chicago: University of Chicago Press.

Davies, J. (1993) 'From household to family to individualism'. In J. Davies (Ed.) *The Family: Is It Just Another Life-Style Choice?* London: Institute of Economic Affairs.

Dearden, R.F., Hirst, P.H. and Peters R.S. (Eds) (1972) *Education and the Development of Reason,* London: Routledge.

Dennis, N. and Erdos, G. (1993*) Families Without Fatherhood,* London: Institute of Economic Affairs.

Dostoyevsky, F. (1881) *The Brothers Karamazov,* trans. C. Garnett, London: Heinemann, 1912.

Drewe, S. (2001) *Socrates, sport and students: a philosophical enquiry into Physical Education and Sport,* Lanham, MD: University Press of America.

Droste-Hülshoff, A. von (1842) *Die Judenbuche: ein Sittengemälde aus dem gebirgichten Westfalen,* Stuttgart: Reclam.

Etzioni, A (Ed.) (1988) *The Essential Communitarian Reader,* Lanham MD: Rowman and Littlefield.

Etzioni, A. (1993) *The Spirit of Community: Rights, Responsibilities and the Communitarian Agenda,* New York: Crown.

Feinberg, J. (1970) The nature and value of rights, *Journal of Value Enquiry,* 4, pp. 243-59.

Feinberg, J. (1980) 'The child's right to an open future'. In W. Aiken and H. Lafollette (Eds) *Whose Child?* Totowa, New Jersey: Littlefield Adams.

Fish, S. (1989) *Doing What Comes Naturally: Change, Rhetoric and the Practice of Theory in Literary and Legal Studies,* Durham, NC: Duke University Press.

Flew, A. (1972) 'Sincerity, criticism and monitoring', *Journal of Philosophy of Education,* 13, pp. 141-48.

Flew, A. (1975) *Thinking about Thinking,* Glasgow: Fontana/Collins.

Flew, A. (1976) *Sociology, Equality and Education,* London: Macmillan.

Foucault, M. (1973) *The Birth of the Clinic: an Archeology of Medical Perceptions,* trans. A. Sheridan, New York: Pantheon.

Gagné, R.M. (1970) *The Conditions of Learning,* London: Rinehart and Winstone.

Gallie, W.B. (1956) 'Essentially contested concepts', *Proceedings of the Aristotelian Society,* Vol. 56, pp.160-73

Gamm, H.J. (1970) *Kritische Schule,* München; List Verlag.

Gardner R., Cairns J. and Lawton D. (Eds) (2000) *Education for Values,* London: Kogan Page.

Gardner, J.P. (1990) 'What lawyers mean by citizenship'. In F. Morrell (Ed.) *Encouraging Citizenship: Report of the Commission on Citzenship,* London: HMSO.

Gellner, E. (1998) *Nationalism,* London: Phoenix.

Gert, B. (1998) *Morality,* NewYork and Oxford: Oxford University Press.

Gilligan, C. (1982) *In a Different Voice,* Cambridge MA: Harvard University Press.

Griffin, J. (1986) *Well-being,* Oxford: Clarendon Press.

Gutman, A. (1992) Introduction to A. Gutman and C. Taylor, *Multiculturalism and the Politics of Recognition,* Princeton, NJ: Princeton University Press.

Gutman, A. and Taylor, C. (1992) *Multiculturalism and the Politics of Recognition,* Princeton NJ: Princeton University Press.

Habermas, J. (1991) *Communication and the Evolution of Society,* Cambridge: Polity Press.

Halstead M. and Taylor, M. (Eds) (1996) *Values in Education and Education in Values,* London: Falmer Press.

Hare, R.M. (1963) *Freedom and Reason,* Oxford: Clarendon Press.

Hart, W. (1998) Nussbaum, Kant and conflicts between duties, *Philosophy,* 73/286, pp. 609-18.

Haydon, G. (1997) *Teaching about Values: a New Approach,* London: Cassell.

Hegel, W.F. (1807) *Phänomenologie des Geistes,* trans. A.V. Miller, as *Hegel's Phenomemology of the Spirit,* Oxford: Oxford University Press, 1990.

Himmelfarb, G. (1995) *The Demoralisation of Society: from Victorian Virtues to Modern Values,* London: Institute of Economic affairs.

Hirst, P. (1972) *Moral Education in a Secular Society,* London: University of London Press.

Hobbes, T. (1642) *De Cive, translated as* 'The Citizen'. In *Thomas Hobbes Man and Citizen,* ed. B. Gert, London: Harvester, 1972.

Hobbes, T. (1651) *Leviathan,* ed. C.B. Macpherson, Harmondsworth: Penguin, 1971.

Houlgate, L.D. (1979) 'Children, paternalism and rights to liberty'. In O. O'Neill and W. Ruddick (Eds), *Having children: philosophical and legal reflections on parenthood,* New York: Oxford University Press.

Hugo, V. (1862) *Les Misérables,* Paris: Garnier 1957.

Hume, D. (1740) *A Treatise of Human Nature,* Ed. E.C. Mossner, Harmondsworth: Penguin.

Hume, D. (1748) *An Enquiry Concerning Human Understanding,* Oxford: Oxford University Press, 1999.

Hursthouse, R. (2001) *On Virtue Ethics,* Oxford: Oxford Univesity Press.

Ignatieff, M. (1994) *Blood and Belonging: Journeys into the New Nationalism,* London: Vintage.

Inman, S. and Buck, M. (Eds) (1995) *Adding Value?* Stoke -on-Trent: Trentham Books.

Kant, I. (1785) *Fundamental Principles of the Metaphysic of Ethics,* trans. T.K. Abbott, London: Longmans, 1962.

Kant, I. (1788) *Critique of Practical Reason,* Indianapolis: Bobbs-Merrill, 1956.

Kierkegaard, S. (1834) *Fear and Trembling,* trans. A. Hannay, Harmondsworth: Penguin, 1985.

Kim, J-N and Wringe C. 'Well-being, virtue and education', *Seoul University Journal of Eucational Research, 32/2, pp. 225-38.*

Kohlberg, L. (1968) 'Stage and sequence: the cognitive-developmental approach to socialisation'. In D. Goslin, (Ed.) *Handbook of Socialisation,* New York: Rand McNally.

Kymlicka, W. (1999) 'Education for Citizenship'. In J.M. Halstead and T.H. McLaughlin, *Education in Morality,* London: Routledge.

Ladd, J. (1985) *Ethical Relativism,* Lanham MD and London: University Press of America.

Lamb, S. (1997) 'Sex education as moral education: teaching for pleasure, about fantasy and against abuse' *Journal of Moral Education,* 26/3, pp. 301-315.

Levinas, E. (1978) La pensée de l'être et la question de l'autre, *Critique,* 369, pp. 187-97.

Lickona, T. (1991) *Education for Character: How our Schools can Teach Respect and Responsibility,* New York: Bantam Books.

Lickona, T. (1996) Character Education, *Journal of Moral Education* , 25, 1. pp.93-100.

Locke, J. (1689) *Second Treatise of Government,* ed. P. Laslett in *Locke's Two Treatises of Government,* Cambridge: Cambridge University Press, 1960.

Lockwood, A.L. (1997) 'Character Education: searching for a definition'. In A. Molnar (Ed.) *The Construction of Children's Character,* Chicago: Chicago University Press.

Lyotard, J-F. (1979) *La Condition Postmoderne: Rapport Sur le Savoir,* Paris: Editions de Minuit.

MacIntyre, A (1982) *After Virtue,* London: Duckworth.

MacIntyre, A. (1988) *Whose Justice? Which Rationality,* London: Duckworth.

Marshall, T.H. (1950) *Citizenship and Social Change,* Cambridge: Cambridge University Press.

McLaughlin, T.H. and Halstead, J. M. (1999) 'Education in character and virtue'. In J.M.Halstead and T.H. McLaughlin, *Education in Character and Virtue,* London: Routledge.

Meakin, D. (1981) 'Physical Education: an agency of moral education?', *Journal of Philosophy of Education,* 15, pp. 241-253.

Midgeley, M. (1994) 'Duties concerning islands'. In P. Singer, (Ed.) *Ethics,* Oxford: Oxford University Press.

Milgram, S. (1974) *Obedience to Authority: an Experimental View,* London: Tavistock.

Mill, J.S. (1861) 'Utilitarianism'. In J.S. Mill, *Utilitarianism, Liberty, Representative Government,* London, Dent, 1910.

Mill, J.S. (1869) 'The subjection of women'. In J.S. Mill, *On Liberty, Representative Government, The Subjection of Women* Ed. g. M. Fawcett, London: Oxford University Press, 1912.

Milne, A.J.M. (1968) *Freeedom and Rights,* London: Allen and Unwin.

Moore, C.E. (1903) *Principia Ethica,* Cambridge: Cambridge University Press.

Mount, F. *The Subversive Family,* London: Cape.

Mulgan, G. (1997) *Connexity: How to Live in a Connected World,* London: Chatto and Windus.

Murdoch, I. (1970) T*he Sovereignty of the Good,* London: Routledge.

Murray, C. (1996) 'The emerging British underclass'. In R. Lister (Ed.) *Charles Murray and the Underclass,* London: Institute of Economic Affairs.

National Curiculum Council (1990a) *Curriculum Guidance 3: The Whole Curriculum,* York: National Curriculum Council.

National Curiculum Council (1990b) *Curriculum Guidance 8: Education for Citizenship,* York: National Curriculum Council.

Nietzsche, F. (1885) *Also Sprach Zarathustra,* trans. R.J. Hollingdale as *Thus Spake Zarathustra,* Harmondsworth: Penguin, 1961.

Noddings, N. (1984) *Caring: a Feminine Approach to Ethics and Moral Education,* Berkeley and Los Angeles: Chicago University Press.

Noddings, N. (2002a) *Educating Moral People,* New York: Teachers' College Press

Noddings, N. (2002b) *Starting at Home: Caring and Social Policy,* Berkeley and London: California Universty Press.

Oakeshott, M. (1962) *Rationalism in Politics and Other Essays,* London: Methuen.

O'Hear, A. (1992) 'Respect and the dangers of an unfettered "critical spirit" in education'. In D. Anderson (Ed.) *The Loss of Virtue,* London: Social Affairs Unit.

O'Keeffe, D. (1992) 'Diligence abandoned: the dismissal of traditional virtues in the school'. In D. Anderson, *The Loss of Virtue,* London: Social Affairs Unit.

Ollendorff, R. (1971) 'The rights of adolescents'. In P. Adams et al. *Children's Rights,* London: Elek Books.

Paine, T. (1792) *The Rights of Man,* Harmondsworth: Penguin, 1969.

Pascal, B. (1657) *Lettres Provinciales,* trans. A. J. Krailsheimer as *Provincial Letters,* Harmondsworth: Penguin, 1967.

Peters, R.S. (1974) *Psychology and Ethical Development,* London: George Allen and Unwin.

Phillips, M. (1997) *All Must Have Prizes,* London: Little Brown.

Piaget, J. (1932) *The Moral Judgement of the Child,* London: Routledge.

Pincoffs, E. (1986) *Quandaries and Virtues,* Kansas: University Press of Kansas.

Pritchard, M. (1996) *Reasonable Children,* Kansas: University Press of Kansas.

Purpel, D. (1997) 'The politics of character education'. In A. Molnar (Ed.) *The Construction of Children's Character,* Chicago: Chicago University Press.

Qualifications and Curiculum Authority (1999) *The National Curriculum Handbook for Primary/Secondary Teachers,* London: Qualifications and Curriculum Authority.

Racine, J. (1677) *Phèdre.* In J. Racine, *Théâtre,* Paris: Hazan.

Rachels, J. (1999) *The Elements of Moral Philosophy,* Boston: McGraw Hill.

Ranson, S. (1994) 'Towards education for democracy: the learning society'. In S. Tomlinson (Ed.) *Educational Reform,* London: Rivers Oram.

Raths, I.E. Harmin, M. and Simon, S.B. (1966) *Values and Teaching,* Columbus, OH: Merrill.

Rawls, J. (1973) *A Theory of Justice,* London: Oxford University Press.

Rawls, J. (1985) 'Justice as fairness: political, not metaphysical', *Philosophy and Public Affairs,* 14/3, pp. 223-51.

Raz, J. (1986) *The Morality of Freedom,* Oxford: Oxford University Press.

Reiss, M. (1997) 'Teaching about homosexuality and heterosexuality', *Journal of Moral Education,* 26/3, pp. 343-352.

Richards, J. R. (1980) *The Sceptical Feminist,* Harmondsworth: Penguin.

Rorty, R, (1989) *Contingency, Irony and Solidarity,* Cambridge: Cambridge University Press.

Rorty, R. (1979) *Philosophy and the Mirror of Nature,* Princeton NJ: Princeton University Press.

Rousseau, J.J. (1762) *The Social Contract,* Harmondsworth: Penguin, 1969.

Ryle, G. (1958) 'On forgetting the difference between right and wrong'. In A.I Melden (Ed.) *Essays in Moral Philosophy,* Washington: University of Washington Press.

Ryle, G. (1972) 'Can virtue be taught?' In R.F. Dearden, P.H. Hirst and R.S.Peters, *Education and the Development of Reason,* London: Routledge and Kegan Paul.

Sandel, M. (1982) *Liberalism and the Limits of Justice,* Cambridge: Cambridge University Press.

School Curriculum and Assessment Authority (1996a) *Education for Adult Life: the Spiritual and Moral Development of Young People,* London: School Curriculum and Assessment Authority.

School Curriculum and Assessment Authority (1996b) *Consultation on Values in Education and the Community,* London: School Curriculum and Assessment Authority.

Schools Council (1971) *The Schools Council/Nuffield Foundation Humanities Curriculum Project,* London: Methuen.

Schubert, W. H. (1997) 'Character education from four perspectives on curiculum'. In A. Molnar (Ed.) *The Construction of Children's Character*, Chicago: Chicago University Press.

Schumpeter, J. A. (1954) *Capitalism, Socialism and Democracy*, London: Allen and Unwin.

Scruton, R. (2002) A *Short History of Modern Philosophy*, London: Routledge.

Seaton, N. (1991) *Higher Standards and More Choice: a Manifesto for our Schools*, London: Campaign for Real Education.

Shaw, B. (1891) *The Quintessence of Ibsenism*, London: Scott.

Singer, P. (1993) *Practical Ethics*, Cambridge, Cambridge University Press.

Slote, M. (1992) *From Morality to Virtue*, New York: Oxford University Press.

Smart, J.J.C. and Williams, B. (1973) *Utilitarianism, For and Against*, Cambridge: Cambridge University Press.

Smith, R. and Standish P. (Eds) (1997) *Teaching Right and Wrong*, Stoke-on-Trent: Trentham Books.

Steutel, J. (1997) 'The virtue approach to moral education: some conceptual clarifications', *Journal of Philosophy of Education*, 31/3, pp. 395-408.

Straughan, R. (1988) *Can We Teach Children To Be Good?* London: Allen and Unwin.

Talbot, M. (1999) 'Against relativism'. In J.M. Halstead and T.H. McLaughlin, *Education in Morality*, London: Routledge.

Talbot, M. and Tate, N. (1997) 'Shared values in a pluralist society'. In R. Smith and P. Standish (Eds) *Teaching Right and Wrong*, Stoke-on-Trent: Trentham Books.

Taylor, C (1992)'The politics of recognition'. In A. Gutman and C. Taylor, *Multiculturalism and the Politics of Recognition*, Priceton, NJ: Princeton University Press.

Tönnies, F. (1887) *Gemeinschaft und Gesellschaft* trans. J. Harris as *Community and Civil Society*, Cambridge: Cambridge University Press, 2001.

Walzer, M. (1983) S*pheres of Justice*, New York: Basic Books.

Warnock, G.J. (1971) *The Object of Morality*, London: Methuen.

Warnock, M. (1993) 'Good teaching'. In R. Barrow and P. White (Eds) *Beyond Liberal Education: Essays in Honour of Paul H. Hirst*, London: Routledge.

Weil, S. (1957) 'La personne humaine'. In S. Weil, *Ecrits de Londres*, Paris: Gallimard, trans. R. Rees as 'Human personality' in R.Rees (Ed.), S. Weil, Selected Essays, 1934-1943, Oxford: Oxford University Press.

White, J. (1970) 'Indoctrinatiomn; a reply to I.M.M. Gregory and R. Woods' *Proceedings of the Philosophy of Education Society of Great Britain*, 8/2, pp. 59-80.

White, J. (1990) *Education and the Good Life*, London: Kogan Page.

White, J. (1997) 'Three proposals and a rejection'. In R. Smith and P. Standish (Eds) *Teaching Right and Wrong*, Stoke-on-Trent: Trentham Books.

Williams, B. (1985) *Ethics and the Limits of Philosophy*, London: Fontana.

Wilson, J. (1972) *Practical Methods of Moral Education*,London: Heineman.

Wright, L. (1987) 'Physical Education and moral development' *Journal of Philosophy of Education*, 21, pp. 93-101.

Wringe, C. (1981) *Children's Rights: a Philosophical Study*, London: Routledge.

Wringe, C. (1992) 'The ambiguities of education for active citizenship', *Journal of Philosophy of Education*, 26/1, pp. 29-38.

Wringe, C. (1998) 'Citizenship beyond the nation state: Europe and the world', *Talking Politics*, 11/1, pp. 17-20.

Wringe, C. (1999) 'Being good and living well', *Journal of Philosophy of Education*, 32/2, pp. 267-93.

Wringe, C. (2000) 'The diversity of moral education', *Journal of Philosophy of Education*, 33/3 pp. 659-72.

Wringe, C. (2003) 'Measuring moral development', *Prospero*, 9, pp. 39-46.

Zimmerman, S. (1992) Family Policies and Family Well-Being, London: Sage.

INDEX

Abortion, 127

Abraham, 21, 88, 121

Absolutes, see moral absolutes

Absolutism, 98

Action based and agent based moral
theories, 62

Actions, involuntary, 15

Adams, P. 120

Advisory Group on Citizenship, 79,
147, 166

Anderson, B. 153

Anderson, D. 3

Anscombe, E. 28, 63, 96

Apartheid, 22

Archard, D. 119, 124

Aristotle, 16, 34, 63-65, 68, 72, 74,
95, 97, 100, 101, 142, 143, 153,
161

Arnold, M. 96

Arnold, P. 169

Arrachnee, 21

Ayer, A.J. 26

Bailey. C. 36, 37

Barrow, R. 44-45

Barzun, J. 134

Baudrillard, J. 26, 97

Bellah, R. 74

Bentham, J. 43-47, 58, 110

Berger, B. 3

Blake, N. 7

Bond, E. 40

Bourdieu, P. 12, 34

Browning, R. 110

Buck, M. 10

Burke, E. 16, 76, 138

Callan, E. 146, 149

Caring, 83-93; disadvantage of
defining as a feminist theory,
88; natural and ethical caring,
87; shortcomings as an ethical
theory, 88-93; see also Gilligan,
C. and Noddings N

Carr, D. 10, 169

Casuistry, 22

Chandler, D. 31

Character Counts Coalition, 5

Character Education Partnership, 5

Character Education, 70-73; as a
synonym for moral education,
70; British and American
versions of, 70; deficiencies of,
71-72; origins in America, 70;
positive contribution, 71

Choice/choices, 14-15, 17; liberal and
communitarian views of, 74-76

Cicero, 100

Citizenship, 19, 142-158; active
citizenship157; as a reciprocal
moral relationship, 142-143;
citizenship and protest, 148-
149; citizenship education and
pluralism, 144-146; global
citizenship, 152-158;
responsibilities of citizens, 149-
151; similarities and
differences between ancient and
modern citizenship, 143-147;

Clarke, W. 58

Communitarianism (popular) 79-82;
Communitarian Network, 5;
Communitarian Movement, 79-
81; doctrines, 76-78; lack of
philosophical rigour, 80-82;
links with and differences from
philosophical
Communitarianism, 79, 81-82;
support of European politicians,
80

Communitarianism, (philosophical)
74-79; community involvement